Respect for the Jews

Respect for the Jews

*Collected Works
Volume 4*

FRANZ POSSET

With a Foreword by Yaacov Deutsch

WIPF & STOCK · Eugene, Oregon

RESPECT FOR THE JEWS
Collected Works, Volume 4

Copyright © 2019 Franz Posset. All rights reserved. Except for brief quotations in critical publications or reviews, no part of this book may be reproduced in any manner without prior written permission from the publisher. Write: Permissions, Wipf and Stock Publishers, 199 W. 8th Ave., Suite 3, Eugene, OR 97401.

Wipf & Stock
An Imprint of Wipf and Stock Publishers
199 W. 8th Ave., Suite 3
Eugene, OR 97401

www.wipfandstock.com

PAPERBACK ISBN: 978-1-5326-7090-9
HARDCOVER ISBN: 978-1-5326-7091-6
EBOOK ISBN: 978-1-5326-7092-3

Manufactured in the U.S.A.   SEPTEMBER 20, 2019

Cover: "Synagogue and Church in Our Time," by Joshua Koffman, 2015, commissioned by Saint Joseph's University in Philadelphia to mark the fiftieth anniversary of the 1965 Second Vatican Council Declaration *Nostra Aetate* (Declaration on the Relation of the Church to Non-Christian Religions) and the 1967 founding of the university's Institute for Jewish-Catholic Relations. The sculpture depicts Synagogue and Church as study partners (photo provided by Philip A. Cunningham, PhD, Institute for Jewish-Catholic Relations at Saint Joseph's University).

Contents

List of Illustrations | vii
Foreword by Yaacov Deutsch | xiii
Abbreviations | xv

    Introduction | 1

1 A Fifteenth-Century Bible Codex in Hebrew with a Picture of the Crucifixion and with Two Monastic Figures, Saint Dominic and Saint Bernard | 17

2 Who Is "the Strongest and Most Skilled Protector of This Oppressed Language"? | 36

3 "Search the Scriptures/scriptures" (John 5:39) according to Johann Reuchlin | 60

4 God's Language, Catholic Praise of the Sacred Language of the Jews during the Early Reformation, with Georg Witzel's Speech in Praise of the Hebrew Language | 83

5 "The Hebrews Drink from the Source, the Greeks from the Rills, and the Latin People from the Puddle" | 198

6 Hebrew Translations of Christian Prayers on the Eve of the Reformation | 211

7 In Search of an Explanation for the Suffering of the Jews | 236

8 In Search of the Historical Pfefferkorn | 252

9 "We Love This People" | 271

Bibliography | 273
Index of Personal Names | 283
Index of Biblical References | 289

List of Illustrations

Introduction:

Fig. 0.1. Anthonius Margaritha, *Der gantz Jüdisch Glaub mit sampt ainer gründtlichen vnd warhafften anzaygunge / Aller Satzungen / Ceremonien / Gebetten / Haymliche vnd offentliche Gebreüch / deren sich dye Juden halten / durch das gantz Jar / Mit schönen vnd gegründten Argumenten wyder jren Glauben. Durch Anthonium Margaritham Hebrayschen Leser der Löblichen Statt Augspurg / beschriben vnd an tag gegeben* (Augsburg: Steiner, 1530). Online: https://books.google.com.br/books?id=8hRUAAAAcAAJ&printsec=frontcover&#v=onepage&q&f=false.

Chapter 1:

Fig. 1.1. First full-page miniature with historiated Hebrew initial ב (*bet*) in the Hebrew Bible; fifteenth century. Florence, Biblioteca Medicea Laurenziana, MS Conv. Sopp. 268, folio 1r. From: Posset 2015, Fig. 3.

Figs. 1.2–12. Details (of Fig. 1.1) with the historiated initial ב (*bet*).

Fig. 1.13. Fra Angelico. San Marco Museum, Florence. Online: https://upload.wikimedia.org/wikipedia/commons/c/c7/Fra_Angelico_-_Saint_Dominic_Adoring_the_Crucifixion_-_WGA00562.jpg.

Fig. 1.14. Detail of Fig. 1.1.

Fig. 1.15. *Amplexus Bernardi*, Cistercian Abbey, Florence. From: James France, *Medieval Images of Saint Bernard of Clairvaux*, 2007, no. WA22.

LIST OF ILLUSTRATIONS

Chapter 2:

Fig. 2.1. Title Page of *De Arte Cabalistica*. Online: https://www.martayanlan.com/pages/books/3018/johannes-reuchlin/de-arte-cabalistica-libri-tres.

Fig. 2.2. Pope Clement V (died 1314), *Clementis Quinti Constitutiones* (Basel 1511). MDZ, Signatur: 2 J.can.f. 52-3#Beibd.1. Online: https://bildsuche.digitale-sammlungen.de/index.html?c=viewer&bandnummer=bsb00018940&pimage=2&v=100&nav=&l=en.

Fig. 2.3. *Codex Reuchlin 1* (also called "Reuchlin Bible"). From: Badische Landesbibliothek, 688 folios; Karlsruhe, Germany, here folio 2v; Posset (2015) 203, Fig. 6.

Fig. 2.4. Reuchlin, *De praeparatione hominis*, fol. A 2v. From: Münster, Universitäts- und Landesbibliothek, Sign.: COLL. ERH. 4 (Photo ULB Münster); Posset 2015b, Fig. 3.

Fig. 2.5. Reuchlin's letter to Rudolf Agricola of 1484/1485. Selestat, ms. 332b (=K892 k). Photo: Library Sélestat, France.

Fig. 2.6. TAB: Thomas Anshelm of Baden: Second printer's mark. From: Stadtarchiv Pforzheim, Sig. T Reu 36 070; *Anwälte der Freiheit! Humanisten und Reformatoren im Dialog*. Begleitband zur Ausstellung im Reuchlinhaus Pforzheim, 20. September bis 8. November 2015. Im Auftrag der Stadt Pforzheim, ed. Matthias Dall'Asta. Heidelberg: Winter, 2015, 170, Fig. 2.

Fig. 2.7. Third printer's mark, 1520, by Thomas Anshelm of Baden (initials TAB); colophon in Anshelm's print of Martin Luther's *Von den guten werken, ain gantz nützlich büchlin dem layen zuo lessen / durch D. Martinum Luter zuo Wittenberg gepredigt* (Hagenau: Anshelm, 1520). Austrian National Library, Vienna. Online: books.google.de/books?id=FB9RAAAAcAAJ&hl=de&peg=PT116#v=onepage&q&f=false.

Fig. 2.8. *Liber S. Athanasii De Variis Quaestionibus* (Reuchlin's book about Athanasius on Various Questions); Posset 2015, 741, Fig. 28. MDZ, Signatur Res/4 P. gr. 10 (image no. 55). Online: http://reader.digitale-sammlungen.de/de/fs1/object/display/bsb11227983_00055.html.

LIST OF ILLUSTRATIONS

Chapter 3:

Fig. 3.1. Evangelist John dictates to Prochoros under the inspiration of the Holy Spirit. Reuchlin's Greek Codex of the New Testament (Basel). Codex Basilensis A. N. IV. 2, folio 265v. University Library Basel. Online: https://www.google.com/search?q=Codex+basilensis+A.N.+IV.+2-+Folio+265v&source=lnms&tbm=isch&sa=X&ved=0ahUKEwjS6NP-o8L-dAhUQTawKHQIDDFUQ_AUIDygC&biw=1250&bih=697#imgrc=s4B4e-Wrf_BQoM:.

Fig. 3.2. Sample page from Johann Reuchlin, *Principium libri Ioannis Reuchlin . . . de rudimentis hebraicis* (*The Rudiments of Hebrew*). Pforzheim: Thomas Anshelm, 1506. Online: https://www.library.illinois.edu/rbx/exhibitions/Reuchlin/gallery.html.

Fig. 3.3. *Codex Reuchlin 2*, folio 1r. 36x27 cm, 96 folios; Badische Landesbibliothek, Karlsruhe, Germany; Posset 2015, 204, Fig. 7.

Fig. 3.4. Bishop Paul of Burgos, ca. 1350–1435. Online: https://upload.wikimedia.org/wikipedia/commons/a/a9/Pablo_de_Santa_Maria.jpg.

Fig. 3.5. De-luxe edition of Paul of Burgos' *Scrutinium*, Strasbourg, ca. 1474; MDZ. Online: http://daten.digitale-sammlungen.de/bsb00076968/image_5.

Fig. 3.6. Johann Pfefferkorn, *Ich bin ain Buechlinn der Juden veindt*. Online: https://archive.org/details/bub_gb_y_pSAAAAcAAJ/page/n3.

Fig. 3.7. Jacob von Hoogstraeten, *Destructio Cabale*, Cologne: Quentel, 1519. MDZ, Online: http://daten.digitale-sammlungen.de/0002/bsb00022770/images/index.html?id=00022770&groesser=&fip=sdasxssdaseayaeayayztseayaxdsydxdsydyzts&no=9&seite=1.

Fig. 3.8. Daniel Bomberg. Online: http://1.bp.blogspot.com/-zcqJPyXRyww/VSAB6IF4VtI/AAAAAAAABc8/ePRXSLBG2WA/s1600/sfarim74_O1.jpg.

Fig. 3.9. Bomberg's Rabbinic Bible (edition of 1524/1525). Online: https://www.google.com/search?q=http://www.indiana.edu/~rcapub/v21n1/p5.html&source=lnms&tbm=isch&sa=X&ved=0ahUKEwjGrtbA1cLeAhVk_IMKHSiGA-8Q_AUIEygB&biw=1238&bih=697#imgrc=68uDl3jV9JvlEM:.

LIST OF ILLUSTRATIONS

Fig. 3.10. Bomberg's first Talmud print. Online: http://www.seder-olam.info/seder-olam-g45-renaissance.html.

Chapter 4:

Fig. 4.1 Autograph letter from Martin Luther to Georg Buchholzer, 1543. Online: https://commons.wikimedia.org/wiki/File:Martin_Luther_letter_september_1543_b.png.

Fig. 4.2. Matthaeus Adrianus, *Oratio quam Lovanii habuit, de linguarum laude* [*Oratio de linguarum laude*]. MDZ, Online: https://books.google.com/books/about/Oratio_quam_Lovanii_habuit_de_linguarum.html?id=imm7YbnXoBcC.

Fig. 4.3. Robert Wakefield, a page from his speech. Online: https://www.google.com/search?q=Oratio+de+laudibus+et+utilitate+trium+linguarum&source=lnms&tbm=isch&sa=X&ved=0ahUKEwiMza7Kq5reAhVi6YMKHcFvA4oQ_AUIDigB&biw=1242&bih=697#imgrc=jAITif8empT7AM:.

Fig. 4.4. Portrait of Georg Witzel. British Museum, number 1862,0208.235. Online: http://www.britishmuseum.org/research/collection_online/collection_object_details.aspx?objectId=1452730&partId=1&people=20794&peoA=20794-1-6&page=5.

Fig. 4.5. Georg Witzel, *Oratio* (1534). MDZ, Online, http://reader.digitale-sammlungen.de/de/fs1/object/display/bsb10998438_00005.html.

Fig. 4.6. Georg Witzel's *Encomium* (1538). Online: http://daten.digitale-sammlungen.de/~db/0003/bsb00035934/images/.

Chapter 5:

Fig. 5.1. Johannes Aurifaber: *COLLOQVIA Oder Tischreden Doctor Martini Lutheri so er in vielen jaren die Zeyt seines Lebens gegen Gelehrten Leuthen auch hin vnd wider bey frembden Gesten vnd seinen Tischgesellen gefuehret* (1567). Online: https://iiif.deutsche-digitale-bibliothek.de/image/2/f3977ea7-dbf0-4a7c-bcea-2c58246508dd/full/!440,330/0/default.jpg.

LIST OF ILLUSTRATIONS

Chapter 6:

Fig. 6.1. Four pages with the entire Our Father (and the Holy Holy Holy) in Manutius' grammar book of 1500 (Stuttgart copy). Folios 11v–12r and 12v–13r. Online: http://www.wlb-stuttgart.de/sammlungen/alte-und-wertvolle-drucke/bestand/inkunabeln/inkunabel-rarissima-und-unikate/aldus-manutius/.

Fig. 6.2. The Our Father in Marschalk's reprint, *Introductio ad litteras hebraicas Vtilissima Alphabetum*. Erfurt: Marschalk, 1502. Staatsbibliothek Berlin, image no. 12. Online: http://digital.staatsbibliothek-berlin.de/werkansicht?PPN=PPN815418078&PHYSID=PHYS_0012&DMDID=DMDLOG_0001.

Fig. 6.3. The Our Father in Tissardus. MDZ, Online: http://www.mdz-nbn-resolving.de/urn/resolver.pl?urn=urn:nbn:de:bvb:12-bsb10163789-9.

Fig. 6.4. The Our Father, upper detail of Pfefferkorn's broadsheet. Cologne: Landen, 1508. Göttingen University Library. See the whole page in chapter 8, fig. 8.5, of this volume.

Fig. 6.5. The Our Father in Adrianus, *Libellus Hora faciendi pro Domino, scilicet filio Virginis Mariae, cuius mysterium in prologo legenti patebit*. Tübingen: Anshelm, 1513. MDZ, Online: http://reader.digitale-sammlungen.de/de/fs1/object/display/bsb10984588_00016.html.

Fig. 6.6. Virgin Mother and Child. MDZ, Online: http://reader.digitale-sammlungen.de/de/fs1/object/display/bsb10984588_00013.html.

Fig. 6.7. Portrait of Adrianus praying the rosary, and as itinerant with stick and spur. MDZ, Online: http://reader.digitale-sammlungen.de/de/fs1/object/display/bsb10984588_00012.html.

Fig. 6.8. Portrait of Johann Bo[e]schenstain by Hieronymus Hopfer, ca. 1530. British Museum, number 1845,0809.1479. Online: https://www.mutualart.com/Artwork/Portrait-of-Johannes-Boschenstein—Profe/28FD9E72434FF0F7.

Fig. 6.9. The Our Father in: Boeschenstain, *Elementale introductoriu[m]*. Augsburg: Erhard Öglin, 1514. MDZ, Online (image no. 11): https://reader.digitale-sammlungen.de/de/fs1/object/display/bsb10981642_00011.html.

Fig. 6.10. Table of contents of Boeschenstain's trilingual texts. MDZ, Online (image no. 24): https://reader.digitale-sammlungen.de/de/fs1/object/goToPage/bsb10981642.html?pageNo=24.

Chapter 7:

Fig. 7.1. *Doctor iohanns Reuchlins tütsch missiue, warumb die Jude[n] so lang im ellend sind*. Online: https://sammlungen.ulb.uni-muenster.de/hd/content/pageview/677734.

Chapter 8:

Fig. 8.1. Detail, single leaf of 1516, with a poem in German against Pfefferkorn. *Einzelblatt Mp 19671 Mappe 344*. Germanisches Nationalmuseum, Nuremberg; Photo: Georg Janssen.

Fig. 8.2. Portrait of Iohann Pfefferkorn by Hieronymus Hopfer. Herzog Anton Ulrich Museum, Virtuelles Kupferstichkabinett, Braunschweig, HHopfer AB 3.53 Inv. Nr. 7331. Online: http://kk.haum-bs.de/?id=h-hopfer-ab3-0053.

Fig. 8.3. *Der Joeden spiegel*, 3 September 1507 (P 2299). University and City Library of Cologne. Online: https://www.deutsche-digitale-bibliothek.de/item/I3UPEOIBITNZVST7CYTXIDDBDZHSYPQ3.

Fig. 8.4. Single folio print of Pfefferkorn's three texts including the Hebrew Version of the Lord's Prayer, Hail Mary, and Creed. Cologne: Johannes Landen, 1508. Niedersächsische Staats- und Universitätsbibliothek Göttingen. Online: 2 TH POLEM 564 / 81 RARA: *Titel: Pater noster [und] Credo; Lateinisch u. hebräisch transkribiert. Verfasser: Pfefferkorn, Johann.* Online: https://gdz.sub.uni-goettingen.de/id/PPN856961124.

Every effort has been made to contact all copyright holders. In the event of any omissions or errors the author asks the copyright holders to inform him so that the correct credits may be included in future editions.

Foreword

THE JEWS PLAYED AN important role in the theological writings of Christian scholars in the medieval and the early modern period. For the most part, these writings presented a wide range of negative opinions and perspectives: Jews were described as blindfolded and therefore as people who cannot see and understand the true meaning of the biblical text; they were portrayed as Christ killers who not only did not recognize Jesus as the Messiah but opposed him and were responsible for his crucifixion. In addition, Christians examined Jewish texts, and in later periods Jewish rituals and practices, in order to reveal Jewish hatred toward Christianity and to demonstrate the superstitious nature of the Jewish religion. There are hundreds, if not thousands, of medieval and early modern texts that comprise the *Adversus Judaeos* literature. In contrast, the number of texts that show sympathetic and positive attitudes toward Jews and Judaism is small. Moreover, theses writings are rarely discussed and in many cases are completely ignored.

Franz Posset published his monumental biography of Johannes Reuchlin in 2015. His current publication, *Respect for the Jews*, focuses on Christian attitudes toward Jews in the Jewish relations in the fifteenth and sixteenth centuries. In many ways this new composition is a continuation and elaboration of issues that pertain to Reuchlin, but as Posset demonstrates, these topics are also characteristic of the thinking of other fifteenth- and sixteenth-century scholars.

By concentrating on early modern Christian theologians and thinkers who showed kind, considerate, and in some cases even friendly and congenial attitudes toward Jews, the current volume underlines the complexity of Christian approaches to Jews and Judaism in the early modern period allowing for a more nuanced account of this period.

The articles in this volume relate to some well-known figures such as Reuchlin and Luther, but at the same time also illuminate more obscure and almost unknown texts and figures, some of whom have not received any attention and others who have not been studied in the context of attitudes toward Jews and Judaism. Thus, Posset discusses a fifteenth-century Bible Codex in Hebrew that has an image of the crucifixion, and several Hebrew translations of Christian prayers. He also provides an English translation of the German theologian Georg Witzel's *Praise of the Hebrew Language* that has never been undertaken before. Another important contribution of this volume is the use of images that not only illustrate the topics discussed but also allow Posset to offer new insights about the use of Hebrew by Christians in the fifteenth and sixteenth centuries and more broadly about Christian attitudes toward Jews in that period. We are fortunate to have this volume and can only look forward to Posset's future research.

—Yaacov Deutsch

    Head of the History Department
    David Yellin College
    Jerusalem

Abbreviations

CR	*Corpus Reformatorum*, vols. 1–28 (Melanchthon), edited by Carolus Gottlieb Bretschneider et al. Halle: C. A. Schwetschke, 1834–1860
CSEL	*Corpus Scriptorum Ecclesiasticorum Latinorum*
LW	*Luther's Works.* American edition. 75 vols. St. Louis: Concordia; Philadelphia and Minneapolis: Fortress, 1955–
MDZ	Munich Digitalisation Zentrum (online)
n.	note
RBW	*Johannes Reuchlin Briefwechsel*, edited by Heidelberg Akademie der Wissenschaften and City of Pforzheim, vols. 1–4, Stuttgart-Bad Cannstatt, 1999–2013
SW	*Johannes Reuchlin Sämtliche Werke*, edited by Widu-Wolfgang Ehlers, Hans-Gert Roloff, and Peter Schäfer. Stuttgart-Bad Cannstatt: Frommann-Holzboog, 1996–
WA	[*Weimarer Ausgabe*] *D. Martin Luthers Werke: Kritische Gesamtausgabe*, Weimar: Hermann Böhlaus Nachfolger. Graz: Akademische Druck und Verlagsanstalt, 1883–2009
WA.B	*Briefe* (Letters)
WA.TR	*Tischreden* (Table Talk)
WA.DB	*Deutsche Bibel* (German Bible). (Example: WA 1: 2.3–4 means volume 1, page 2, lines 3–4; usually followed by the number of the Table Talk or Letter).

Introduction

I know my adversaries are dismayed because I have called them [the Jews] our fellow citizens. Now I would want them to go berserk even more, their guts may burst open because I say that the Jews are our brothers.

So said Johann Reuchlin in his *Defensio* of 1513.¹ His words are often drowned out in the rough sea of the numerous anti-Jewish utterances of his time. In the sixteenth century Reuchlin was known as "the strongest and most skilled protector of this oppressed language" (i.e., Hebrew), according to his contemporary Father Georg Witzel (1501–1573), who became Martin Luther's later adversary.² Reuchlin liked the drift of the philosemitic-sounding adage: "The Hebrews Drink from the Source, the Greeks from the Rills, and the Latin People from the Puddle."³ In the same train of thought Georg Witzel stated: "But don't you now want to drink from the so very sweet font after you have had a taste from the Greek rills? You would not be so stupid as to prefer secondary and third-class versions to the original?"⁴

This collection of studies may accompany my book on one of the most influential, but not very well-known, Catholic humanists: *Johann Reuchlin (1455–1522): A Theological Biography*,⁵ which was awarded the 2016

1. SW 4-1: 344.19–22.
2. Böning 2004, 100.
3. The saying is often attributed to Reuchlin, but more likely it is the anonymous intellectual property of the Renaissance humanists; see Posset 2015b, 159–65.
4. *Sed heus, igitur non vis e fonte dulcissimo bibere, posteaquam in gustum dati tibi sunt Graeci rivuli? Eliges ne amens pro prototypo deuterotypon, aut etiam tritotypon?* See chapter 4.
5. Posset 2015.

Monsignor Harry C. Koenig Award for Catholic Biography of the American Catholic Historical Association.

Some of the studies assembled here were delivered at various conferences in recent years: "A Fifteenth-Century Bible in Hebrew with a Picture of the Crucifixion" was presented at the International Medieval Congress in Kalamazoo in 2015 (now chapter 1). My discovery of the "miniature"[6] depicting the crucifixion on the front page of a late medieval Hebrew codex in Florence goes back to my research on the iconography of Saint Bernard of Clairvaux. During a visit in Florence in May 2014 I was granted access to this highly unusual Hebrew codex at the Biblioteca Medicea Laurenziana (MS Conv. Sopp. 268). The creation and the financing and also the preservation of such a luxurious codex in Florence would not have been possible without a certain degree of respect for the Jews and their holy book. The codex under consideration may have been a proud "show and tell" object, highly prized by the Medicis.

Chapters 2 and 3 were given originally as lectures in Wroclaw, Poland, in spring of 2017: (a) "'Search the Scriptures/scriptures' (John 5:39): The Hebrew Scriptures and the Catholic Theology in the Eyes of Johann Reuchlin," at the Pontifical Faculty of Theology, April 25.

(b) "The Jews, Their Sacred Language and the Holy Name of God in the Eyes of Johann Reuchlin," at the Third International Conference on Christian Hebraism in Eastern and Central Europe, April 27, 2017. The image, which is included in chapter 2 (fig. 2.5), is never seen before in an English/American publication. I am grateful to the City Library of Sélestat, Alsace, France, (known in German as Schlettstadt) for allowing the picture to be published.

Part of chapter 4 is the enlarged version of the paper "Respect for the Jews and for God's Language: Catholic Praise of the Sacred Language of the Jews during the Early Reformation," which was presented at the American Catholic Historical Association meeting at Emmitsburg, Maryland, April 14, 2018. This study features the still extant speeches of Catholic scholars in praise of the Hebrew language as the means by which God communicates with humanity. Those speeches include the public lectures of the English scholar Robert Wakefield (d. 1537); the Swiss Catholic humanist Nicolaus Winmann (ca. 1500–ca.1550); the Spanish Hebraist Matthaeus Adrianus (ca. 1470–1521), who worked in German lands; and the German

---

6. A technical term in iconography; "miniature," from the Latin *minium*, i.e., red-lead or vermilion, came to mean any picture in an illuminated manuscript.

ex-Lutheran Georg Witzel (1501–1573). They all echo Johann Reuchlin's pioneering works.

In chapter 4 Georg Witzel's "Speech in Praise of the Hebrew Language" is offered for the first time in an English translation on facing pages taken from the sixteenth-century original.

In chapter 5 we take a look at the adage "The Hebrews Drink from the Source, the Greeks from the Rills, and the Latin People from the Puddle," a saying that was picked up among others by Martin Luther in a Table Talk in 1532. The original version of this chapter was delivered at the conference on Lutheranism and the Classics in 2014 in Fort Wayne, Indiana.[7] Luther employed the adage not in order to attack the Catholic Latin-speaking world for drinking, metaphorically speaking, dirty swamp water, but in order to show his high esteem for the Hebrew language. I presuppose that in this case of a handed-down Table Talk, which was taken up during conversations at Luther's dinner table, actually represents his authentic conviction. When one utilizes Luther's Table Talk, great caution is in order because the sayings that were handed down are not seldom erroneous and tainted. Usually, I consider Luther's Table Talk as secondary literature.[8]

The contribution "In Search of an Explanation for the Suffering of the Jews: Johann Reuchlin's Open Letter of 1505,"[9] was awarded the *Franz-Delitzsch-Förderpreis* in Germany in 2015. It is now chapter 6.

Chapter 7 represents a by-product of my research on Johann Pfefferkorn (d. 1521) as a self-appointed missionary to the Jews; it deals with Hebrew translations of Christian prayers on the eve of the Reformation. They were used somewhat removed from their original purpose, i.e., for praying, by making them teaching tools for training in a foreign language (Hebrew).

Chapter 8 is the paper which was delivered at the international workshop on Johann Pfefferkorn's Campaign against the Jews: Antisemitism and Ethnography in the Sixteenth Century, held on February 24–25, 2015, in Uppsala, Sweden. The contributions are published in *Revealing the Secrets of the Jews: Johannes Pfefferkorn and Christian Writings about Jewish Life and Literature in Early Modern Europe*.[10] The various contributions to the

---

7. With minor differences first published in Posset 2017b.

8. Posset 2011, 30–31. My suggestion to consider Luther's Table Talk as some sort of "secondary literature" is confirmed by the most recent critical study of Klitzsch 2016, 147–99.

9. First published in *Studies in Christian Jewish Relations* 5 (2010) 1–11.

10. Adams and Heß 2017, 43–60.

conference in Uppsala can furnish valuable building blocks for a full, critical biography of Pfefferkorn, which is yet to be written. Such an enterprise could be undertaken as soon as Pfefferkorn's writings become available as part of the critical edition of Reuchlin's (!) collected works.[11] Only this chapter in the collection at hand is concerned with antijudaism/proto-antisemitism, namely that of the notorious Johann Pfefferkorn, who was Reuchlin's formidable adversary. This chapter presents a Christian convert's explicit "dis-respect" for his former coreligionists, a phenomenon which was so very prominent in those times.

Except for chapter 8, the studies assembled here may be considered contributions for evidence of some provocative, early philosemitic elements within a world and a society that was filled with Christian proto-antisemitism in the early sixteenth century. I use the generally accepted definition of philosemitism as an "interest in, respect for, and an appreciation of the Jewish people, their Bible and their history." My intention here is not to offer a comprehensive investigation into philosemitism[12] (nor into antisemitism) in the sixteenth century, but to highlight some friendliness, or at least some respect, toward the Jews—on a stage that is dominated by the gloomy and terrifying backdrop of hate and persecution.

The Reformer Martin Luther was the megaphone on that stage. In order to better understand the historical traces of philosemitism which are to be shown here, it is necessary, in this introduction, to reflect a bit on Luther's antisemitism. This Reformer had no respect for the postbiblical Jews (nor, by the way, for what he called "the papists"). At one point he used the expression "synagogue of Satan" (*synagoga Sathanae*, in Latin) in a series of forty propositions (*propositiones*) which, however, were not directed against the Jews as one might expect from the expression he used, but against the Church of Rome.[13] Luther made both entities his enemies who, in his view, belong to the devil. In his eyes Jews and papists were despicable. They are, along with "the Turks," the "unholy threesome" and prime enemies of his

---

11. SW 4-2: *Johannes Pfefferkorns Schriften* (in preparation).

12. Karp and Sutcliffe 2011, with the contribution by Abraham Melamed, "The Revival of Christian Hebraism in Early Modern Europe," 49–66, quoting from Reuchlin's *De arte cabalistica libri tres Leoni X. dicati* [Three books on the art of the Cabala dedicated to Leo X]: . . . *nihil[que] nostrum esse in philosophia, quod non ante Iudaeorum fuerit* (in my own, more literal, translation: ". . . and there is nothing in philosophy which is our own that previously would not have belonged to the Jews"); SW 2-1: 176.15–17.

13. *Propositiones adversus totam synagogam Sathanae et universas portas inferorum*, WA 30-2: 420–24 (of 1530).

gospel.¹⁴ Not only that; just about everybody who did not agree with Luther was in his eyes a devil. After the fallout between Luther and Erasmus of Rotterdam, the latter was now a devil, too;¹⁵ so was the revolutionary Thomas Müntzer (1490–1525) and also the rioting peasants of the 1520s. In return, Müntzer called Luther "the devil's arch-chancellor" and the "godless Wittenberg flesh."¹⁶ The "enthusiasts" (Luther called them *Schwärmer*), who were supporters of the Reformation but did not bow to the leader in Wittenberg, were possessed by the devil, too.¹⁷ Those examples show that the demonization of one's enemies was customary then, yet perhaps more so with Luther than with any others.

We still have to reflect more on Luther, as it is usually with regards to him that the sharp distinction is made between antijudaism and antisemitism. However, such a distinction is helpful only to a certain degree, especially when one emphasizes that the term "antisemitism" was coined only in the nineteenth century and that Luther supposedly was more of an "antijudaist" because of his theology. The research on this subject, in particular on Luther's shocking hate of the Jews, has continued to mushroom in the twenty-first century, due to the focus on his bad attitude toward the Jews during the past so-called "Luther Decade" of 2007–2017.

In the course of my own studies on "Luther and the Jews" I came to the conclusion that one cannot lopsidedly assign some sort of antijudaism to Luther on the basis of his theological position (and thus, perhaps excuse or explain his hate of the Jews on religious grounds), while in doing so one may avoid altogether any ideological association of Luther and racial antisemitism. However, the theologically based antijudaism took on traits of racial proto-antisemitism, and may make such a distinction rather useless when it comes to Luther. An acceptable solution was found by the authors of the Declaration by the Church Council of the Evangelical Lutheran Church in America (April 18, 1994) when speaking of antijudaism and "its modern successor," antisemitism.¹⁸

For evidence of my working hypothesis of an actual intermingling of antijudaism and proto-antisemitism in Luther's works, one may read a passage from Luther's *The Jews and Their Lies* where Luther expressed his

---

14. Schramm and Stjerna 2012, 8.
15. Walter, "Erasmus of Rotterdam," 506, with reference to Luther's letter no. 2093.
16. Vogler, "Thomas Müntzer's Heritage," 431.
17. Stayer, "Luther and the Radical Reformers," 471.
18. Schramm and Stjerna 2012, 211.

conviction that the corrupt Jewish "nature and life" (*natur und leben*) is permanently ingrained in them and cannot be changed (which constitutes a racist view):

> They have such venomous hate against the Gentiles from childhood on, instilled in them by their parents and rabbis, and they still are soaking it up without ceasing, so that, speaking with Psalm 109, it penetrates blood and flesh, bone and marrow, and has become completely their nature and life [*gantz und gar natur und leben worden ist*]. And since flesh and blood, bone and marrow, cannot be changed, their pride and envy cannot be changed either. They have to stay that way and perish, if God does not perform highly specialized miracles.[19]

Evidently, according to Luther, Jews cannot change their own "nature and life." Such a conviction explains the Reformer's disappointment with the failure of the Christian efforts of the missionizing of the Jews: they cannot be converted. The Jews are children of the devil, and "the devil and his followers are impossible to convert, and anyways, [such missionizing] is not ordered [by God]."[20] Luther appears to be surprised that the medieval learned Spanish Jewish convert Paul of Burgos (ca. 1350–1435), later a bishop, whom he cited regularly and in a positive way, actually had become a Christian—by the grace of God. Luther called the Spaniard's conversion *seltzam*[21] (*seltsam*, in High German, i.e., "rare," "strange," "wonderful," perhaps "weird" or "odd").

The historical Luther believed that the real Jews are possessed by the devil. They are stuck with their blood and circumcision.[22] Due to their nature and circumcision they commit their evil deeds which are recorded in the history books. Crimes such as poisoning wells, kidnapping children, torturing them to death with tools like awls (*zpfrimed, zepfrimet*) or sharp combs (*hecheln*) have happened, Luther wrote, "at Trent and Weissensee etc," all of which the Jews deny as he very well knows.[23] "The Jews" according to Luther are miserable, incorrigible people; they apply scandalous

---

19. WA 53: 481.23–29; see also 490.10–13, on raising their children as criminals. For more on Luther's use of Ps 109, see below.

20. WA 53: 510.27–28.

21. WA 53: 491.14.

22. WA 53: 482.12.

23. WA 53: 482.12–14; 53: 520.13; Trent in today's northern Italy; Weissensee in Berlin.

interpretation of the Scriptures; they have venomous intentions; they are revengeful, bloodthirsty liars, applying sorcery tricks of Satan. They are an evil, cursed, blinded, and whorish people. Since they are possessed by the devil they deserve to be hanged seven times higher than ordinary criminals.[24]

Such hateful opinions contain not only elements of theological antijudaism (which would primarily be concerned with issues of Scripture interpretation and with blasphemy on the part of the Jews against the Triune God of the Christians), but they show also traces of racial proto-antisemitism when considering Luther's saying about the "nature and life" of the Jews. Therefore, one cannot really uphold the differentiation of antisemitism and antijudaism when it comes to Luther's thinking about his contemporaneous Jews. Two recent authors (both are Lutheran church historians), Eric W. Gritsch with his *Martin Luther's Anti-Semitism* (2011) and Thomas Kaufmann with his *Luther's Jews: A Journey into Anti-Semitism* (2017), had no qualms about applying the notion "antisemitism" to Luther. Having said this, one must stress at the same time that for Luther the main issue was not the Jews' ethnicity or "race," but their blasphemy of the Triune God. Luther is not simply a modern racial antisemite. His rejection of the Jews is based more on religion than on race.[25] But his antijudaism contains elements of antisemitism.

At times the distinction of tolerance and toleration is offered in trying to understand Luther within the early sixteenth century, but to no avail. He was neither in favor of tolerance nor of toleration of the Jews. It was impossible for him to tolerate (German, *dulden* or *leiden*) the Jews because to him they always were the blasphemers ridden by the devil. They might be infectious and therefore needed to be shunned and exiled. Although Luther did not wage a war of religion against the Jews with weapons, he certainly waged war with his pen. Sometimes one may hear that "tolerance" was the child of the Reformation. This is not the case. According to Heinz Schilling in his Luther biography of 2013, "plurality and tolerance" were not the children, but at best the great-grandchildren of the Reformation.[26] "At best"—may be; but really? Was Luther and the Lutheran Reformation really tolerant of anybody who did not agree with him/them? Sorry to say:

---

24. WA 53: 502.9–10.
25. Schramm and Stjerna 2012, introduction, 34.
26. Schilling 2013/2017.

Luther was not the father, nor the grandfather, nor the great-grandfather of religious tolerance.

There is no way around but to admit together with Klaus Wengst that Protestantism has to live with its "birth defect," i.e., Luther's intolerance of the Jews.[27] And, Protestants have no choice but to distance themselves from it and Luther in this regard, time and again. All too quickly is Luther's hate of the Jews excused with the fallacious idea that he was simply a "man of his time," living in a milieu which was saturated with anti-Jewish attitudes. In contrast to that, one must look to other "children" of that time who did not feel the same need to viciously attack the Jews in the way Luther did. Those other authors of Luther's time had the courage to swim against the currents, whereas Luther did not. The best-known countercultural example of that time is Johann Reuchlin, whose blessed memory was preserved by the Jewish leader Josel from Rosheim (ca. 1480–1554/1555) in his memoirs, *Sefer ha-miknah* (*Sefer ha Miqnah*). Having the controversy between Pfefferkorn and Reuchlin in mind, Josel praised Reuchlin as "one of the wise men of the nations," and a "miracle within a miracle" because due to Reuchlin's efforts, the books of the Jews were returned to them; and, it was the work of a Christian: "And God showed us a miracle within a miracle, to send a good man, Doctor Reuchlin, from the sages of the nations."[28] The same Josel had nothing good to say about Luther. In Josel's view, Emperor Charles V was fighting the Lutherans and saved the Jews "from, this new religious movement, established by a priest named Martin Luther, an unrighteous person, who intended to annihilate and kill all the Jews, juveniles as well [as] old ones. Blessed be the Lord who invalidated his intention."[29]

Josel's contra-positioning of Luther and Reuchlin is striking. Reuchlin was ready to enter friendly conversations with Jews, Luther no longer was, if he ever really had been. Both, Reuchlin and Luther, had reacted to requests by contemporaneous local lords who asked them for advice on how to deal with their local Jews. Reuchlin wrote his response in 1505 in the form of an open letter to an unknown nobleman, on what kind of issues should be discussed with them in a friendly atmosphere (see chapter 6). Luther, too, was approached by a nobleman, by the name of Wolfgang Schlick of Falkenau in Moravia. However, Luther's response was far from

---

27. Wengst 2014.

28. Posset 2015, 866.

29. I used the translation conveniently provided in Weinstein, "Jews and Lutheranism," 646.

recommending friendly conversations. Luther composed an aggressive pamphlet "Against the Sabbatarians" in 1538, after having been informed by Count Schlick, whom he calls "his good friend," that the Jews with their *geschmeis* (vermin, rabble; modern German: *Geschmeiß*) were making inroads at various places.[30] A second time Luther wrote to Schlick, this time sending him his book *On the Jews and Their Lies*, which was published in 1543. In it "one novel element in Luther's rhetorical arsenal" emerged, i.e., Luther now accepting the old stereotype against Jews poisoning wells, ritual murder of Christian children, etc.[31]

Having sketched here Luther's proto-antisemitism and his refusal to further speak with Jews, I nevertheless cannot make friends with the thesis that Luther's proto-antisemitism is supposedly the unsettling problem that lies "at the heart" of Luther's theology; specifically, of his doctrine of justification and of his christocentrism. One may doubt that Luther's antijudaism/proto-antisemitism would be central or essential to his writings and that "the recognition of the centrality of antijudaism in Luther's works is still a desideratum."[32] True, Luther's hate of the Jews is still not generally known, and in this regard it still is necessary that this element of the historical Luther's life and work be acknowledged. However, this desideratum must be distinguished from the thesis that Luther's hate of the Jews would have to be considered "central" (or, essential) for his teachings (admittedly, it is not negligible either). If such centrality were indeed the case, then the chief article of Luther's theology, or, the core of his theology, on which the church stands and falls (as Luther insisted), could necessarily be demonstrated and articulated only by a recourse to Luther's blatant hate of the Jews (theologically called "antijudaism"), which, however, is not the case. And, the Lutheran Churches' rejection of Luther's historical proto-antisemitism does not mean that they committed theological suicide or would have given up their identities as Lutheran congregations anywhere in the world. And, in terms of a Catholic-ecumenical consideration in this regard, one must stress that the recent articulation of Luther's theology of grace/justification, as found in the *Joint Declaration on the Doctrine of Justification* of 1999, signed by the Catholic Church's Pontifical Council for Promoting Christian Unity and the Lutheran World Federation, would have to (as a logical consequence of the centrality thesis) include or incorporate at least a

---

30. WA 50: 312–37, here 312.8–12.
31. Schramm and Stjerna 2012, 164.
32. Helmer, "Luther in America," 1290.

few explicit considerations about "Luther and the Jews"; which, however, it does not.³³ If antisemitism were essential for the understanding of Luther's theology of justification, later Lutheranism would have to operate with that same assumption, but they do not. If Luther's hate of the Jews were central and essential to his thought, I would have to completely reject all of Luther's works (which I do not). Christocentrism, be it Luther's or any others', does not mean antijudaism.

In this context one must take into consideration some exegetical statements about Israel and the Gentiles which can be found in the elder Luther's words of 1544 when he lectured on Gen 38 as follows:

> God wanted to point out that the Messiah would be a brother and a cousin of both the Jews and the Gentiles, if not according to their paternal genealogy, at least according to their maternal nature [Tamar, Ruth, Rahab, and Bathsheba]. Consequently, there is no difference between Jews and Gentiles, except that Moses later separated this people from the Gentiles by a different form of worship and political regime. Moreover, these things were written to make it known to all that the Messiah would gather Gentiles and Jews into one and the same Church [*in unam et eandem Ecclesiam*].³⁴

The Church of Jews and Gentiles!

Luther at times distinguishes between the Jews of old and the later Jews (up to his own time), as one may observe in his pamphlet *On the Jews and Their Lies*. Luther had respect only and exclusively for the "old Jews" (*alte Juden*), not for the "new Jews." For Luther, the *alte Juden* are exclusively the prophets of the Old Testament with their hope-filled message of the Messiah who is to come. They had the proper insight (*verstand*) with respect to the promised Messiah. Those "old Jews" are, therefore, the "right" Jews (*die alten rechten Juden*) and their prophetic insight is the same which "we Christians" have, writes Luther. He apparently adopted the Hebrew prophets' scolding of the Jewish people, but he did not identify with those sinners whom the prophets have scolded. The biblical prophets' criticism

---

33. There is, though, a sentence in the *Joint Declaration* of 1999 (no. 31) which may cause concern to some: "Christ has fulfilled the law and by his death and resurrection has overcome it as a way to salvation." However, one must not read some veiled antisemitism into it. See the discussion in Pettit 2018, 1–12.

34. WA 44: 312.36–42; translated in consultation with the American edition of *Luther's Works*: LW 7:15.

and scolding of their audience (German *Publikumsbeschimpfung*) became fodder for Luther in his attacks against "the Jews" in general. If the Hebrew prophets can attack them, so can Luther.

In contrast to the "old Jews" there are the "new alien Jews" (*die newen frembden Juden*), also called "the present-day Jews" (*die jtzigen Juden*), who are identical with the ignorant Jews of postbiblical times. They are the enemies of Jesus in New Testament times. Being ignorant, they teach the false interpretation of the Scriptures.[35] Time and again he speaks of "the old Jews, their ancestors [*die alte Juden, jre vorfaren*]."[36] When he speaks of "the Jews" in an abbreviated and general way, he usually means the "new alien Jews."

With respect to the sixteenth-century Renaissance times, one reasonably could have expected that the developing scholarly esteem for the Hebrew Bible and the Hebrew language (a respect shared by Luther and others) would gradually morph into some general acceptance of or respect for the practitioners of the Jewish faith, who indeed do cherish both the holy book and the holy language. Such respect created a relatively benevolent attitude toward the Jews with Luther's contemporary Johann Reuchlin. But in this regard Reuchlin was a "rare bird" on the eve of the Reformation in Germany and during its later manifestations. Such transfer and positive attitude from respecting Hebrew books toward contemporaneous Jewish persons (whom Luther called "the new alien Jews," *die newen frembden Juden*) was glaringly absent not only from Luther's mind but also, for instance, from Reuchlin's opponent, i.e., the Catholic author of Jewish descent Johann Pfefferkorn, and their respective supporters. However, Luther never mentioned or openly relied upon Pfefferkorn's works, which had been published between 1507 and 1511.

Luther's literary source was *Der gantz Jüdisch Glaub* (*The Whole Jewish Faith*; see fig. 0.1) of 1530, written by Anthonius Margaritha (Margareta, Margalita, ca. 1490–1542) of Regensburg. By the time Luther was involved with Jewish issues, Pfefferkorn's pamphlets may have been out of print; they evidently had not come to Luther's attention. A comparison between Luther and Pfefferkorn would reveal their congeniality. Luther ladled indirectly from Pfefferkorn insofar as Pfefferkorn's works were the direct source material for Margaritha's book *Der gantz Jüdisch glaub*, from which Luther loved to quote. Here is Margaritha's full title in English translation:

35. WA 53: 450.22—455.38.
36. WA 53: 488.1.

The whole Jewish faith together with a thorough and truthful presentation of all rules, ceremonies, prayers, secret and public customs which the Jews hold throughout the entire year, with beautiful and well-founded arguments against their faith. Described and made public by Anthonius Margaritha, Hebrew lector of the laudable city of Augsburg.

Fig. 0.1. Anthonius Margaritha, *Der gantz Jüdisch Glaub mit sampt ainer gründtlichen vnd warhafften anzaygunge / Aller Satzungen / Ceremonien / Gebetten / Haymliche vnd offenliche Gebreüch / deren sich dye Juden halten / durch das gantz Jar / Mit schönen vnd gegründten Argumenten wyder jren Glauben. Durch Anthonium Margaritham Hebrayschen Leser der Löblichen Statt Augspurg / beschriben vnd an tag gegeben* (Augsburg: Steiner, 1530).

Margaritha is rightly characterized as "Luther's chief witness."[37] Margaritha's book was eagerly excerpted by the Reformer in 1542 for his verbal abuse with which he called for the physical abuse of the Jews. Margaritha actually reused Pfefferkorn's illustrations from *The Jewish Confession* of 1508 in his own book of 1530, *The Whole Jewish Faith*,[38] which Luther highly recommended in 1543 for further information on the devilish practices (*Teufelswerck*) of the Jews.[39] Luther chose to copy abundantly from the anti-Jewish literature of his time. Nobody forced him to do that. Furthermore, he also opted out of collaborating, for instance, with Reuchlin in the attempts of rapprochement of Christians and Jews. Luther apparently ignored Reuchlin's concept of the Jews as fellow citizens with whom one must coexist. Most of all, Luther chose not to follow the law of the Church with respect to the Jews, something Reuchlin had inculcated in his *Expert Opinion* to Emperor Maximilian in 1510:

> One should not burn the books of the Jews and one should persuade them to our faith with rational disputations [*durch vernünfftig disputationen*], gently and kindly [*sennftmuetigklich vnd guettlich*], with the help of God.[40]

In his *Defensio* of 1513 Reuchlin reiterated that one has to love one's neighbor, including the Jews. For this attitude Reuchlin referred to Church law, arguing that he favors the Jews because the Church favors them in the sense that they receive special treatment by not being considered "heretics" and by being tolerated:

> What about the [position of the] Church? Does she not favor the Jews, she who could expel them, but instead tolerates them benignly out of her singular piety (not so with heretics)? ... Also, that they are to be persuaded, not impelled, and that they are to be dealt with "rather with reasoning and kindness in order that they—provoked in this way—want to follow us, not run away from us. In this way we can demonstrate from their books what

---

37. Stephen G. Burnett, "Luther's Chief Witness: Anthonius Margaritha's *Der gantz Jüdisch glaub* (1530/1531)," in Adams and Heß 2017, 183–200.

38. Pfefferkorn's illustrations are shown in Rummel 2002, figs. 2–5. Those pictures were reused by Margaritha, see image nos. 39, 41, 46, 50 in MDZ, http://daten.digitale-sammlungen.de/~db/ausgaben/thumbnailseite.html?fip=193.174.98.30&id=00024581&seite.

39. See below in chapter 4.

40. SW 4-1: 64.7-11; Posset 2015, 360; a slightly different translation is provided by Wortsman 2000, 87.

we say, and convert them, with God's help, to the bosom of Mother Church." So says the Church in her canon *Qui syncera [Codex Iuris Canonici (Decretum Gratiani* I, 45, 3)] and in the canon about the Jews, distinction 45 [*canone de Iudaei Codex Iuris Canonici (Decretum Gratiani* I, 45, 5).[41]

Both Luther and Pfefferkorn ignored Reuchlin in this regard and his hint at the law of the Church concerning the Jews.

There is also a conspicuous political parallel between Pfefferkorn and Luther with respect to the attempts of enlisting ladies of the higher nobility for their anti-Jewish crusades. Pfefferkorn approached Kunigunde of Bavaria (1465-1520) who was Emperor Maximilian's widowed, younger sister, for her assistance in obtaining the imperial *Mandate of Padua* in order to carry out his plan of the destruction of all Jewish books within the empire.[42]

More indirect in his approach than Pfefferkorn, Luther thought of Mary Queen of Hungary and Bohemia (1505-1558), to whom he dedicated one of his booklets in 1526, titled "Four Comforting Psalms Addressed to the Queen of Hungary."[43] In his commentary on Psalm 109, the last of the four psalms of comfort, which is basically a prayer of a person falsely accused, Luther took the opportunity to attack the betrayer of Christ, i.e., Judas, and his people, the Jews: "David composed this psalm about Christ, who speaks the entire psalm in the first person against Judas, his betrayer, and against Jewry/Judaism as a whole [*widder das gantze Juedenthum*], proclaiming their ultimate fate."[44] Luther is convinced that Jews cannot be converted because their stubbornness has become part of their nature (*es ist zur natur worden*).[45] Jewry/Judaism (*das Juedenthum*), as we call the Jewish people (*das Juedische volk*), will not (cannot) be converted.[46]

In the given historical context of the early sixteenth century, it remains conspicuous that not all sympathizers of Luther at that time joined in Luther's anti-Jewish tirades. They may not even have been aware of his hate of the Jews, especially not during the early years of the Reformation. They, including Luther's sympathizers who remained Catholic, preferred

---

41. SW 4-1: 338.24—340.10; Posset 2015, 463-64.
42. Posset 2015, 313-14.
43. *Vier tröstliche Psalmen an die Königin von Ungarn*, WA 19: 542-615.
44. WA 19: 595.4-7 (on Ps 109:8).
45. WA 19: 606.21—607.5 (on Ps 109:18).
46. WA 19: 608.30-31 (on Ps 109:19).

to focus, and together with Luther, on the proclamation of the Evangelical Truth (*evangelica veritas*).[47]

All the more is one tasked today to differentiate and to bring out the contrast between the spokesmen of proto-antisemitism, such as Pfefferkorn, Margaritha, and Luther on the one side, and some of their less known contemporaries on the other side who respected the Jews (i.e., Reuchlin and others who are featured in chapter 4). They demonstrate at times a remarkable esteem for the Jews, their Bible, and the Hebrew language. Their respect for the Jews is intimately connected to their respect for the Word of God in the Scriptures as, for instance, Reuchlin told the emperor in his *Expert Opinion* of 1510: "I do not know of any other nation on this earth that takes greater pains to faithfully spell the Sacred Scriptures than do the Jews."[48] Such respect for the Jews and their sacred Scriptures was admired by Reuchlin, whereas Luther rejected such a connection since he held the Word of God high, but not the Jews as the transmitters of the Word of God in the Scriptures.

In order to better appreciate the respect for the Jews by a minority in the early sixteenth century, it is necessary, here, to point out the overpowering disrespect for the Jews (to put it mildly) by men like Luther, Pfefferkorn, and Margaritha (the latter, as said, as Luther's source). Connected with Luther's and others' disrespect is their lack of any self-critical examination of conscience with respect to their own position toward the Jews.[49] Such disrespect has to form for us the dark backdrop against which authors like Reuchlin brightly stand out.

Luther's attitude toward his contemporary Jews is still upsetting today, but is nevertheless a part of the portrait of the historical Luther. In a way, then, this collection of studies wants to be understood not only as a companion volume to my book *Johann Reuchlin* (2015), but also to *The Real Luther* (2011) in which—with its focus on the young Luther—the topic of the elder Luther's repulsive attitude toward the Jews was not treated. Much

---

47. Posset 2015c.

48. SW 4-1: 55.24–26; Posset 2015, 343, 353.

49. Bernhard Lohse, an eminent Luther scholar, meritoriously pointed out: "What is absent here in Luther is the self-critical question as to whether the picture he was drawing of the Jewish religion actually applied." In Lohse 2011, with an excursus at the end of his book: "Luther's Attitude toward the Jews," here 345. However, Lohse simultaneously and unfortunately excused Luther as a child of his time: "Luther did not subject his judgements [about the Jews] to critical examination. In this regard, he was captive to the views of his time" (ibid).

has been written about a contrast between the young and the old Luther's attitude toward the Jews.[50] After examining the source material, one must conclude, however, that there was little change and no major developments in Luther's view of postbiblical Jews. Rather, his aversion against them went from bad to worse.

The present volume 4 of my *Collected Works* is issued now with the picture shown on its book cover that depicts synagogue and church as study partners—hopefully to the pleasant surprise of the onlooker. The volume is offered in the spirit of Pope Francis's statement at the occasion of the blessing of this sculpture in Philadelphia:

> Dialogue and friendship with the Jewish people are part of the life of Jesus' disciples. There exists between us a rich complementarity that allows us to read the texts of the Hebrew Scriptures together and to help one another mine the riches of God's word.[51]

---

50. For a recent example, see Mansch and Peters 2016, 200, 305–9.

51. Quoted from "Synagoga and Ecclesia in Our Time," Institute for Islamic, Christian, Jewish Studies, https://icjs.org/%E2%80%9Csynagoga-and-ecclesia-our-time%E2%80%9D.

1

A Fifteenth-Century Bible Codex in Hebrew with a Picture of the Crucifixion and with Two Monastic Figures, Saint Dominic and Saint Bernard

Fig. 1.1. First full-page miniature with historiated Hebrew initial ב (*bet*) in the Hebrew Bible; fifteenth century. Florence.

Fig. 1.2. Detail with the historiated initial ב (*bet*), with two names added in Latin. The monastic figure on the right in a white cowl, although called S. Thomas (Aquinas), is Bernard of Clairvaux. The figure on the left is St. Dominic.

A FIFTEENTH-CENTURY BIBLE CODEX IN HEBREW

THE PURPOSE OF THIS study is to unfold a mix of motifs in a picture on parchment on the first page of a complete Bible that is written in Hebrew letters[1] and to figure out the possible *Sitz im Leben* and the wider historical context in which such a miniature could come into existence. The miniature is one of the most unusual Christian book illuminations, first of all because it is found in a Hebrew Bible in which even the New Testament is included in Hebrew. This manuscript may actually be the only Bible written in Hebrew letters that shows a Christian depiction on the opening page. The codex belonged to the Dominican friary in Fiesole, near Florence, dated the fifteenth century. This friary was the home of Fra Angelico (ca. 1395–1455) before he transferred to the Dominican friary in Florence; but the miniature may not be the famous friar's.[2] Second, equally strange is the inclusion of the figure of Saint Bernard of Clairvaux in a Bible of the Dominican order.

This oddity was confusing already to a later Dominican user of this Bible who tried to identify the figure in white with Saint Thomas of the Dominican order, as he added the name of Saint Thomas in the caption (fig. 2), mistakenly as we shall see. For the unwrapping of the elements displayed in this miniature the close relationship between spirituality and iconography has to be taken into consideration.

1. The Historiated Hebrew Initial B

The opening picture is the historiated initial of the Hebrew letter ב ("B," *bet*) (fig. 1.3) for בראשית (*bereshit*, "In the beginning") which is the first word of the Hebrew Bible, Gen 1:1. The Hebrew wording of Gen 1:1 is continued in the right column (Hebrew is read from right to left) comprising seven lines, then continued in the left column with also seven lines.

---

1. MS Conv. Sopp. 268, folio 1r, with a total of 317 folios; present location: Bibliotheca Medicea Laurenziana, Florence; first published in 1990 in *Bernardo di Chiaravalle nell'arte italiana dal XIV al XVII seculo*, ed. Laura Dal Prà (Milan: Electa, 1990), fig. 123; France 2007, no. MA267; Hammer 2009, 316–17.

2. Hammer 2009, 316.

The Hebrew Letter B

Fig. 1.3. The Hebrew letter B (bet) (left). The main scene is contained within the letter B (right).

Fig. 1.4. Five empty roundels in the baseline of the Hebrew letter B indicate the incompleteness of the miniature.

Fig. 1.5. The upper five finished roundels with images of creation story according to Gen 1 and 2. (Note: the color of the creator's garment changes from brown and blue working clothes to regal red for the Sabbath rest).

A FIFTEENTH-CENTURY BIBLE CODEX IN HEBREW

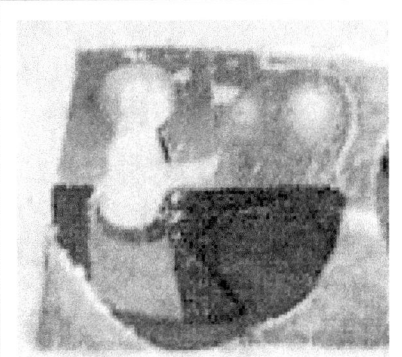

Fig. 1.6. First Roundel: Gen 1:1–5. The roundel is distorted; from chaos to cosmos. The first day of creation.

Fig. 1.7. Second Roundel: Gen 1:6–13. The second and third day of creation: water and sky; dry land with vegetation, water flowing at the feet of the creator.

Fig. 1.8. Third Roundel with the Crucified directly under it. Gen 1:14–31. The fourth day: light coming in from the right side. Below: Christ Crucified, the light of the world.

 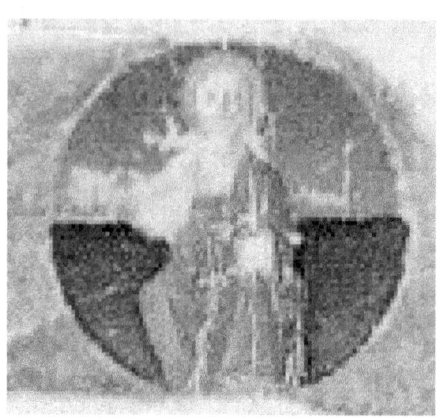

| Fig. 1.9. Fourth Roundel: Gen 1:28–31. The fifth and sixth day: The Creator blesses creation. | Fig. 1.10. Fifth Roundel: Gen 2:1–3. The Seventh Day: Sabbath Rest. |

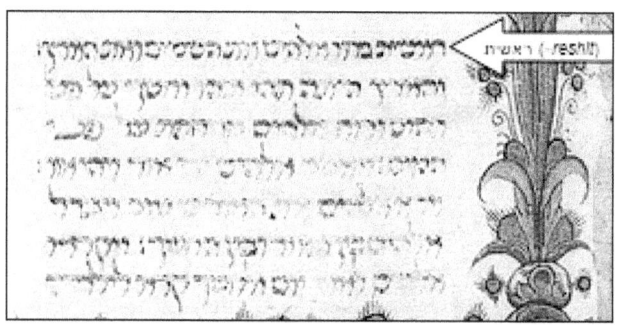

Fig. 1.11. *[B]ereshit*: the first Hebrew word of the book of Genesis.

A concise description of the image is offered by James France: "Fifteenth-century Hebrew Bible with an opening image of the Crucifixion by a Florentine miniaturist, with the Virgin on the left and St John Evangelist on the right, and, kneeling below them, St Dominic and Bernard."[3] It is a full-page illustration that depicts in its upper part the known motif "The Crucifixion with Mary and John." At the foot of the cross, a skull is exposed which may be seen also in the Crucifixion by Fra Angelico or in the Florentine fresco of the School of Pietro Perugino (1506), at the Cistercian Abbey Cestello (now

---

3. France 2007, no. MA267 (showing only the miniature, i.e., a detail of the complete page). Hammer 2009, 316–17, provides the full page.

Santa Maria Maddelena dei Pazzi, Chapter House) (see fig. 1.13),[4] and as such it is not unusual for images of the crucifixion. This aspect in crucifixion images denotes the medieval legend that Christ's cross was actually placed upon the grave of Adam.[5]

Mary and John are standing under the cross in the traditional positions within an elaborate landscape. Untraditional is John's gesture. He holds his right hand to his cheek or chin—a hint for resting or sleeping. The artist may have wanted to evoke the association and the reminder that John being the Beloved Disciple had rested at Christ's side at the Last Supper. John's conspicuous gesture is shown in a similar way in an Austrian fresco of ca. 1480 as part of "The Crucifixion with Mary and John" into which the *Amplexus Bernardi* is incorporated.[6]

Two monastic figures kneel at the feet of Mary and John. At first sight one notices the Latin caption for the illustration referring to the kneeling figures assumed to be two Dominican friars, *S. Dominic[us]* (left) and *S. Thomas* (right), even though the color of their cowls differs and would indicate two different religious orders (fig. 1.2). The Latin caption was definitely added at a later time by a less learned Dominican brother.[7] The illumination does, indeed, show Saint Dominic (1170–1221) on the left. But the figure on the right is mistakenly identified as Saint Thomas. In reality it is Saint Bernard (1090–1153), who is recognizable by the white cowl, which is Bernard's attribute.

The basic composition of the miniature is the traditional motif of "The Crucifixion with Mary and John." Mixed into this composition are two other motifs: (a) Saint Dominic under the cross, and (b) Saint Bernard under the cross. The figure of Dominic appears as if cut and pasted into the basic composition of the crucifixion scene because he kneels outside the "frame" within which Bernard is placed. Dominic's placement may be indicative of an originally separate motif/composition that was "copied" for and integrated into the miniature here. The depiction of Dominic under the

---

4. France 2007, no. WA22; see also no. DR18, and no. WA22; Dal Pra 2007, no. 20 (painted by Sperandino di Giovanni, 1506). The sinopia for this fresco is reproduced in Posset, *Amplexus Catalogue*, no. 45.

5. Entry "Skull," in Diane Apostolos-Cappadona, *Dictionary of Christian Art* (New York: Continuum, 1994), 308.

6. *In situ* at the Cistercian abbey of Rein in Styria, Austria; see *Amplexus Catalogue*, no. 19.

7. Hammer 2009, 316.

cross is well known from Fra Angelico's "Calvary with Saint Dominic"[8] and his fresco titled "Saint Dominic Adoring the Crucifixion" (fig. 1.13).

Fig. 1.12. Saint Dominic Adoring the Crucifixion. Detail from Hebrew Bible (Fig. 1.1).

Fig. 1.13. Saint Dominic, Adoring the Crucifixion, by Fra Angelico. San Marco Museum, Florence.

There is general consensus that in the miniature the figure on the right is Saint Bernard. In the following we focus primarily on the Bernard figure in trying to come up with an explanation as to why Bernard was entered into this particular picture. We must refrain from a detailed consideration of the entire page that includes in the lower, decorated border a roundel with the Man of Sorrows with a crown of thorns, standing in a sarcophagus.[9] Also unexplained must go a series of five unfinished roundels (below the miniature) which form the base line of the Hebrew letter ב.

---

8. The painting is reproduced, for instance, in *Dictionary of Christian Art*, fig. 64.

9. On this motif, see *New Perspectives on the Man of Sorrows*, ed. Catherine R. Puglisi and William L. Barcham. This book focuses, however, primarily on Venice.

Fig. 1.14. Saint Bernard Adoring the Crucifixion. Detail from Hebrew Bible (fig. 1.1).

Fig. 1.15. *Amplexus Bernardi*, with skull under the cross. Fresco attributed to the School of Pietro Perugino, early sixteenth century. Florence, Cistercian Abbey.

In our miniature Bernard's body posture is distinct from Dominic's, whose hands appear to be folded in adoration. Dominic is looking up to the Crucified. The picture shows eye contact not only between Dominic and the Crucified, but also between Dominic and John. Mary, too, looks at John or gazes in his direction. When considering who is looking at whom, Bernard's figure is the odd man out as he does not look at anybody and nobody is looking at him. Bernard has his head bowed and with his halfway open arms is ready either to prostrate before the crucifix, or more likely, to point with his hands toward Christ while still humbly holding down his head as he is about to get up in order to receive the embrace of the Crucified. The manner in which Bernard is shown is a hint at the fact that there is a motif incorporated into this scene that had its own independent existence in the history of the Bernard iconography. The way the Bernard figure is positioned may very well depict a moment prior to the "Embrace by the Crucified" and thus it would represent an aspect of the *Amplexus Bernardi* motif.[10] The story of the Embrace is told in *Vita S. Bernardi*: Bernard, who is prostrated before a crucifix in front of an altar, is being embraced and enfolded by the Crucified, who has taken his hands off the crossbeam.[11] He has no crown of thorns, just like it is shown in some of the earliest *Amplexus* images.[12]

What we see in this Florentine miniature is not the *Amplexus* because Christ at that moment is not looking at Bernard and his hands remain nailed to the beam, whereas in the *Amplexus* images the Crucified would have taken one or both arms off the crossbeam in order to embrace Bernard. Nevertheless, the miniature is inspired by the Cistercian, Bernardine cross-centered spirituality, at least as far as the incorporation of the Bernard-figure into "The Crucifixion with Mary and John" is concerned. That the typical, explicit *Amplexus* motif could not have been mixed into the present picture may have something to do with the fact that in fifteenth-century Florence the *Amplexus* motif was not known at all. The first Italian *Amplexus Bernardi* picture would not arrive in Florence until 1506.[13] But apparently, by the fifteenth century, when the miniature in the Hebrew Bible under consideration here was produced, Bernard's cross-centered spirituality had become known in Florence alongside the cross-centered spirituality of the Dominican order of which the figure of Saint Dominic under the cross gives witness.

2. Open Questions

Since this Hebrew Bible is a manuscript, it may have come into existence before any prints of Hebrew Bibles were available in the second half of the fifteenth century; for example in 1488, when the *Biblia Hebraica* was printed by the Soncino Press in Italy.[14] The Jewish community in Florence

10. The origins of this motif and its dissemination in the late Middles Ages is studied in Posset 1998, 289–314.

11. *Amplexus Catalogue*, 251.

12. Out of sixty-two artistic representations that were studied in my *Amplexus Catalogue*, a few depict the Crucified without the crown of thorns, in particular the earliest two manuscript illuminations (no. 1 and no. 2).

13. *Amplexus Catalogue*, no. 45.

14. The first complete Hebrew Bible was published by Joshua Solomon ben Israel Soncino at the Soncino Press in 1488. Between two hundred and three hundred copies were printed. Johann Reuchlin purchased a copy in Rome in 1492 for six gold coins, a year's salary for a government clerk.

was formally founded in 1437. The following questions arise: Was this Bible produced in this historical situation, perhaps of the first half of the fifteenth century? Was it used for dialogue or for polemic between Christians and Jews? In the fifteenth century, two developments came together (in following Eugenio Garin [1909–2004]): (a) The number of Jews in Italy increased, who taught Hebrew to Christian scholars; (b) The number of Jews who became Christians also increased.[15] Is the miniature part and product of a "convert culture"? Is the Hebrew Bible with the Christian miniature a product of these developments? A more precise date for the coming into existence of this Bible would be most helpful.

Was this Bible used for the purpose of Christian missions to the Jews—locally or nationally, or internationally? Was this Bible written by Jews who were commissioned by the Dominicans? Or, were there capable Dominican friars (perhaps converts) who were skilled to write the Bible in Hebrew? Were other Jewish converts to the Christian faith involved in the production of this Bible? Since the Medici family of Florence was closely linked to the Jews of Florence, did this family have anything to do with the funding and production of this luxurious Bible?

The time period under the early Medici rule was marked not only by relative calm, but also by intense cultural exchanges between Hebrew and Christian scholars. In 1477 Lorenzo the Magnificent (1449–1492) prevented an attempt to expel the Jews from the city, which had resulted from anti-Jewish feelings aroused by some preacher of the Franciscan order. Lorenzo protected the Jewish community.

At the Medici court there was Giovanni Pico della Mirandola (1463–1494), a young religious humanist, who was interested in the Jewish Cabala and its usefulness for Christian theology. At that same court one also finds for a certain period of time a Sicilian scholar of Jewish decent by the name Flavius Mithridates (Wilhelmus Raymundus Romanus, ca. 1450–ca. 1490).[16] During his first journey to Italy, in spring 1482, the German Count Eberhard of Württemberg (1445–1496), who was accompanied by the Christian Hebraist and later defender of Jewish books Johann Reuchlin, was received by Lorenzo de' Medici in Florence. During his second journey through Italy in 1490 Reuchlin visited with the mentioned Pico in Florence. Reuchlin felt confident when in 1491/1492 he sent his younger brother,

15. Garin 1996, 361–83.
16. Idel 2011, 192–95.

Dionysius, to Florence for study purposes. Evidently, this city was conducive to what he wanted his brother to learn and soak up.[17]

As said, the Christian miniature with the historiated initial B (*bet*) is unique with respect to its incorporation into a Bible codex that was written entirely in Hebrew. The additional question arises: Is there a connection between the Cabalistic speculations (made popular in Florence) concerning the Hebrew Letter B and the miniature under review here? What is the Cabalistic interpretation of this letter? Part of an answer to this question relies on Rabbi Menachem Recanati (around 1300), an Italian Cabalist and commentator of the Pentateuch. He saw the letter *bet*, which follows *alef* (the first letter of the Hebrew alphabet), as the cause of all things: "You will find that this letter [i.e., *bet*] makes/creates everything." This sentence, by the way, is quoted by Reuchlin in his *Art of the Cabala*, book 3.[18]

Furthermore, Pico della Mirandola offered this philosophical-cabalistic interpretation of Gen 1:1 (*bereshit*): "In the beginning the Father in the Son, through the Son as the beginning, the repose and the end, created the head of the fire and the foundation of the great human being with a good covenant."[19] The Son is "head" or "beginning" or principle of the world and simultaneously the life and foundation of the good covenant. Thus, the first word of Genesis contains a cabalistic-christological message,[20] which is unfolded in salvation history including the crucifixion as shown in the miniature.

3. The Miniature in the Historical Context of the Bernard Iconography, the Civic Cult of Bernard in Florence, and of the "Bernard Renaissance"

Why would the Bernard-figure be included in the picture? Is the exceptional Florentine miniature in the Hebrew Bible a fruit of this Bernard revival? First of all, it is a very rare occurrence that a depiction of Bernard is found in a medieval Bible edition, and in a Hebrew one at that. There is only one medieval *Latin* Bible codex, known as the *Paris Bible*, dated second half of

---

17. Posset 2015, 60–70, 93–98.

18. SW 2-1: 438.1–4.

19. *In principio pater in filio / per filium principium quies et finis creavit caput ignis et fundamentum magni hominis foedere bono*; Giovanni Pico, *Heptaplus*, ed. Garin 1942, 378–79.

20. Black 2006, 215–16.

the thirteenth century, which contains an illumination that likely depicts Saint Bernard, but as the expositor of the creation story.[21]

Those two Bibles, the Hebrew and the Latin edition, are the exception to the rule according to which the Bernard images are found primarily in liturgical books and breviaries of the Cistercian order, or, at times, in "commentaries" on biblical books.[22] In a manuscript titled *Commentarius in Apocalypsin* from England, ca. 1243, Bernard does appear, but in the company of other abbots and monks.[23] This "Commentary on the Apocalypse" of the Franciscan friar Alexander has a description of the foundation of Cîteaux, the early growth of the Order and of the role of Bernard in its expansion. In the group of the abbots, Bernard may be the second from the left who, according to tradition, had a short beard.[24]

The depiction of Bernard as a teacher or preacher[25] can be expected in editions of Bernard's own "commentaries," i.e., his famous sermons about the Song of Songs, in one case holding a distinctly red book.[26] One may also see a full-page miniature in a Florentine codex of ca. 1474–1480, titled *Commentarium super Cantica Canticorum*, showing the Virgin Mary, who dictates something that Bernard writes down as he is sitting at a stone desk, with a pen in his right hand (the *Dottrina* motif, see below).[27] Having said this, one may conclude that in medieval Bible editions the Bernard figure is rarely shown.

Thus, the fact that Saint Bernard appears in a Florentine late medieval Hebrew Bible is further food for thought, and it leads to the investigation of the theme of "Bernard and Florence." One wonders whether the "Bernard Renaissance"[28] blossomed also in late medieval Florence. The "Bernard

21. The unusual initial in the book of Genesis is a seven-part illustration of the creation. This Bible ended up in the German abbey of Eberbach; see France 2007, no. MA050; Hammer 2009, 234–35.

22. The concept of "commentary" in medieval and also in later times is vague; Hagen 2016, 13–38.

23. Hammer 2009, 146–47.

24. France 2007, no. MA058.

25. Hammer 2009, 212–13; 216–17; 218–19; 224–25; 238–39; 240–41; 242–43; 246–47; 248–49. Hammer's entire chapter 4 is dedicated to pictorial representations of Saint Bernard in editions of his works, 169–299; especially in editions of *On Consideration*.

26. France 2007, no. MA244; Hammer 2009, 68–69.

27. France 2007, no. MA243; Hammer 2009, 372–73.

28. Bernd Hamm, who coined the expression "Bernard Renaissance" as the result of his studies in late medieval spirituality, Hamm 1982, 193.

Renaissance" is known as a historical-spiritual period in late medieval Germany (which also impacted Martin Luther).[29] Is the exceptional Florentine miniature in the Hebrew Bible a fruit of this Bernard revival? This appears to be the case, since depictions of Bernard abound in late medieval and Renaissance Florence,[30] whereas, generally, Bernard had a relatively low profile in Italy.[31] One simple explanation for Bernard's popularity is that he is one of the four patron saints of Florence, besides John the Baptist, Victor, and Zenobius.[32] But how can one explain that specifically this French Cisterican monk became one of Florence's patron saints?[33] There are four plausible reasons:

First, Bernard had early on intervened in favor of the Italian Pope Innocent II during the schism of Anaclete, an act that turned Bernard into a man of international significance. Second, a legend of unknown origin was in circulation according to which Bernard was supposed to have composed a letter which teaches how to live (*Dottrina del vivere*), also known as Letter to Raymond. The pseudo-Bernardine text was illustrated by the Florentine Rustici[34] as it had enhanced Saint Bernard's fame as a spiritual director to laypersons (see below with respect to the other drawings by the Florentine goldsmith Rustici). Bernard's authentic letters and treatises had made him already the advisor of rulers who had consulted him for guidance on public affairs. This may have been the case also for the leaders in the city-state of Florence.

This brings us to the third reason for the high esteem of Saint Bernard not only in Florence but in all of Italy: It is due to the impact of Bernard's five books *On Consideration* in the late Middle Ages, including its influence on Dante Alighieri (1265–ca. 1321), Petrarch, Marsilius of Padua, and Egidio of Rome.[35] Fourth, the Cistercians were represented around and in

---

29. Theo Bell 1993; Posset 1999/2018.

30. Alison Luchs, *Cestello: A Cistercian Church of the Florentine Renaissance* (New York: Garland, 1977) 111–12; A. Luchs, "Alive and Well in Florence: Thriving Cistercians in Renaissance Italy," *Cîteaux* 30 (1979) 109–24; Goffredo Viti, *San Bernardo e i Cistercensi in Umria* (Florence: Certose di Firenze: 1995).

31. France 2007, 249.

32. France 2007, 251. I am grateful to Theo Bell for hints on Bernard and Florence.

33. Melinda Kay Lesher, "St. Bernard of Clairvaux and the Republic of Florence in the Late Middle Ages," *Cîteaux* 35 (1984) 258–67.

34. France 2007, 250.

35. Lesher, 264; France 2007, 250.

the city; i.e., since 1236 in Settimo.[36] One of the monks of Settimo even had a seat on the city council of Florence. He was the only cleric among the four city leaders; the other three were laymen.[37] In this milieu in and around Florence it is not all too surprising then that the "civic cult of Bernard in Florence"[38] could emerge. The city administration was located in the Palazzo della Signora (now called Palazzo Vecchio) with the Chapel of the Priors. The cornerstone of this chapel was laid on the feast day of Saint Bernard in 1298 and was dedicated to him. An altarpiece was painted in 1486 by Filippino Lippi (ca.1457–1504): The Virgin is enthroned with the Child on her knee. She is flanked by John the Baptist and Victor on the left, and Zenobius and Bernard on the right, i.e., the patron saints of Florence.[39]

Of the greatest influence in Florence had been Dante. He shaped the image of Bernard as a teacher about the Virgin Mary with the famous prayer of Bernard in Canto 33 of the *Divine Comedy*, and he was of influence on the unique iconographic motif invented in Florence: *La Dottrina*, i.e., Bernard receiving his wisdom from the Virgin Mary, or *The Vision of Mary*. In *La Dottrina* Bernard has a vision of the Virgin (depicted without the Child), as Bernard sits or kneels while simultaneously writing.[40] This motif has no basis in any specific literal source. It is the creation of the Florentines. *La Dottrina* is "unrecorded anywhere else in Europe."[41]

A wider knowledge about Bernard at that time was based primarily on the various stories in *The Golden Legend*, which is the most likely literary source for non-Cistercian persons seeking information about Bernard. In this tradition, Bernard as a devotee of Mary is fostered, especially in the chapter on "The Ascension of the Lord,"[42] whereby this particular passage is based upon a pseudo-Bernardine concept of intercession before God the Father.[43] The visual expression of Bernard as venerator of Mary is

36. Luchs, *Cestello: A Cistercian Church of the Florentine Renaissance*.

37. Lesher, 265.

38. France 2007, 251, 252.

39. France 2007, 251, no. PA148.

40. France 2007, nos. PA119, PA155, PA160, MA012, MA243, MA266.

41. There are 32 *La Dottrina* images. Only eight of them are from before ca. 1450; France 2007, 253.

42. *The Golden Legend*, trans. William Granger Ryan, 2 vols. (Princeton: Princeton University Press, 1993), 1:298; Steven Botterill, *Dante and the Mystical Tradition: Bernard of Clairvaux in the* Commedia (Cambridge: Cambridge University Press, 1994), 124–28; France 2007, 240–41.

43. Posset 1999/2018, 310–14. The source of the concept is Ernald of Bonneval

found, for example, in the Florentine fresco of 1496 by Pietro Perugino (ca. 1450–1523) which shows the crucifixion with several figures including the Virgin standing on the left and Bernard kneeling beside her.[44]

All this fits well with the overarching and comprehensive emergence of the "Bernard Renaissance" in late medieval Europe, a phenomenon that thus can be evidenced first for Florence in the fourteenth century (with Dante in particular) and further on, from the fifteenth-century in the Christian art world, including the painting by Fra Filippino Lippi titled *The Vision of Saint Bernard*. The painting was commissioned for a chapel in the Benedictine church of Le Campora outside the city walls. Another indicator for the "Bernard Renaissance" in Florence is the fresco in the chapter room of the Cistercian Cestello abbey (now Santa Maria Maddalena dei Pazzi) with the first Italian *Amplexus Bernardi* picture which thus finally had arrived in 1506 in Florence,[45] after a long history of development of this particular motif that can be traced from ca. 1340 in a Cistercian monastery for women in southwest Germany (Wonnental).[46]

Further evidence for the "Bernard Renaissance" comes from the numerous Florentine book illuminations in which Saint Bernard is celebrated. In Gabriel Hammer's eminent collection of medieval European book illustrations one finds numerous miniatures which show Bernard and which have an immediate connection to Florence. In the Cistercian *Graduale Sanctorum*, dated ca. 1315–1335, one of the earliest pictorial representations of Bernard in Florentine book illustrations is found. It shows Bernard with the Holy Spirit in the form of a dove.[47] Another early Florentine image is the one in a manuscript of Bernard's sermons on the Song of Songs: Bernard preaches to monks.[48] The same sermons were copied in Florence at the beginning of the fifteenth century and were adorned with an initial with the same motif of Bernard preaching to monks.[49]

The Florentine Bernard-pictures are not necessarily always of direct Cistercian provenance, but nevertheless most likely influenced by Cistercian spirituality that was present in the Cistercian houses in the region.

(= Arnold of Chartres, d. 1156).

44. France 2007, no. WA28.
45. *Amplexus Catalogue*, no. 45.
46. *Amplexus Catalogue*, no. 1.
47. For examples, see Hammer 2009, 182–83.
48. Hammer 2009, 240–41.
49. Hammer 2009, 246–47.

However, Cistercians in Florence were not the only ones who highly esteemed Saint Bernard and his spirituality and sermons. He was revered also by Florentine laymen and monastic women and men of other orders. However, the two most popular motifs of the Bernard-iconography, the *Lactatio Bernardi* and the *Amplexus Bernardi*, never emerged in late medieval, Florentine book illuminations. The only Florentine *Amplexus* is the fresco of 1506, as said. The following samples of miniatures demonstrate the dissemination of Bernardine/Cistercian works and motifs among Cistercians and non-Cistercians in Florence:

1. The Florentine goldsmith Marco di Bartholommeo Rustici (ca. 1392-1457) wrote and illustrated his manuscript named after him *Codex Rustici* (1447–1448). He drew three Bernard-related pictures. One depicts Bernard's Christmas vision which refers to the story of young Bernard in the *Vita Prima* hagiography[50] The *Codex Rustici* contains Marco's memoirs of his pilgrimage to the Holy Land.[51] Two scenes in the margin are explained by the text below them. On the left a nimbed Bernard is seated and hands a letter to a monk who stands in front of him. The text below in red ink deals with Bernard giving a letter to Raymond.[52] In the third drawing Bernard is kneeling at a desk at which he is writing in an open book. He looks up to the Virgin who appears in a mandorla in a cloud.[53]

2. At about 1474–1480 the Florentine *Commentarium super Cantica canticorum* is being graced with a full-page miniature of the Virgin's apparition to Bernard. However, the book is not commissioned by Cistercians but by the art-lover Duke Federigo da Montefeltro (1422–1482) who financed the production of numerous illuminated books.[54] In the opposite folio (8r) of that codex there is a magnificent border by Francesco d'Antonio del Cherico (d. 1484) or his Florentine school, with figures of the same duke and a very ornate initial "V" that shows Bernard holding a red book.[55]

---

50. France 2007, no. DR14.
51. Hammer 2009, 124–25; France 2007, 250, see also nos. DR14 and DR16.
52. France 2007, no. DR15.
53. France 2007, no. DR16.
54. France 2007, no. MA243; Hammer 2009, 372–73.
55. France 2007, no. MA244; Hammer 2009, 68–69.

3. At about the same time (1475–1477) an Augustinian friar by the name of Domenico Scarperia of the friary of Santo Spirito translated Bernard's *Sermones de tempore* and *Sermones de sanctis* into the vernacular. The final version of the codex was finished in about 1481. In it a miniature in the initial "B" shows the Virgin appearing to Bernard in the library.[56]

4. Other Florentine codices are extant from the fifteenth century, including the *Hymnarium cisterciense* of 1440–1450 with a miniature of the Virgin appearing to Bernard.[57]

5. Notably, Bernard's *Sermones in psalmum "Qui habitat"* were translated into Italian in ca. 1485, decorated with the same motif of the Virgin's apparition, but enhanced by the inclusion of a devil next to Bernard's desk.[58]

6. In the first quarter of the sixteenth century the same motif of the Virgin appearing to Bernard who sits at his desk emerges in a manuscript of an Italian translation of Bernard's Advent sermons for the Franciscan monastery for women in Florence, written by Sister Ubia Dimano, who dated its completion with March 6, 1525.[59] The pictorial representation of Bernard and the Virgin Mary apparently had become popular also in Florence's non-Cistercian circles of the second half of the fifteenth century.

7. The spiritual director for the Cistercian nuns of the abbey San Donato in Polverosa (Florence), by the name of Romolo, who was a Cistercian monk, translated Bernard's seventeen sermons on the psalm *Qui habitat* (Ps 90) into the vernacular in 1546. The codex is adorned with a full-page illumination in which Bernard recommends Sister Caritas (who arranged the production of the codex) to the Virgin who appears in the clouds with Baby Jesus.[60]

Since we have no precise date for the Hebrew Bible with the miniature that includes Saint Bernard, it is impossible to correlate it to any of the book

---

56. France 2007, no. MA271; Hammer 2009, 378–79.

57. Hammer 2009, 370–71; for the same motif see also Hammer 2009, 384–85 (a *Breviarium cisrterciense* of ca. 1460–1470); 382–83 (of the end of the fifteenth century).

58. Hammer 2009, 374–75.

59. France 2007, no. MA077; Hammer 2009, 380–81.

60. Hammer 2009, 482–83.

illuminations just mentioned. Nevertheless, from the study of late medieval Florentine book illuminations that were created for vernacular editions of Bernard's sermons one can confirm that there was, indeed, a "Bernard Renaissance" in Florence, which made an impression not only on the religious orders in the area, including the Benedictines, Augustinians, Franciscans, and the Dominicans (who in the title page of their Hebrew Bible included Saint Bernard under the cross), but also in lay circles. The "Bernard Renaissance" was thus not just a phenomenon within the monastic tradition of the Cistercian order, but was a respectable phenomenon outside Cistercian walls. Not only were Bernard and his works, including pseudo-Bernardine ones, highly esteemed in the territory of Florence, by both male and female religious orders, and most significantly, also by laypeople, but he was popular also across the Alps, in German-speaking lands, as is known from the widespread use of Bernard's works in religious and lay circles alike, especially in the late fifteenth and early sixteenth century. The popularity of Bernard's cross-centered spirituality showed its precipitate most clearly through the dissemination of the Bernard-iconography outside the Cistercian order at that time.[61] This cross-centered spirituality had entered also into the fifteenth-century miniature of the Hebrew Bible of the Florentine Dominicans, even though it was Bernard's Marian devotion that may have dominated the "civic cult of Bernard" in Florence. All in all, the miniature under consideration here is a combination of at least three motifs: "The Crucifixion with Mary and John," "Saint Dominic Adoring the Crucified," and St. Bernard prostrated before the Crucified who will embrace him. There is no doubt that the entry of the name of Saint Thomas was mistaken and that Saint Bernard is the proper identification in this miniature.

---

61. Demonstrated for the *Amplexus* motif in Posset, *Amplexus Catalogue*, with sixty-two artistic representations, a number which J. France increased to seventy-two (in 2007) and which still will increase as research on it continues. Another colored woodcut of the *Amplexus Bernardi* came to my attention which is included in a gospel book of 1516, published in Basel: *Das Plenarium oder Ewangely buoch*.

2

Who Is "the Strongest and Most Skilled Protector of This Oppressed Language"?[1]

Or, The Jews, Their Sacred Language, and the Holy Name of God in the Eyes of Johann Reuchlin (1455–1522)

LET ME START WITH a commemoration of the persecution of the Jews in Breslau/Wroclaw in the fifteenth century. This event is mentioned during the sixteenth-century controversy between Johann Reuchlin (1455–1522) and Johann Pfefferkorn (1469–1521); in Pfefferkorn's letter of 1516 to the archbishop of Cologne, Hermann von Wied (1477–1552). In it five locations were listed of alleged incidents of desecrations of communion hosts and its horrible consequences for the accused Jews: at Bratislavia (*sic*; i.e., Breslau in Silesia; today Wroclaw, Poland; in 1453), Passau on the Danube (in 1477), Sternberg (in 1492), Berlin (in 1510), and the earliest one listed for Deggendorf (in 1336).[2]

---

1. *De Capnione quid attinet referre, quem totus orbis, ut linguae huius oppressae vindicem fortissimum iuxta ac peritissimum sucipit, colit, amat?* (Böning 2004, 100).

2. The letter to the archbishop is printed in Pfefferkorn's *Defensio*, image nos. 6–9; Posset 2015, 303. With respect to the persecution in Breslau/Wraclaw, see *De persecutione Iudaeorum Vratislaviensium a[nno] 1453*, http://www.geschichtsquellen.de/repOpus_01961; Rubin 1999/2004, 119–26, https://books.google.com/books?id=rhvmCdXXsSQC&q=breslau#v=onepage&q=wroclaw&f=false; Joldersma, 15–16; Dinzelbacher 2013, 163–78; Mühle 2015, 108. With respect to the case of Berlin 1510, see Mende 2011.

Reuchlin may not have been aware of the persecution at Breslau as it had occurred a few years prior to his birth.³

The Hebraist Reuchlin was well known in Breslau through Ambrosius Moibanus (Mecodiphrus or Moyben, 1494–1554) who was born and died in Breslau, an early Lutheran scholar. Moibanus wrote that Dr. Johann Reuchlin is unjustly being defamed by the enthusiasts (*Schwärmer*) as a heretic and as the father of all heresy because he brought the holy language (Hebrew) to the German lands.⁴ Apparently, Reuchlin was known in Breslau of that time primarily as an expert in the Hebrew language—and not so much as an expert in the *Art of the Cabala* and in Cabalistic methods of Scripture interpretation. Historical sources mention that he had visited Reuchlin in Tübingen, but more likely it was in Stuttgart.⁵ Reuchlin and Moibanus share an interest in the origins of religion. The young Moibanus composed a poem on this subject.⁶ Moibanus saw Reuchlin as the victim of both, the ecclesiastical conservatives and the radical enthusiasts. In 1537 Moibanus wrote his book *Glorious Commission of Jesus Christ, Our Lord and Savior* [Mark 16:15] (*Das herrliche Mandat Jesu Christi unseres Herrn und Heilands*) against the enthusiasts (to which Luther contributed the preface).⁷

1. Reuchlin's Respect for the Jews and Their Books

1.1. Who Was Johann Reuchlin?

For a more objective image of him, his correspondence can now be consulted, which is available in the critical edition of 4 volumes.⁸ His publications include the early Cabalistic work *De verbo mirifico* (*The Wonder-Working Word*) of 1494 and the textbook *Rudimenta Hebraica* (*Rudiments of Hebrew*) of 1506. From 1510 he was involved in defending the books of the Jews, including the Talmud. In 1512 he published a literal translation of the *Seven Penitential Psalms* from Hebrew into Latin. In 1517, the year which

---

3. No mention of the persecution at Breslau is found in the four volumes of the critical edition of Reuchlin's correspondence.

4. Konrad 1891, 48.

5. Konrad 1891, 14; Stupperich 1984, 148–49.

6. Konrad 1891, 12–13.

7. WA 50: 119–20. Luther's preface now in English in LW 60:149–51.

8. RBW 1-4 (Stuttgart-Bad Cannstatt, 1999–2013).

marks Luther's Reformation, Reuchlin published *The Art of the Cabala* which he dedicated to Pope Leo X.[9] With these works Reuchlin demonstrates his capacities as an expert in Hebrew and Greek, and also as a biblical humanist, lay theologian, religious philosopher, and as a budding expert in the Cabala. He wrote two comedies, *Sergius* and *Henno* (1496/1497). In 1518 he wrote his last book on Hebrew philology, with an appendix on music notes, *De accentibus et orthographia linguae hebraicae* (On accents and orthography of the Hebrew language). He was widely supported by the humanists of Europe.

Throughout the time of the early Lutheran Reformation, Reuchlin remained faithful to the Catholic Church. He always wrote with the awareness of being a Roman Catholic author, wanting always to be in agreement with the teachings of the Church. Reuchlin wrote to Archbishop Uriel von Gemmingen on October 6, 1510, that with his writings he wanted to have written only what is admissible by the holy Christian Church.[10] In a letter which was published later in the *Letters of Illustrious Men*, in 1519, he expressed his wish not to be "averted" from Christ and that he maintained to believe whatever the holy Church, the pillar and firmament of the truth, believes. What the Church expounds of the Sacred Scripture, he too expounds and confesses. If ever he would have said something to the contrary, he gladly would change his mind "so that the uncontaminated faith would preserve her [the Church's] integrity in me."[11] In 1521 the pious Reuchlin joined the local *Salve Regina Confraternity* in Stuttgart.[12] This is a little-known fact from the end of his life. In the eyes of a contemporaneous Florentine observer, Bartolomeo Cerretani (1475–1524), Reuchlin, with his book on the *Art of the Cabala*, is "the unique philosopher and theologian of our time."[13]

Since we do not have a historical portrait painting of Reuchlin, we must rely on other kinds of images that tell us something about him, besides, of course, the contents of his books and correspondence. One such historical image, which can teach us something about him, is the title page of the original edition of the book he published five hundred years ago. It

---

9. SW 2-1. The English translations are my own, in consultation with the German edition and with the English version in Goodman 1983.

10. RBW 2: 160.57–58 (no. 171).

11. RBW 2: 204–205.55–63 (no. 184), originally of October 28, 1511, to a Dominican friar by the name of Arnold von Tongern; Posset 2015, 398.

12. Posset 2015, 806–7.

13. Bartolomeo Cerretani; Posset 2015, 14.

shows Reuchlin's Bible-based coat of arms which calls for a brief explanation: *Johann Reuchlin of Pforzheim, doctor of law, The Art of the Cabala in three books dedicated to [Pope] Leo X (Latin: Ioannis Reuchlin Phorcensis LL Doc[toris] De Arte Cabalistica Libri tres Leoni X. dicati.*

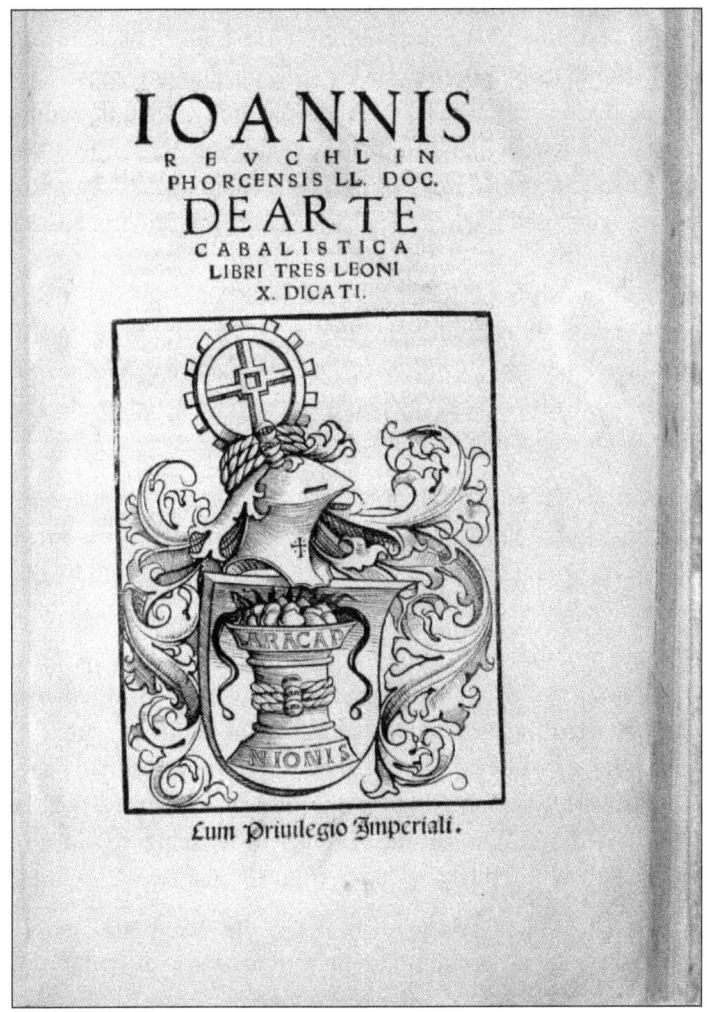

Fig. 2.1. Title Page of *De Arte Cabalistica*, with Reuchlin's Coat of Arms.

At the occasion of being received into the ranks of the nobility in 1492, Reuchlin obtained his coat of arms (fig. 2.1). It shows a blue-grey shield with a golden altar, from which smoke is rising from red-hot burning coals. "Smoke" is, of course, a hint at his name in German, "Little Smoke," derived from the German *Rauch* with its diminutive form *Räuchlein*, or *Reuchlin* in early new high German spelling. The imperial diploma detailed that the coat of arms has to have the inscription *ARA CAPNIONIS*, with his humanistic name, "altar of Capnion [Reuchlin]," written with capital letters onto the rim and bottom of the round altar. The altar is to be girded with grey-blue and golden bands (*tenia*).[14] The biblical backdrop for it is Exod 30:1–8 with its instructions on building an altar of incense. The three bells on the three ropes around the altar may be symbols that hint at the vestments of the Jewish high priest at the temple services in Jerusalem according to Exod 28:33 and Exod 39:25 ("bells of pure gold"). Paradoxically, the lay theologian used a symbol of priestly vestments and functions for his coat of arms.[15]

Burn all Jewish books? This was the question of the day. On this issue, Reuchlin in 1510 composed his *Expert Opinion* for the emperor: *Recommendation Whether to Confiscate, Destroy and Burn All Jewish Books*. During that controversy over the books of the Jews Reuchlin declared the following about respecting the Jews and their books:

1. We are instructed by canon law (*9. dis. c. ut veterum*) to refer back to the original Jewish texts [the Old Testament]. This is convincing proof that the Christian Church still considers them to be the most dependable source.[16]

2. We are prohibited by canon law (*c. sicut iudaeis ex de iu.*; "Just as to the Jews") from confiscating the Jews' possessions, whether money or valuable things encompassed under the rubric "pecunia" (*1. q. 3 totum*). And whoever acts in defiance of this decree shall be relieved of his worldly honors and his position or be banned (i.e., excommunicated), until he has made sufficient recompense to the injured party.[17] Reuchlin thus concluded from Church law:

   > One should not burn the books of the Jews and one should persuade them to our faith with rational disputations [*durch*

---

14. RBW 1: 433.145–48 (appendix III: *Ernennungsurkunde zum Hofpfalzgrafen*, October 24, 1492).
15. Posset 2015, 109–10.
16. Wortsman 2000, 76.
17. Wortsman 2000, 84–85.

vernünfftig disputationen], gently and kindly [*senfftmuetigklich vnd guettlich*], with the help of God."[18]

He relied on the so-called Clementine canons (named after Pope Clement V [reigned from 1305–1314]); they were available in print since 1491. Another print was made in Basel in 1511 (see fig. 2.2).

Fig. 2.2. Pope Clement V (d. 1314), *Clementis Quinti Constitutiones* (Basel 1511). Title Page by artist "VG" (engraved on top of the throne; i.e., Urs Graf).

18. SW 4-1: 64.7–11; Posset 2015, 360; slightly different translation in Wortsman 2000, 87.

In following ecclesiastical law Reuchlin favored a gentle approach in the attempt of leading "the Jews into our camp, while holding to the dictates of canon law (*c. qui sincera et. c. de iudae. 45. dis.*)." He concludes his Expert Opinion of 1510 by quoting the Church's law once more:

> [In canon law] the following is expressly stated: "We should, therefore, deal with them [the Jews] in such a way as to so move them with logical arguments and gentleness of manner that they would rather join us and not flee from us, so that with God's help and the testimony of their own books, we may succeed in converting them to the cause of our Mother, the Christian Church." This is more or less, the gist of the canon law (*dicto. ca. qui sincera*), upon which I base my opinion concerning the treatment of the Jews ...
>
> From the two aforementioned articles of law, the "Clementine" and the Distinction of the Decree," we may derive the conclusive judgment in this entire matter, namely: That we should not burn the Jews' books, and that through logical discourse, we should convince them with gentle persuasion and kindness and with God's help to accept our Faith.[19]

Reuchlin, the law expert, simply wanted to clarify for the emperor the official position of the Church in dealing with the Jews and their books: Respect them and their books! In later years Reuchlin solidified his position toward the Jews as he very forcefully declared:

> "The Jewish faith is none of our business";[20] in utilizing 1 Cor 5:12 (where Saint Paul says: "What business is it of mine to judge outsiders ...") and arguing for the preservation of the Talmud.
>
> "The Jew is as worthy in the eyes of our Lord as am I"[21]
> —advocating equal human dignity for all.

The Jews are "fellow citizens," and:

> "I know my adversaries are dismayed because I have called them [Jews] our fellow citizens. Now I would want them to go berserk even more, their guts may burst open because I say that the Jews are our brothers."[22]

---

19. SW 4-1: 64.7-11; Wortsman 2000, 86-87.

20. ... *vnd gat [geht] vns ir glaub nichtz an*, with Reuchlin's reference to the gloss: *glo. penul. in cle. i. de usur*; SW 4-1: 48.34—49.5; Wortsman 2000, 64; Posset 2015, 348-49.

21. *Der iud ist vnsers herr gots alls wol als ich*, SW 4-1: 59.20; Wortsman 2000, 80; Posset 2015, 357.

22. *Defensio*, 1513, SW 4-1: 344.19-22.

How did Reuchlin come to this position? There are several contributing factors:

1. He arrived at it through the careful study of the Church's laws concerning the Jews.
2. Another factor was his personal experience with a learned Jew in 1492 at the court of the "King of the Jews" as Emperor Frederick III (reigned 1440–1493)[23] was nicknamed for his kindness to the Jews. Jacob Jehiel Loans (d. 1505? Loans's surname refers to the French city, Louhans) was the personal physician of the emperor. He became Reuchlin's Hebrew teacher. The nineteenth-century biographer of Reuchlin, Ludwig Geiger (1848–1919), called Reuchlin's encounter with Dr. Jacob Jehiel Loans, the learned Jew at the imperial court, "a moment of world-historical significance."[24] Dr. Loans arranged for Reuchlin at the end of his service at the imperial court in Linz to receive a valuable Hebrew Bible manuscript as a farewell gift from the emperor, now known as *Codex Reuchlin 1*, or the *Reuchlin Bible* (fig. 2.3).

---

23. Posset 2015, 108.
24. Geiger 1871, 105.

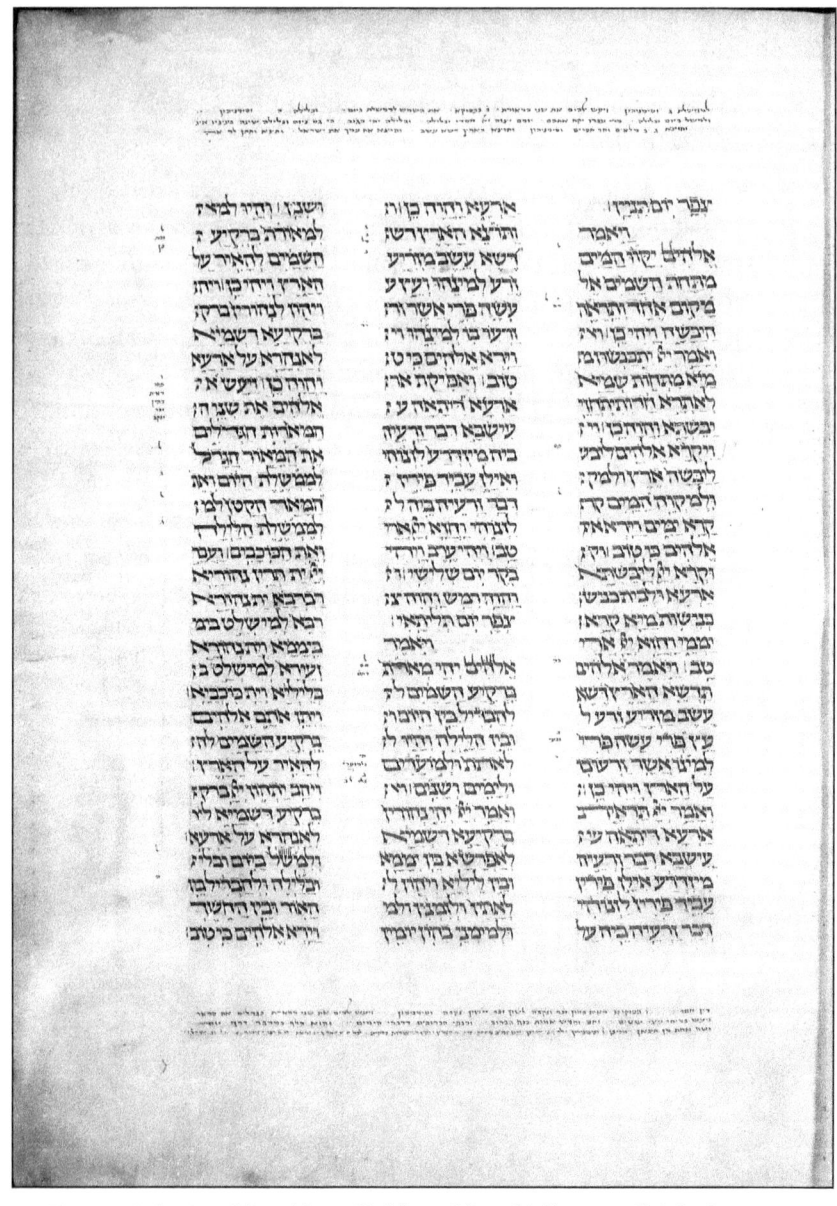

Fig. 2.3. *Codex Reuchlin 1* (also called "Reuchlin Bible"); Farewell Gift of Emperor Frederick III. Hebrew Bible with Aramaic translation (*Targum Onkelos*), parchment, twelfth/thirteenth century; shown here is folio 2v.[25]

25. Posset 2015, 112–13.

3. *Ad fontes*, A third factor may be seen in Reuchlin's cultural-historical studies by which he came to the insight that only the Jews ladle from the pure sources. Reuchlin respected the Jews because they drink from the sources, whereas the Greeks from the rivers or rills and the Latin people from the swamp[26] (fig. 2.4).

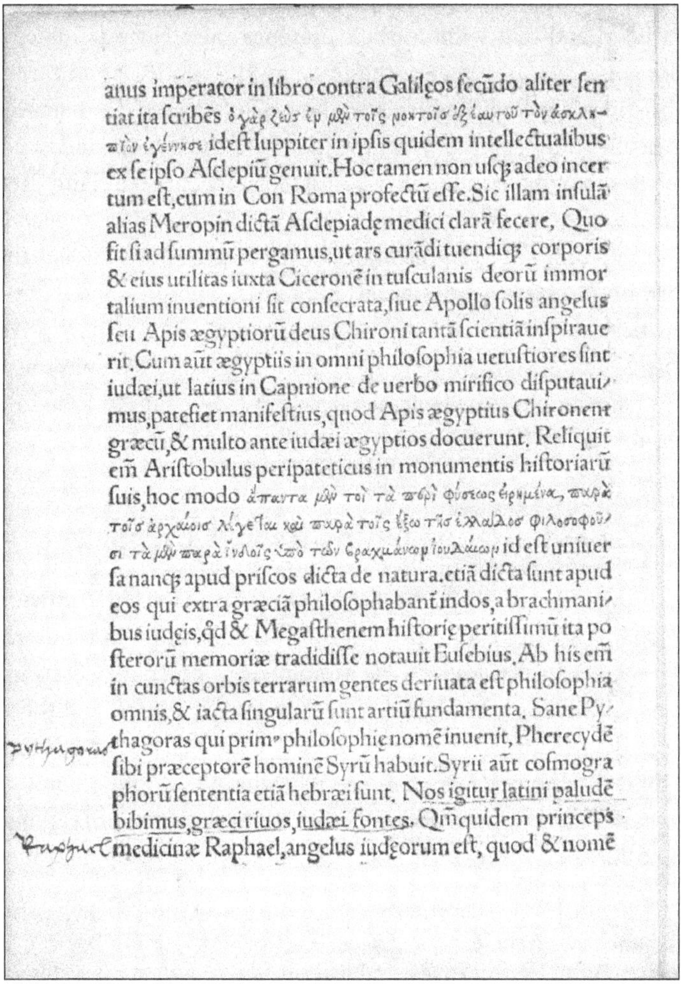

anus imperator in libro contra Galilęos ſecũdo aliter ſen
tiat ita ſcribẽs ὁ γὰρ ζεὺς ἐν μὲν τοῖς νοητοῖς ἐξ ἑαυτοῦ τὸν ἀσκλη-
πιὸν ἐγέννησε idest Iuppiter in ipſis quidem intellectualibus
ex ſe ipſo Aſclepiũ genuit. Hoc tamen non uſq; adeo incer
tum eſt, cum in Con Roma profectũ eſſe. Sic illam inſulã
alias Meropin dictã Aſclepiadę medici clarã fecere, Quo
fit ſi ad ſummũ pergamus, ut ars curãdi tuendiq; corporis
& eius utilitas iuxta Ciceronẽ in tuſculanis deorũ immor
talium inuentioni ſit conſecrata, ſiue Apollo ſolis angelus
ſeu Apis ægyptiorũ deus Chironi tantã ſcientiã inſpiraue
rit. Cum aũt ægyptiis in omni philoſophia uetuſtiores ſint
iudæi, ut latius in Capnione de uerbo mirifico diſputaui-
mus, patefiet manifeſtius, quod Apis ægyptius Chironem
græcũ, & multo ante iudæi ægyptios docuerunt. Reliquit
eñ Ariſtobulus peripateticus in monumentis hiſtoriarũ
ſuis, hoc modo ἅπαντα μὲν τοι τὰ περὶ φύσεως εἰρημένα, παρὰ
τοῖς ἀρχαίοις λέγεται καὶ παρὰ τοῖς ἔξω τῆς ἑλλάδος φιλοσοφοῦ-
σι τὰ μὲν παρὰ ἰνδοῖς ὑπὸ τῶν βραχμάνων ἰουδαίων id eſt uniuer
ſa nanq; apud priſcos dicta de natura. etiã dicta ſunt apud
eos qui extra græciã philoſophabant indos, a brachmani-
bus iudęis, q̃d & Megaſthenem hiſtorię peritiſſimũ ita po
ſterorũ memoriæ tradidiſſe notauit Euſebius. Ab his eñ
in cunctas orbis terrarum gentes deriuata eſt philoſophia
omnis, & iacta ſingularũ ſunt artiũ fundamenta. Sane Pythagoras qui prim⁹ philoſophię nomẽ inuenit, Pherecydẽ
ſibi præceptorẽ hominẽ Syrũ habuit. Syrii aũt coſmogra
phorũ ſententia etiã hebræi ſunt. Nos igitur latini paludẽ
bibimus, græci riuos, iudæi fontes. Qm̃quidem princeps
medicinæ Raphael, angelus iudęorum eſt, quod & nomẽ

Fig. 2.4. Reuchlin, *De praeparatione hominis*, fol. A 2v; at the bottom of the page, with the underlining of the proverbial saying: "*Nos igitur latini paludē bibimus, graeci riuos, iudaei fontes.*"

26. *Nos igitur latini paludem bibimus, graeci rivos, iudaei fontes*, Reuchlin's Preface, *De praeparatione hominis* (1512); Posset 2015b, 159–65.

Reuchlin feared that with the expulsion of the Jews they would no longer be available as resource persons. In the preface of his *Rudiments of Hebrew* (1506) he complained about the persecution of the Jews in Spain and Germany, as they were forced to seek residence elsewhere and to turn to the *Agareni* (Saracens, Arabs, Moslems).[27] He feared that with the exodus of Jews from Christian lands they could no longer function as experts to be consulted and that without their presence their Hebrew Bibles would soon be gone, too. In his view the Jews are the needed book carriers for the Christians. He, in following the church fathers and Thomas Aquinas, whom he mentions explicitly, saw the Jews with their books and in particular their Hebrew Bible in the service-role for the Christian faith. Reuchlin explained to the emperor in 1510 in his *Expert Opinion (Recommendation)* as he warned him not to let the books of the Jews be burned: "For the Jews are our book carriers, copyists, and librarians, who preserve those books from which we can present the witness for our faith."[28] In *The Wonder-Working Word* Reuchlin praised the Hebrew language as simple, unspoiled, holy, and concise. It is the language in which God communicated without a translator face to face.[29]

2. Admiration for the Hebrew Language

The Hebrew language "must be kissed tenderly and embraced with both arms" (to his brother Dionysius).[30] With this conviction in mind he composed his *Rudiments of Hebrew*. He promoted the study of Hebrew in order to understand the original Word of God in the Scriptures, and thus to get to the Hebrew Truth.

Divine Scripture originated directly from the "mouth of God" (*os dei locutum est*).[31] One must study the Bible "until the voice of God becomes clear and the text of the most holy Scripture is opened up and offered to

27. ... *atque ad Agarenos divertere*; preface 1 for *De rudimentis*, RBW 2: 37. 89-92 (no. 138) with n28. The designation *Agareni* is derived from Agar (= Hagar in Gen 16) being descendants of her, the maid of Abraham. The Arabs claim their origin from Hagar's and Abraham's son Ishmael. *Agareni* are the Saracens of the Middle Ages.

28. SW 4-1: 52.28-29; Wortsman 2000, 70; Posset 2015, 339.

29. *De verbo mirifico*, Book II, SW 1-1: 162.36-39. On other aspects of Reuchlin's thinking in this regard, see Wolfson 2005, 7-41.

30. To Dionysius = Preface 1 for *De rudimentis*, RBW 2: 35.27-28 (no. 138); Posset 2015, 254-55.

31. Preface 1 for *De rudimentis*, RBW 2: 35.15 (no. 138).

us."[32] Therefore, Count Mirandola said in his *Conclusions*: "*Quaelibet vox virtutem habet in magia, in quantum dei voce formatur*" (Each word has power in magic in so far as it is formed by the voice of God).[33]

For the proper understanding of the Scriptures one must know Hebrew precisely because this is the language in which God has spoken. From this divine font all theology has gushed forth (*a quo fonte omnis theologia scaturivit*).[34] "The Hebrew alphabet: what is more sacred than this *sacramentum*? What is more enjoyable than this *sacramentum*?" Nothing is better than to get to "know God's foreseeing and to enter into God's secrets [*abdita*]."[35] In following the church father Jerome, Reuchlin saw in the Hebrew language the venue to God's mysteries and therefore a means of grace, a "*sacramentum*." Hebrew is essential for the relationship with God, as Reuchlin wrote to Nicolaus Ellenbog OSB (1481–1543), monastic humanist (*Klosterhumanist*) at the Benedictine Abbey Ottobeuren on March 19, 1510:[36]

> After I have tried various other studies, nothing from among all other languages that I have learned connects me more to God than practicing the reading of the Sacred Scriptures in Hebrew. For whenever I read Hebrew it seems to me that God Himself is speaking with me as I think that this language is the means God and angels use in dealing with human beings.[37]

Reuchlin continued with an autobiographical confession:

> When I do that I am shaken by some sort of shudder [*horrore*] and terror [*terrore*], not however without ineffable joy that follows this awe or rather such numbness, a joy which I really would like to call wisdom of which the divine Hebrew verse [*eloquium*] says: "The fear of the Lord is the beginning of wisdom" [Ps 110:10 / 111:10; Prov 1:7].[38]

---

32. *De Arte Cabalistica*, SW 2-1: 514.39—515.1.

33. Goodman reads: "Any sound has power for magic in so far as it is formed from the sound of God" (337).

34. Preface 1 for *De rudimentis*, RBW 2: 35.22 (no. 138); Posset 2015, 254–55.

35. Comments at the end of Book III of *De rudimentis*; RBW 2: 45.281-83 (no. 138); Posset 2015, 262–63.

36. On Ellenbog, see Posset 2005, 155–71.

37. RBW 2: 130.8–13 (no. 162).

38. RBW 2: 130.13–17 (no. 162).

Reuchlin's grammar book was meant not only for beginners of the study of Hebrew, but also for scholars of other disciplines. In his conviction, the knowledge of Hebrew is a necessary precondition also for the "arcane discipline of Pythagoras and the art of the Cabala" and for the oldest philosophy of the venerable ancient ones.[39] Reuchlin followed Giovanni Pico della Mirandola (1463–1494) in this regard.[40]

Reuchlin's praise of the Hebrew language inspired others to do the same. They composed eulogies of their own:

1. Matthaeus Adrianus (ca. 1470–1521), *Oratio de linguarum laude* (Wittenberg: Grunenberg, 1520), about Latin, Greek, and Hebrew.
2. Robert Wakefield (d. 1537), *Oratio de laudibus et utilitate trium linguarum: Arabicae, Chaldaicae et Hebraicae*, 1524/1528; he was successor of Reuchlin in Tübingen, then Hebraist in Cambridge.
3. Georg Witzel (1501–1573), *Encomium sanctae linguae. Oratio in Laudem Hebraice linhguae*, 1534.

Witzel said this about Reuchlin (i.e., Capnion):

> What shall I say about Capnion to whom the entire world looks up, honors and loves him as the strongest and also the most knowledgeable protector of this oppressed language?
>
> *De Capnione quid attinet referre, quem totus orbis, ut linguae huius oppressae vindicem fortissimum iuxta ac peritissimum suscipit, colit, amat?*[41]

3. The Holy Name of God Saves

Reuchlin's study of the grammar and the language of the Jews always had a theological component: In the preface of his Hebrew grammar, *The Rudiments of Hebrew* (1506), he declared that this grammar will be most useful for the study of the "name of the highest God" (*nomen dei summi*).[42] With this theme, we come now to Reuchlin's early letter to Rudolf Agricola (1444–1485) of 1484/1485, an original source of the highest value (fig. 2.5).

---

39. Preface 1 for *De rudimentis*, RBW 2: 37.105—38.115 (no. 138); Posset 2015, 257.
40. Posset 2015, 263.
41. Böning 2004,100.
42. RBW 2: 38.114 (no. 138).

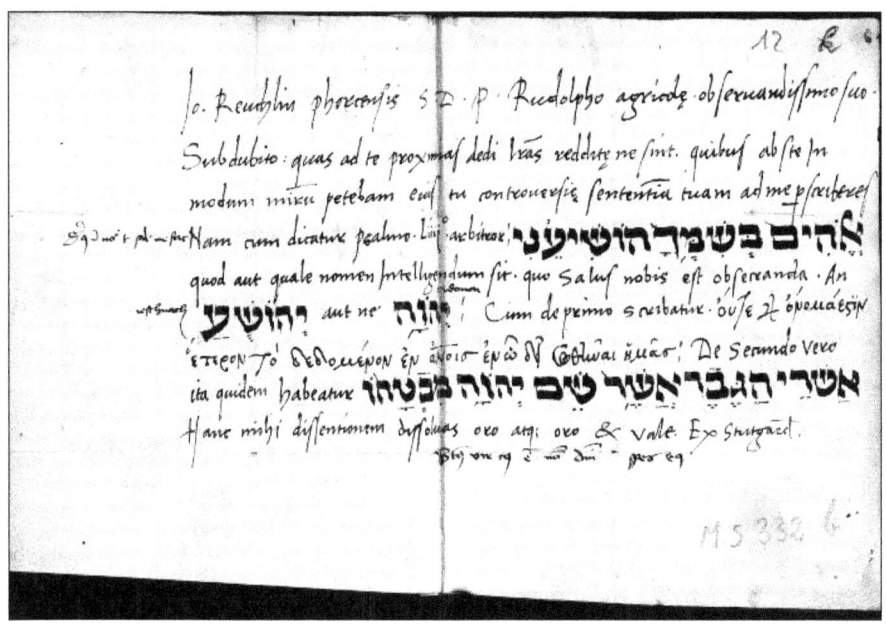

Fig. 2.5. Reuchlin's letter to Rudolf Agricola of 1484/1485, ms. 332b (= K892 k). The autograph is written in Latin, Greek, and Hebrew.

Already in 1484/1485, at about the age of thirty, Reuchlin in his correspondence with the humanist Rudolf Agricola had brought up the topic of God's saving name.[43] In this very short letter Reuchlin quotes *psalmus LIIII* (Ps 54:3; thus not using the Vulgate numbering 53:3). In this verse the divine name *Elohim* is used: "O God [*Elohim*], by your name save me." He quotes the verse in Hebrew including his vocalization: אֱ[ל]הִים בְּשִׁמְךָ הוֹשִׁיעֵנִי (*E[l]ohim, beshimeka hoshieni*). Reuchlin's autograph has the Hebrew word for "God" אֱהִים (*Eohim*) without the letter ל (*lamed*), and thus not in the usual spelling, i.e., אֱלֹהִים. Why? We do not know.

He asks Agricola: exactly which divine name is meant that would be the saving name? Is it יְהוֹשֻׁעַ (Yehoshuah) which is the Hebrew wording for the name of Jesus, stemming in terms of etymology from ישע (yasah, "to save," "to help") as in Matt 1:21, "and you are to name him Jesus, because he will save his people"; or, is it יְהוָֹה (Yehouah) which, according to Reuchlin's vocalization, is to be pronounced "Yehouah" (not "Yahueh").[44]

43. RBW 1: 47–50 (no. 13), here 48.7–8; Posset 2015, 150. The autograph is kept at Sélestat, France, Municipal Library, ms. 332b (=K892 k); Posset 2015, 71n141.

44. In the recent German translation of Letter no. 13, the questionable wording

Reuchlin explicitly has the vocalization "o" for the letterוֹ (waw) whereas the standard spelling in the Hebrew Bible does not. Thus, Reuchlin in his letter provided the vocalization for the *Tetragrammaton* not quite as it is found in the critical edition of the *Biblia Hebraica*. The vocal "point" over the letter וֹ (waw) makes the difference for the pronunciation.

Reuchlin: יְהֹוָה

Biblia Hebraica: יְהוָה

With "Yehoshuah" Reuchlin means "Jesus" of whose name one reads in the New Testament, Acts 4:12b (a verse which Reuchlin quotes in Greek): "nor is there any other name [under heaven] given to the human race by which we are to be saved." This verse in Saint Peter's speech is important to Reuchlin, who cites it again in his book *The Wonder-Working Word* of 1494.[45] With respect to the second name, "Yehouah," Reuchlin has the divine name, the *Tetragrammaton*, in mind as given in Ps 40:5, "Happy is the man who trusts in the name of יְהֹוָה [Yehouah, the Lord]."[46] Reuchlin ends his short letter with the urgent request to solve this issue for him.

This letter was not known to Ludwig Geiger, the nineteenth-century editor of Reuchlin correspondence and who was his biographer, born in 1848. Here, therefore, my translation:

> Jo[hann] Reuchlin of Pforzheim sends many greetings to his highly to be respected Rudolf Agricola.
>
> I am not sure whether you have received the letter which I recently had sent you. In it I beseeched you to write to me your opinion in full about the following controversy. When it is said in, I believe, Psalm 54 [verse 3, in Hebrew letters]: "O *Elohim*, by your name save me," what or which name is meant here in which our salvation is to be expected; is it יְהוֹשֻׁעַ [Yehoshuah] or rather יְהֹוָה [Yehouah]? For, with respect to the first [Yehoshuah], it is written: "nor is there any other name [under heaven] given to the human race by which we are to be saved" [Acts 4:12, in Geek letters], whereas to the second [Yehouah] there is this [verse] to be had: "Happy is the man who trusts in the name of Yehouah [יְהֹוָה]" [Ps 40:5,

---

of "Jahwe" is given; *Johann Reuchlin Briefwechsel Band 1 1477-1505. Leseausgabe in deutscher Übersetzung von Adalbert Weh* (Stuttgart-Bad Cannstatt, 2000), 53. It should be "Jehova."

45. SW 1-1: 402.37—404.13; Posset 2015, 150.

46. מִבְטַחוֹ יְהֹוָה שָׂם אֲשֶׁר הַגֶּבֶר אַשְׁרֵי.

in Hebrew letters]. Please, please solve this variance for me. Fare well! From Stuttgart.[47]

Reuchlin did not receive a response as far as one can tell from the available source material. From the time of this correspondence with Agricola in 1484 or 1485, throughout his life, Reuchlin was preoccupied with the theme of the divine saving name.

In book 2 of the *Wonder-Working Word* of 1494 Reuchlin returns to the topic of the name of God. The name of God with the four letters (*Tetragrammaton*) was not invented by human beings, but was revealed by God and therefore it is a holy and venerable name. The name was revealed to Adam and Eve, to Abraham, Isaac and Jacob, and most of all to Moses; also the Prophet Isaiah proclaimed it (in Isa 25:1 and 63:16).[48] The name was unpronounceable.

In following Pico della Mirandola, Reuchlin was convinced that help was coming from the Cabalistic interpretation of the Hebrew name of the second person of the Trinity, Jesus. The four-letter name of God in Deut 28:10 (*Yehouah*) becomes pronounceable and understandable when one inserts the Hebrew letter ש (*shin*) in the middle and thus arrives at the name "Yehoshuah." The *Tetragrammaton* [of Deut 28:10] becomes thus also audible to all the nations, "who will stand in awe of you" (Deut 28:10b). This insight comes from the "Cabala of the Hebrews" (*iuxta Cabalam Hebraeorum*) יהשוה. All this is being taught by the Cabalists. Reuchlin continues: The Father of our Lord Jesus Christ instills in us the knowledge of the true name of his Son and of our Savior.[49]

Sometimes it is assumed that Reuchlin learned directly from Pico's deliberations in 1486 that by the insertion of the Hebrew letter *shin* one receives the name "Jesus" in Hebrew: יהשוה. However, the letter to Agricola under consideration here is dated one or two years earlier, so that Pico could not have been of direct influence on Reuchlin in this regard. It is difficult to decide whether Reuchlin came up with this idea all on his own, or whether he relied on other sources without mentioning them, such as Paul of Burgos.[50]

Why is it that from all the Hebrew letters, this one (*shin*) has to be inserted? According to Reuchlin, in his *Wonder-Working Word*, the Hebrew

47. From fig. 5 (autograph), RBW I: 48.
48. SW 1-1: 240.24–25; Posset 2015, 135.
49. SW 1-1: 370.17-30; Posset 2015, 148.
50. On this, see Posset 2015, 72–73.

consonant *shin* is the first letter of the Hebrew word for "oil," שמן (*shemen*), and it is also contained in the Hebrew word for Messiah, "the anointed one," who is Christ.[51] In Jesus' Hebrew name the letter *shin* is found in the middle of what is God's name (*Yehouah*). This letter, *shin*, therefore, designates the mediator. The incarnation of God in the man Jesus makes him the mediator between God and humanity.[52] See fig. 2.6 with the letter *shin* lowered in order to underscore the divine lowering in the incarnation.

> God has been revealed progressively in human history.[53] God is revealed
>
> 1. to the ancient ones in Three Letters SDI (Sadai),
> 2. to the biblical fathers in Four Letters YHUH (Yehouah),
> 3. "and to us, the sons" in the Five Letters YH-Sh-UH (Yehoshuah, Jesus).

Reuchlin's printer applied these insights from *The Wonder-Working Word* of 1494 to the graphic design of his identification device (the printer's second mark, or logo) sometime in 1506/1507.

---

51. SW 1-1: 354.22—356.7; Posset 2015, 147.
52. SW 1-1: 368.37—370.1; Posset 2015, 147.
53. SW 1-1: 402.34-37; Posset 2015, 150. Martin Rösel, *Adonaj—warum Gott "Herr" genannt wird*. Forschungen zum Alten Testament 29 (Tübingen 2000), without any mention of Reuchlin.

Fig. 2.6. TAB: Thomas Anshelm of Baden: Second Printer's Mark, influenced by Reuchlin.

The printer's new logo mirrors Reuchlin's teaching in *The Wonder-Working Word* about the name of Jesus in Hebrew, i.e., the *Pentagrammaton*, יהשוה, with the letter *shin* being lowered (fig. 2.6) as a hint at the divine *kenosis* in the incarnation.[54] The third version looks like this:

54. I.e., the "renunciation" of the divine nature, at least in part, by Christ in the incarnation; about the printer's various devices; shown here is the second version of 1506–1507, which was in use to about 1516, see Posset 2015, 285–87. Afterward, the third and final version was used which was designed by Hans Baldung Grien. This final logo shows two angels each holding a banderole with Jesus's name in Greek and Hebrew.

Fig. 2.7. Third Printer's Mark. Jesus' name in Greek and Hebrew. The design is inspired by Reuchlin's theology of the name of God and of Jesus. Woodcut by Hans Baldung Grien who might have adapted the concept from Albrecht Dürer's "Three Genii." This printer's device is used as colophon in Anshelm's print of a book by Martin Luther: *Von den guten werken, ain gantz nützlich büchlin dem layen zuo lessen / durch D. Martinum Luter zuo Wittenberg gepredigt* (Hagenau: Anshelm, 1520).

Here (fig. 2.7), the Hebrew name of Jesus is given with the non-vocalized spelling (the *Pentagrammaton*): יהשוה. There is a problem, however: The proper Hebrew spelling of the name of Jesus is: יְהוֹשֻׁעַ (Yehoshuah), whereas

WHO IS "THE STRONGEST ... PROTECTOR OF THIS OPPRESSED LANGUAGE"?

Reuchlin has the spelling with the ending ה: יְהֹשֻׁוָה (Yehoshuah, with vowels), יהשוה (without vowels, as shown in printer's logo); different ending, but both are pronounced and sound the same! The printer kept the spelling as he learned it from Reuchlin's idiosyncratic spelling of the Hebrew name of Jesus ending with ה (heh), not with ע (ayin), as the proper name of Jesus would be spelled in Hebrew. Did Reuchlin not know the difference in spelling? He probably did, but spelling was not of the highest importance to him. Reuchlin was interested in the way the words sound, as he is operating orally most of the time so that the different spelling in print does not come into play as a primary concern. Despite the different spelling at the end, the last syllable of the name of God in the *Tetragrammaton* and that of the Hebrew name of Jesus do sound the same.[55] That's what counts in Reuchlin's view: with which name, or with which sound, are we to "call" out to the saving God, not in which spelling we write it.

In his *Art of the Cabala* of 1517 Reuchlin provides additional reasoning about the Hebrew consonant ש [*shin*] being inserted in the middle of the divine name: This letter represents in Cabalistic thinking the word "in mercy" / "in mercies." The insertion of the letter ש [*shin*] leads the Cabalist to the name of God as YH-in-mercy-UH, which again makes the name of Jesus: Yehoshuah. This was a revelation given already to Adam—according to Cabalistic teaching and its technique of *gematria* (gimatria) for Scripture interpretation. Gematria is about the numerical value of Hebrew letters, and is also a system of interpretation by substituting for a particular word another word whose letters give the same numerical sum. Accordingly, God wanted to be called by the letter *shin*, = 300, which in the art of the Cabala is the equivalent of "in mercy." The numerical equivalent of the letter ש (*shin*) being 300 is equal to the numerical value of the six Hebrew letters of the expression "in mercies": ברחמים (BeRaH-MYM = 2 + 200 + 8 + 40 + 10 + 40 = 300). According to the Cabalistic *gematria* the two are thus interchangeable.

>letter ש (*shin*) = 300.
>ברחמים "in mercies" (BRHMYM)
>= 2 + 200 + 8 + 40 + 10 + 40 = 300.

It is the "most holy and highest revelation."[56] "On the letter *shin*, any Cabalist who knows anything about Cabalistic *gematria* will agree that the

---

55. Posset 2015, 133.
56. SW 2-1: 86.38–39; Posset 2015, 670.

numerical value of the letter *shin* [= 300] comprises the other four letters, YHUH, and that it also possesses the same properties of clemency and mercy."[57]

Reuchlin's search for the name of God had no end. In 1518 he was again occupied with the way the known religions of the world refer to God, as we may see in his book about Saint Athanasius's various questions. He returned to the initial issue, namely to his letter to Agricola in which he quoted Ps 54:3: "O God [*Elohim*], by your name save me." Here in 1518 he elaborated on the Hebrew word for God, *Elohim*, and how he found it in ten languages.[58]

Reuchlin assumed the text to be authentic Athanasius, but it is pseudepigraphy. One of the most interesting comments he made is found with respect to the expressions for "God" in the ten languages with which he was familiar, starting with the Hebrew *Elohim*. Reuchlin provides the original characters of the languages if he knew them (see fig. 2.8).

---

57. SW 2-1: 33–38.
58. See fig. 28 in Posset 2015, 741 (showing the entire page).

Fig. 2.8. *Liber S. Athanasii De Variis Quaestionibus* (Reuchlin's book about Athanasius on Various Questions, folio G iii; with Reuchlin's commentary on the word "God" in ten languages.

The size of the Ethiopian and Arabic letters takes up three lines.

The Ethiopian letters are perhaps copied from J. Potken's book of 1513. For a later edition, see online: *Psalterivm In Qvatvor Lingvis, Hebraea, Graeca, Chaldaea, Latina* (Cologne, 1518), MDZ, image no. 96 in Potken 1518. There is, however, no resemblance to what Reuchlin shows in his Athanasius; image no. 57.

1. אלהים, Elohím (original Hebrew and Latin transliteration).
2. Eloha, in Chaldean (Ethiopian), with the original characters carved for this page.
3. Alla, in Arabic, with the original characters carved for this page.
4. Artziburtzis, in Armenian (given in Latin transliteration.
5. ZEYC, [Zeus] given in original Greek only.
6. DEVS, in Roman (i.e., Latin).
7. THEVTH, in Teuthonic (*sic*, Reuchlin explains that this is Egyptian, too, according to Plato).
8. Dieu, in Gallic (French).
9. Dio, in Italian.
10. Got, in Alemanic (German).

Conclusion

Reuchlin, the father of Christian Hebraism since the Renaissance time, was an eminent scholar not only of the Hebrew language, but also of the history of religion and the philosophy of religion, a lay theologian concerned about the true name of God. Somewhat exaggerated, his work in Christian Cabala has been called "a kind of gnosis" (Moshe Idel)[59] (there is a kernel of truth in this, although "gnosis" may have a bad reputation in Catholic circles). In his scholarly search Reuchlin always was concerned about being in agreement with the Catholic Church and its ecclesiastical law (canon law). By reading the Cabalistic tradition as a Catholic thinker, Reuchlin developed a Catholic, Cabalistic philosophy "for Christ" (Lewis W. Spitz).[60]

---

59. Idel 1997, 14–15.
60. Spitz 1956, 1–20.

Therefore, the big difference between Reuchlin's Catholic Cabala and the Jewish sources he utilized consists in his reinterpretation of them in terms of the Catholic doctrine of salvation. Reuchlin in doing research in this way came to appreciate most highly the sacred language of the Jews, who are his fellow citizens and "brothers." And, most of all he had high regards for the methods of the Jewish Cabalists in approaching the name of God.

When reading the Sacred Scriptures in the language of God, i.e., in Hebrew, Reuchlin felt as though he was having a religious experience, as he had written to the Benedictine monk Ellenbog in 1510, which I repeat as my conclusion:

> After I have tried various other studies, nothing from among all other languages that I have learned connects me more to God than practicing the reading of the Sacred Scriptures in Hebrew. For whenever I read Hebrew it seems to me that God Himself is speaking to me as I think that this language is the means God and angels use in dealing with human beings.

3

"Search the Scriptures/scriptures" (John 5:39) according to Johann Reuchlin

JOHN 5:39 MAY BE read in basically two ways, as follows:

1. "You search the Scriptures, because you think you have eternal life through them; even they testify on my behalf."—The verb "search" is taken in the indicative form and the noun "Scriptures" is capitalized in order to signal its meaning: Sacred Scripture, the Hebrew Bible.

2. Search the scriptures, because you think you have eternal life through them; even they testify on my behalf!—The verb "search" is taken in the imperative form and the noun is taken with a small "s" to mean any kind of "scriptures" as writings of the Jews, including the Hebrew Bible.

The Greek original reads:

ἐραυνᾶτε τὰς γραφάς, ὅτι ὑμεῖς δοκεῖτε ἐν αὐταῖς ζωὴν αἰώνιον ἔχειν· καὶ ἐκεῖναί εἰσιν αἱ μαρτυροῦσαι περὶ ἐμοῦ.

The Vulgate version can be read with the two possibilities:

Scrutamini scripturas/Scripturas quia vos putatis in ipsis vitam aternam habere et illae sunt quae testimonium perhibent de me.

This Bible verse made history with Johann Reuchlin during the controversy over the preservation of Jewish books. How did he understand it and how did he want others to understand it, too? The purpose of this study is to shed light on Reuchlin's understanding and use of this verse in the historical-theological context of the Renaissance and early Reformation.

Reuchlin was primarily concerned with how to understand the original Greek word for "scriptures," with capital "S" or small "s"? "Search the scriptures" with small "s" means to Reuchlin both Sacred Scriptures (Hebrew Bible) and the Jewish written tradition including the Talmud. He understood Christ's word to mean all Jewish scriptures. He thus did not exclude other nonbiblical Jewish "scriptures" or to take it exclusively to mean the Hebrew Bible, "the Scriptures."

1. The Historical-Theological Context with a Biographical Sketch of Reuchlin

The revival or rebirth of the study of antiquity in the Late Middle Ages meant simultaneously the recovery of the study of Hebrew and Greek. The motto then was: *Ad fontes*: go back in time and search the sources. With respect to Scripture studies, this concern led Erasmus of Rotterdam (ca. 1466–1536), the prince of the humanists, to the first print of the Greek New Testament in 1516. The study of the two biblical languages, Hebrew and Greek, raised questions about the accuracy of the Latin Bible version which the church father Jerome (347–419) had provided, known as the Vulgate. The humanists did not primarily aim at the replacement of the *Biblia Latina*, but at getting to the proper meaning of it. They, including Martin Luther (1483–1546), wanted to improve the Vulgate on the basis of their expertise in the original biblical languages.[1] One outstanding representative of this "biblical humanism"[2] was Johann Reuchlin.[3]

Two years prior to Reuchlin's birth in 1455 (January 29), Constantinople had fallen to the Turks (1453), which caused a wave of Greek scholars fleeing to the West. In the same year, 1453, Jews were persecuted in Wroclaw (Breslau) for allegedly desecrating communion hosts.[4]

After having attended Latin school in his hometown Pforzheim (1462–1470), Reuchlin, at the age of fifteen, is enrolled at the University of Freiburg, about 150 km to the south. At the age of eighteen Reuchlin

---

1. WA.DB 5 (of 1529).
2. Augustijn 2003; Rummel 2008.
3. Posset 2015.
4. *De persecutione Iudaeorum Vratislaviensium a[nno] 1453*, http://www.geschichtsquellen.de/repOpus_01961; Rubin 1999/2004, 119–26.

becomes the chaperone (in 1473) of the son of the local ruler Carl I of Baden. They both attend the University of Paris (Sorbonne). In Paris Reuchlin has the first opportunity to study Greek. He writes a Greek grammar, *Mikropaideia*, which is lost. It is also the time when the first Hebrew printing presses are established in Italy. In 1481 Reuchlin earns his licentiate in imperial/civil law (*Lic. iur Civ.*) at Poitiers, France.

In 1482 Reuchlin accompanies Count Eberhard the Bearded (1445–1496) to Italy, as legal councilor and translator in the negotiations with Pope Sixtus IV (1414–1484) with respect to the foundation of the University of Tübingen. In Florence Reuchlin has a chance to meet the famous Lorenzo de' Medici (1449–1492). In 1484, back home, Reuchlin attends lectures by Flavus Mithridates (1450–1489) in Tübingen. Mithridates is a Catholic scholar of the Cabala, of Jewish descent.

In 1488 Reuchlin turns to theology as he translates Nestorius and Cyril from Greek into Latin; he also translates Proclus's sermon on the Virgin Mary. In a letter that is extant from that year, i.e., of July 22, 1488, to the Carthusian Prior Jacob Lauber (ca. 1440–1513) at Basel, Reuchlin shows himself a *biblical* humanist as he expresses his determination to turn to the Scriptures and that from now on he would want to study the salvific source texts in the original and disregard all the other worldly writers, historians, poets, and philosophers. Christ's command of "searching the scriptures" is an essential element of the life of a disciple of Christ (*sectator*).[5] It remains significant in terms of biography that already here, in his letter of 1488, the thirty-three-year-old Reuchlin sees himself motivated by Christ's command of "searching the scriptures" (John 5:39). He feels drawn to them like iron to the magnet because eternal life is in them.[6] All the aspects of Reuchlin's life and work have something to do with command in this biblical verse.

---

5. In his letter to Prior Lauber Reuchlin used an unusual expression when he referred to Christ's followers as *sectatores*. To some it may smack of "sectarian," but in classical Latin (Tacitus, Suetonius) it means "members of a philosophical school" and this is what Reuchlin tried to say.

6. Posset 2015, 84.

Fig. 3.1. Evangelist John dictates to Prochoros under the inspiration of the Holy Spirit. Full-page miniature in Reuchlin's Greek Codex of the New Testament (Basel).

As a Catholic scholar he feels compelled to deal with the salvific texts of the "new law" (New Testament), texts which are written by the first followers of Christ (*Christi sectatores*) under the influence of divine "instigation." He uses the Latin verb *instigare* (to instigate)[7] where a professional theologian probably would have used the technical theological term of "divine inspiration" of the Scriptures, i.e., by the Holy Spirit. He may have been mindful of the miniature with this motif shown in the codex he had borrowed from the Dominicans in Basel. The text of the Gospel of John is introduced with a full-page miniature on gold background (fig. 3.1). This page shows the Evangelist John as he dictates to Prochoros, his secretary, what he receives

7. RBW 1: 81–86, here 83.25–30 (no. 26).

as divine inspiration from God, whose hand is shown sticking out of the blue sky in the upper right corner of the main scene. Reuchlin keeps the codex in his possession for the rest of his life, but he makes sure that it would be returned at the time of his death. Indeed, the codex was then returned to the Dominicans at Basel.[8] The twelfth-century codex contains all the parts of the Greek New Testament except that the text of the book of Revelation (Apocalypse) was incomplete.

In spring 1490 he is on his second journey to Italy as chaperone of Ludwig, son of Count Eberhard. In Rome he meets the humanist Ermolao Barbaro (1454–1493), who is the first to call him his humanistic name, *Capnion* (Καπνίων), "Little Smoke." He will use his Greek name for the book title and its leading literary figure: *Capnion, seu, De verbo mirifico* of 1494. On the way home from Rome, he meets the young Count Pico della Mirandola (1463–1494, philosopher) and Demetrius Chalcondyles (1423–1511, Greek scholar) in Florence. Pico further piques his interest in the Jewish Cabala.

In 1492 Reuchlin takes on the role of the ambassador at the court of Emperor Frederick III (reigned 1440–1493) in Linz, Austria. This time is of great significance as Reuchlin meets there the emperor's Jewish physician, Jacob Jehiel Loans. He is Reuchlin's Hebrew teacher and provides him with a valuable Hebrew manuscript from the emperor as a farewell gift. It became known as *Codex Reuchlin 1* (also called "Reuchlin Bible), a Hebrew Bible with Aramaic translation (*Targum Onkelos*), with extraordinary weight of 27 kg.[9] Reuchlin is now in possession of a Bible in Hebrew.

In the 1490s Reuchlin collects material for his first Cabalistic book, *De verbo mirifico* (*The Wonder-Working Word*), which is published by Johannes Amerbach in Basel late in 1494.[10] Reuchlin's first major publication is inspired by the Florentine humanist Giovanni Pico della Mirandola. With it Reuchlin offers his ideas with respect to a "Catholic Cabala." He claims that the ineffable *Tetragrammaton* of God's name (YHVH) has become effable and efficacious in the new form of Jesus's name (YH-Sh-VH). For this book he does not yet use the logo which expresses what he writes in the book.

---

8. Today in the university library, Basel.

9. Parchment, twelfth/thriteenth century, 688 folios. See chapter 2 in this volume (Who Is "the Strongest and Most Skilled Protector of This Oppressed Language"?) with fig. 2.3.

10. Posset 2015, 117–66.

Only later will Reuchlin's publisher Thomas Anshelm use Reuchlin's concept for his printer's logo for numerous book that come of his press.

In 1495, during the imperial diet of Worms, Bishop Johannes von Dalberg (1455–1503) gives Reuchlin the book *Hortus Nucis* (*The Nut Garden*) by the medieval Spanish Cabalist Joseph Gikatilla (1248–after 1305). In 1498–1499 he has the opportunity to travel to Italy a third time, now on behalf of Elector Philip (1448–1508); Reuchlin is ambassador of the Palatinate in Rome. Here he grasps the opportunity to study Hebrew under the renowned Jewish scholar Obadiah Sforno (ca. 1470–ca. 1550). Reuchlin spends a lot of money purchasing Hebrew books in Rome.

With the intensive instruction in the Hebrew language from Jews like Loans at the imperial court in Linz and from Sforno in Rome, Reuchlin is able soon to publish his Hebrew grammar and lexicon for Christians in 1506, *Rudimenta Hebraica* (fig. 3.2). All this work is done in order to be able to properly "search the Scriptures." The first edition is issued in 1500 copies. Four years later, by 1510, only 250 copies have been sold.

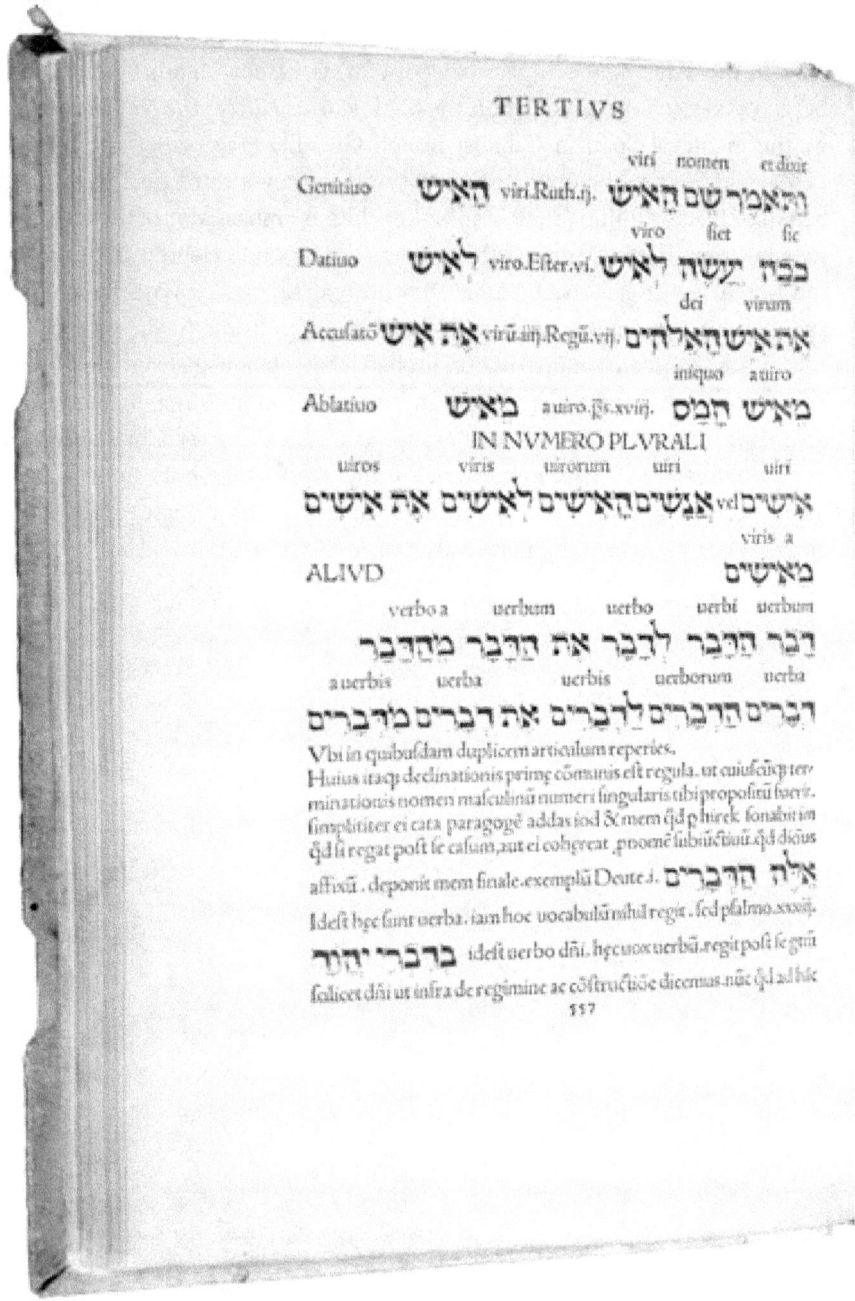

Fig. 3.2. Sample Page from Johann Reuchlin, *Principium libri Ioannis Reuchlin ... de rudimentis hebraicis* (*The Rudiments of Hebrew*). Pforzheim: Thomas Anshelm, 1506.

1.1. Reuchlin's Entanglement in the Battle over Jewish Books

During the battle over Jewish books,[11] the issue of the proper meaning of the "searching in the scriptures" of John 5:39 plays a major role, as Reuchlin's *Expert Opinion* of 1510 for the emperor shows, *Recommendation Whether or Not to Confiscate, Destroy and Burn All Jewish Books*. Reuchlin's answer to the emperor is: NO!

Imperturbably, in 1512 Reuchlin publishes his *Seven Penitential Psalms*: *Joannis Reuchlin Phorcensis LL. doctoris in septem psalmos poenitentiales hebraicos interpretatio de verbo ad verbum* . . . (Tübingen: Thomas Anshelm, 1512),[12] which he has translated from Hebrew into Latin. Driven by the "search of the Scriptures" (John 5:39), he wants people to understand the Psalms from the Hebrew original.

At that time (in 1512) Reuchlin acquires a part of the Talmud (named *Sanhedrin*) as any Jewish texts should help him to better understand the Scriptures. We see him—in his "searching of the scriptures"—to include all Jewish scriptures besides the Scriptures of the Old Testament. This codex (part of the Talmud) is known now as *Codex Reuchlin 2* (fig. 3.3):

---

11. Price 2011; Lorenz and Mertens 2013.

12. Online: MDZ, http://daten.digitale-sammlungen.de/~db/bsb00005533/images/index.html?fip=193.174.98.30&seite=7&pdfseitex=; Posset 2015, 434-46, with the reproduction of the title page (fig. 26).

Fig. 3.3. *Codex Reuchlin 2*, folio 1r. Part of Talmud Tractate Sanhedrin; parchment, between 1400 and 1450. At the bottom of the page shown here Reuchlin entered these words: *Thalmud Ioannis Reuchlin phorcens LL Doctoris* (Talmud of Johann Reuchlin of Pforzheim, Doctor of Laws).

"SEARCH THE SCRIPTURES" ACCORDING TO JOHANN REUCHLIN

In order to better understand Reuchlin in his pursuit of all that is *Hebraica*, one must know that he highly appreciated the famous medieval Spanish bishop Paul of Burgos, of Jewish descent (fig. 3.4), from whose book *Scrutinium scripturarum* he expects to draw support.

1.2. Reuchlin's Reliance on Paul of Burgos

Fig. 3.4. Bishop Paul of Burgos, ca. 1350–1435.

The book, which was famous through the centuries, deals with John 5:39, as already the title indicates: *Scrutinium: Dialogus Pauli et Sauli contra Judaeos, sive Scrutinium scripturarum* (A dialogue between Paul and Saul against the Jews, or: Search of the scriptures). It was written by Bishop Pablo de Santa María (his baptismal name) in 1432–1434, shortly before his death. The key word "search" in the book title is taken from the Vulgate version of John 5:39 (*scrutamini scripturas*), "Search of the scriptures," or "Scrutiny of scriptures." The author, by the Jewish name Solomon ha Levi, had been the most wealthy and influential man of Burgos, a scholar of the first rank in Talmudic and rabbinical literature. He received baptism in 1390. His brothers together with his daughter and four boys were baptized with him. Twenty-five years later, in 1415, he became archbishop of Burgos.[13]

The *Scrutinium scripturarum* is extant in over fifty manuscripts and was published in no less than five editions between 1469 and 1478.[14] After the invention of the printing press, the *Scrutinium* became available in several editions of the fifteenth and sixteenth centuries, printed in Rome 1471, Strasbourg 1474, Mantua 1474/1475; Mainz 1478, Paris 1507 (and after Reuchlin's death, again in Paris in 1535). It was last published in Burgos in 1591. One of the earlier printed editions must have been accessible to Reuchlin, as in the course of time he became very familiar with Bishop Burgos's work. Reuchlin referred to Burgos's *Scrutinium* with the statement about the anti-Christian books such as *Nizzahon* (Nizahon, "Victory," written in 1399) and *Tolduth Jeshua nozri* (*Toldos Jeschu hanozri*, "Life of Jesus"). Reuchlin points out that these books are "considered by the Jews themselves as *apocrypha*," as Paul of Burgos writes in chapter 6 of the second half of his "Scrutinium scripturarum."[15]

---

13. Posset 2015, 260.

14. Reinhardt and Santiago-Otero 1986, 245–48. In recent years, Paul of Burgos received much scholarly attention: His *Scrutinium* has recently been edited in two doctoral dissertations at the Pontifical University of the Holy Cross in Rome: N. Visiers Lecanda, "El Scrutinium Scripturarum de Pablo de Santa María. Parte I: Diálogo imaginario entre el judío Saulo y el cristiano Pablo" (diss. 1998); and Javier Martínez de Bedoya, "La segunda parte del "Scrutinium Scripturarum" de Pablo de Santa María: "El diálogo catequético" (diss. 2002). Detailed consideration of eleven manuscripts in the Bayerische Staatsbibliothek in Munich can be found in Santiago-Otero1987, vol. 1:91–96. Discussion of Yale Beinecke MS 353 can be found in Szpiech 2005, 113–28. A critical edition taking full account of the complex manuscript tradition remains a scholarly desideratum as Ryan Szpiech pointed out, Szpiech 2010, 96–142.

15. SW 4-1: 29.7–14 (*Expert Opinion*), English translation in Wortsman 2000, 34; Posset 2015, 338, 388.

Reuchlin quoted also from Burgos's introduction about the origins of the Talmud before Christ:

> Even before the death of our beloved Lord and long before his birth, the scholars and masters of the Jews wrote much and taught and recorded their teachings in various books and documents. But later, once the Christian faith began to grow, long after our dear Lord's death, and in conformity with the explanation of Rabbi Moses of Egypt [Maimonides] in his Deuteronomy [*Mishneh Torah*; 1,13], they held council and systematically compiled all the writings of their scholars and legal authorities into a single work, as it exists today, and called this collection of the teachings of their masters the Talmud.[16]

John 5:39 became Reuchlin's motivation for all his work, especially in his argumentation of whether or not to confiscate, destroy, and burn all Jewish books early in the sixteenth century, as he wrote in his *Expert Opinion* for the emperor, saying that they should be preserved because Christ said so: "Search the scriptures." Reuchlin declared v. 39 to be "the principal pillar of my argumentation"[17] for the preservation of the Jewish literary tradition:

> In support of my opinion that the Talmud not be burned, I cite the Holy Gospels themselves. For our Lord Jesus Christ said to the Jews: "Search the scriptures; for in them you think you have eternal life: and they are they which testify of me." Since this very passage is the principal pillar [*grundtfeste*] of my argumentation, it is right and fitting to begin here by clearly establishing the precise meaning of each word, so that to bypass the many objections of my opponents, should they choose to raise them in this regard.[18]

These sentences are taken from Reuchlin's *Expert Opinion* for his explanation of the value of the Talmud. Christ himself divided "the scriptures" according to John 5:39 into two: the Bible (*die bibel*) and the books of the masters (*die bücher der maister*)—taken from the German text of Reuchlin's *Expert Opinion*.[19]

---

16. SW 4-1: 40.26—41.2; Posset 2015, 347.

17. [John 5:39] *mein grundtfeste diß ratschlags*; SW 4-1: 38.24; Posset 2015, 346 and 391.

18. SW 4-1: 38.

19. SW 4-1: 39.4–5; Posset 2015, 346.

Reuchlin continued that since Christ himself said that one should search all the scriptures, a book like the Talmud should not be burned. He employed a second biblical quotation for his argumentation of preserving the Talmud and other Jewish books, referring to the books as trees, stating that fruit-bearing trees must not be felled according to Deut 20:19.[20]

Burgos demonstrated that the authentic Catholic beliefs harmonize well with authentic Jewish ones.[21] He elaborated upon exegetical views which he had expressed already in his *Additiones* to the Bible commentaries of Nicholas de Lyra's (ca. 1270–1349, a Franciscan friar). Those "Additions" had become an integral part of all later medieval Latin editions of the commented Bible, *Biblia Latina cum comento*, up to Reuchlin's days.[22]

Burgos attributed to Israel a central role in the history and future of the church, and conceptualized a new "convert" or "converso doctrine" that maintained the singular place of Jewish converts in the unfolding history of salvation. This theological scheme delineated the path from Jewish to Christian beliefs. It also solidified the religious identity of Jewish converts within the Church, allowing them to take great pride in their Jewish lineage.[23] The medieval bishop practiced "Christian Hebraism" by introducing Hebrew linguistic knowledge as the key for the Christian understanding of the Bible. Reuchlin followed him.

Burgos's *Scrutinium* is of importance to Reuchlin for the following reasons:

1. Reuchlin carefully read the *Scrutinium* primarily because he became fascinated by Burgos's demonstration of the truth of the Christian faith, shown from the Talmud.[24] Burgos's ideas about rabbinic traditions and biblical hermeneutics proposed an alternative to the exclusively polarizing representations of Judaism and Christianity. Here now is Reuchlin's decisive view in arguing for the Talmud:

   We may read good and evil writings side by side and examine them; evil writings to rectify them with prudent words, and good writings, which can be found like roses among thorns, to use them and apply them to sacred teaching. Now, there is no one who can

---

20. SW 4-1: 41.6–10; Posset 2015, 347.

21. Yisraeli 2014, 185–215; Yisraeli 2015.

22. See, for example, Franz Posset, *Marcus Marulus and the Biblia Latina of 1489. An Approach to his Biblical Hermeneutics* (Cologne, Weimar, Vienna: Böhlau, 2013).

23. Yisraeli 2015.

24. SW 4-1: 42.6–28; Posset 2015, 388.

say in truth that the Talmud, in which the four higher faculties are described, is completely evil and that one cannot learn anything good from it. For it contains many good medical prescriptions and information about plants and roots, as well as good legal verdicts collected from all over the world by experienced Jews.

Reuchlin continued with his direct reference to Burgos's *Scrutinium*:

And in theology the Talmud offers in many passages arguments against the wrong faith. This can be seen from Bishop of Burgos's books concerning the Bible, which he has written in a praiseworthy and Christian manner, and in the *Scrutinium*, in which he clearly protects our faith on the basis of the Talmud. I noticed and counted in the first part of his *Scrutinium scripturarum* more than fifty passages in which he draws on the Talmud for arguments against the Jews. I do not mention the other part of that book, where he points out many passages in the Talmud which support us Christians.[25]

The opus of Bishop Paul of Burgos was an important theological source for Reuchlin, as he readily admits that Burgos defended the Christian faith with arguments taken from the Talmud.

2. Reuchlin's biblical hermeneutics offered a new view of Scripture interpretation which takes the Hebrew original into serious consideration, yet always remaining within the Catholic frame. Nobody who has read Burgos can deny his merits, Reuchlin continued. When in his train of thought Reuchlin arrived at the issue of the literal interpretation of the Bible he recommended caution. Only simple folks have no sense for higher meanings and want to take everything literally. He cited the historical example against Emperor Julian the Apostate (AD 331–363). Cyril insisted that a text may not always be understood in the literal sense alone, referring to the religious practice of chasing the scapegoat into the desert (Lev 16:10), a ritual which Julian ridiculed. Reuchlin also quoted Jerome on the issue of simplistic literal interpretation. Reuchlin pointed out that at times the Bible and other ancient ways of thinking deliberately cloak their insights in images and in secret code language, similar to alchemists and their technical terms.[26]

---

25. SW 4-1: 42.15–17; Posset 2015, 347–48.
26. SW 4-1: 44.23—46.2.

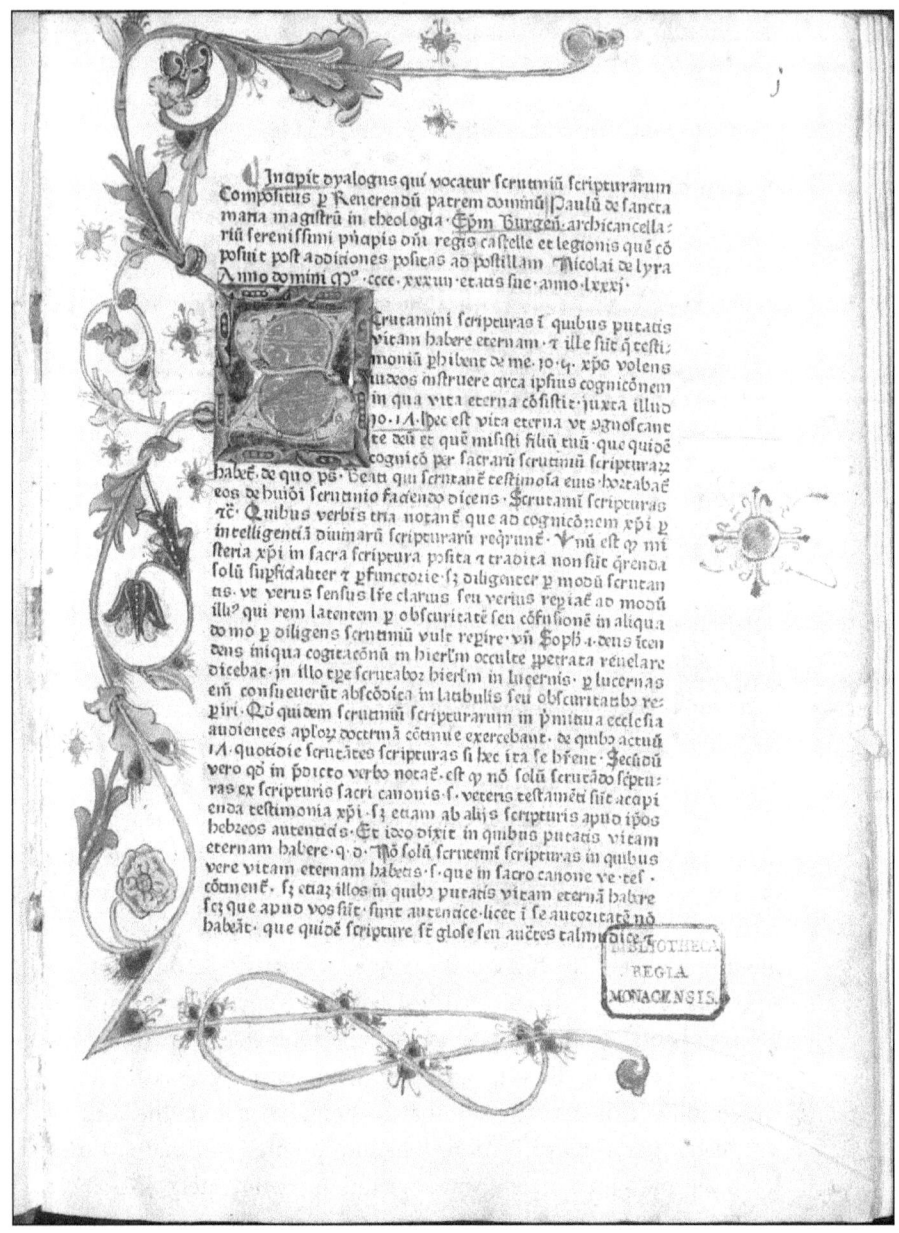

Fig. 3.5. De-luxe edition of Paul of Burgos's *Scrutinium*, Strasbourg, ca. 1474; with references to John 5:39.

3. Most significant is the fact that Reuchlin accepts Burgos's peculiar interpretation of the word "scriptures" in verse John 5:39, namely that the "scriptures" include both the Hebrew Bible and the other writings of the Jews such as the Talmud, as the reader could find this view already expressed on the first page of the bishop's book.

The following two passages are taken from the first page of Burgos's *Scrutinium* (as shown in fig. 3.5):

> Not only are the testimonies for Christ to be accepted from the canonical Scriptures of the Old Testament, but also from the other scriptures which are held authentic with the Hebrews themselves.[27]

Burgos continued in interpreting John 5:39:

> Not only are you to scrutinize those scriptures in which you truly will have eternal life [John 5:39] which are contained in the sacred canonical Old Testament, but also those books in which you believe that you have eternal life, that is, those which are held authentic among you but do not have authority in themselves, which of course are the "scriptures" such as the glosses or the Talmudic authorities ... [28]

Burgos mentioned explicitly the Talmudic authorities (*auctoritates talmudice*).

In following the bishop's thinking, and with the search for the truth of the Scriptures/scriptures and in following Saint Jerome with his concept of the "Hebrew Truth" Reuchlin was not a revolutionary. The concept of the Hebrew Truth (*veritas hebraica*) had been introduced to theology by Jerome.[29] Speaking with Jerome's words, Reuchlin advocated the search for the original well (German *Brunnen*) that the Jews have, and not be content with the runoffs (German *Abflüsse*).[30] Reuchlin took the words of Christ

---

27. ... *quod non solum ex scripturis sacri canonis s. veteris test. sunt accipienda testimonia Christi. sed etiam ab aliis scripturis apud ipsos hebreos autenticis* ... (text from print shown in fig. 5).

28. *Non solum scrutemini scripturas in quibus vere vitam eternam haberetis. quae in sacro canone veteris test. continentur. sed etiam illos in quibus putatis vitam habere. scilicet que apud vos sunt autentice. licet in se autoritatem non habeant. que quidem scripture sunt glo. seu auctoritates talmudice.*

29. The notion "Hebrew Truth" appears to have been coined by Saint Jerome, *Epistola* 57, CSEL 54: 513, 23. In his *Epistola* 106 he used it seven times, CSEL 55: 247–70; Kamin 1992, 243–53; Miletto, 1993, 56–65; Hobbs 1990, 83–99; Oberman 1992, 19–34.

30. SW 4-1: 51.17–19; Posset 2015, 342.

as an imperative: "Search the scriptures," and as such it was taken very seriously in the late Middle Ages and early sixteenth century. Scripture study was the essence of theology.

Of course, Christians had long been using rabbinic materials for polemical, apologetic (and also exegetical purposes). However, the legitimacy and authority of rabbinic traditions was never established in the Church. Bishop Burgos openly advocated the study of rabbinic literature, and delineated new channels for the inclusion of rabbinic literature within Christian scholarship. The Talmud, according to Burgos, was a collection of various teachings from different periods, and it included ancient and authentic traditions that preceded Jesus. Some parts of the Jewish rabbinic literature were essential to the religious context in which Jesus preached and established the church; and thus the Judaism from which Christianity emerged was rabbinic as much as it was biblical. From a conservative Christian perspective it was a bold theory that rabbinic traditions were a powerful tool that can shed a new light on the New Testament (Yisraeli).

With respect to John 5:39 Reuchlin definitely followed Burgos whose entire line of argumentation presupposes that this verse goes beyond the books of the Old Testament. Reuchlin will never give up this position, even under pressure as is evident from Reuchlin's *Eye Glasses* of 1511,[31] *Doctor Johannsen Reuchlins . . . Augenspiegel* (Tübingen: Thomas Anshelm, 1511). With its forty-two pages, Reuchlin now publicly defended Jewish scriptures against their confiscation, as he had argued already in his more or less confidential *Expert Opinion* written was submitted to the emperor.

Since Reuchlin became known as a defender of the writings of the Jews, including the Talmud, on the basis of Christ's command in John 5:39, one of his adversaries quickly labeled him a "Talmudist." It was Professor Ortwin Gratius (ca. 1480–1542), a priest-humanist in Cologne, who set the traditional theologians up "against Johann Reuchlin, the Talmudist."[32] The phalanx formed on the one side with Reuchlin, equipped with Bishop Paul of Burgos's theological support, against an author on the other side, along with his supporters, who pursue exactly the opposite. This adversary was Johann Pfefferkorn (1469–1521), a self-appointed missionary to the Jews.[33] This Catholic lay theologian of Jewish descent defamed the Jews in a pamphlet of 1509, *Ich bin ain Buechlinn der Juden veindt* (*Enemy of the Jews*,

31. Argument 23, SW 4-1: 102.18—104.15; Posset 2015, 350, 410.
32. . . . *contra Joannem Reuchlin Talmudistam*; Posset 2015, 536.
33. See chapter 8.

see fig. 3.6). Pfefferkorn's attacks against the Jews irked Reuchlin so much that he felt compelled to mention it to the emperor in his *Expert Opinion* of 1510, referring to it as follows: "A pamphlet defaming the Jews has recently

Fig. 3.6. Colorized print of Johann Pfefferkorn, *Ich bin ain Buechlinn der Juden veindt*.

been printed."[34] Pfefferkorn found a likeminded theologian in the inquisitor of Cologne, Jacob von Hoogstraeten (ca. 1460–1527). Hoogstraeten, too, submitted an expert opinion to the emperor, but with a position contrary to Reuchlin's.

34. SW 4-1: 34.

The inquisitor Hoogstraeten was Reuchlin's fierce adversary. One of his works against Reuchlin is best known by its first word *Erronee* ("Erroneous [Assertions]") of 1517.[35] In it he listed nineteen *Erroneous Assertions* in the hope of using them for disputations or presentations in Rome in 1516 and 1517, especially during sessions of the ongoing Fifth Lateran Council. "But despite the dogged efforts to have the case placed on the agenda, that venue was never granted to him."[36] He wanted Reuchlin's *argumenta* in the *Eye Glasses* to be excluded from further consideration because they were not really explications but represent a definite contradiction to other statements Reuchlin had made.

The main point of the kerfuffle was Reuchlin's understanding of John 5:39 ("Search the scriptures") with the understanding that all Jewish scriptures are meant, which was the subject of six of Hoogstraeten's nineteen articles. Hoogstraeten knew exactly that this verse was Reuchlin's pillar of argumentation. Hoogstraeten opposed the expansion of the meaning of the verse if it comprises non-biblical "scriptures." He pointed out that Reuchlin's defense of those Jewish "scriptures," including the Talmud, would question the papal condemnations of the thirteenth century. In 1519, Hoogstraeten published another book against Reuchlin, his *Destructio Cabale*; he even included Reuchlin's name on the title page (fig. 3.7).

---

35. Full title: *Erronee assertiones in oculari speculo Io. Reuchlin verbatim posite et conclusiones per magistrum Iacobum de alta platea eisdem obiecte* (Rome: Giacomo Mazzocchi [?], 1517); Posset 2015, 623–24.

36. Price 2011, 185; Price, however, is mistaken in stating that Hoogstraeten attacked the errors in Reuchlin's *Recommendation* (*Expert Opinion*); Price obviously meant Reuchlin's *Eye Glasses*.

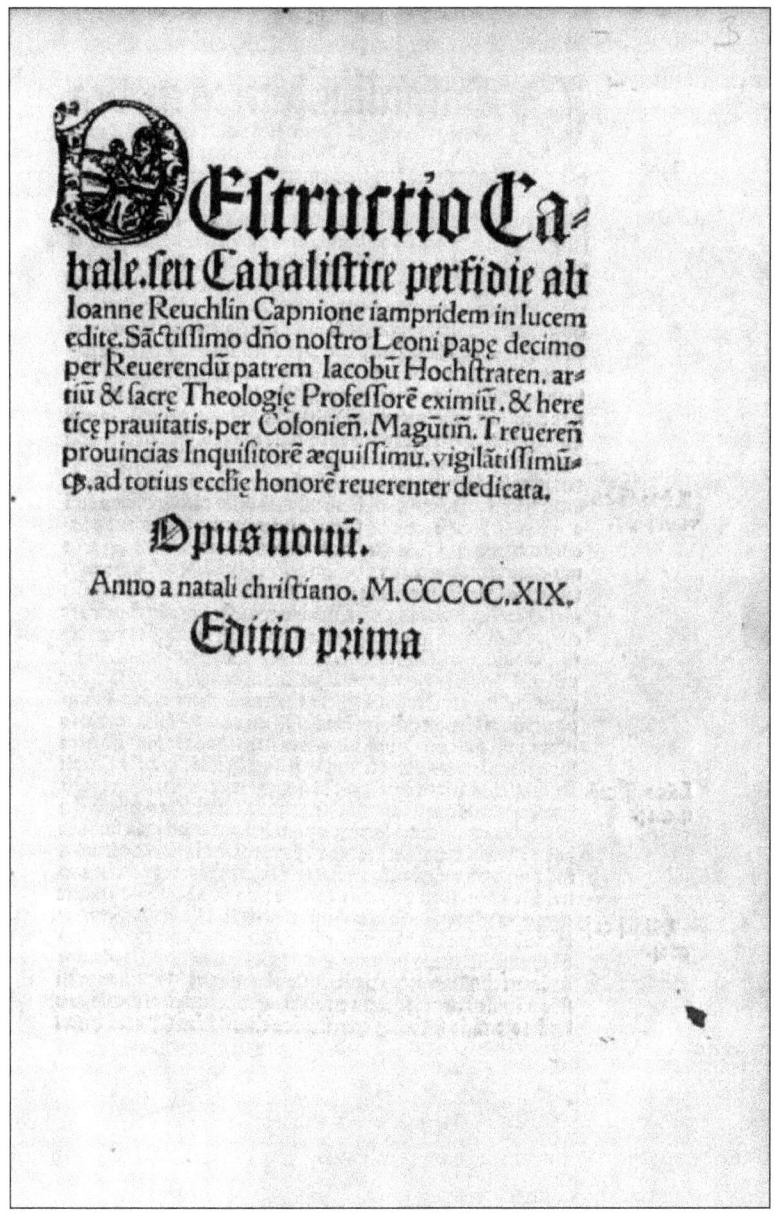

Fig. 3.7. Jacob von Hoogstraeten, *Destructio Cabale*, Cologne: Quentel, 1519.

Quite in contrast to the inquisitor, Reuchlin is in step with papal thinking of that time (with his position concerning the books of the Jews). This can be seen from some most remarkable facts of those years: in 1516/1517 the

Christian printer in Venice Daniel Bomberg (d. ca. 1549) (fig. 3.8) issued the entire Hebrew Bible with comments, in four volumes. Bomberg was one of the most important printers of Hebrew books. He employed rabbis, scholars and former Jews.

Fig. 3.8. Daniel Bomberg.

Fig. 3.9. Bomberg's Rabbinic Bible (edition of 1524/1525). Page showing Gen 1.

Reuchlin purchased the four volumes right away. This opus is known as the first rabbinic Bible (fig. 3.9), i.e., the Bible with commentaries by rabbis. Reuchlin's copy was destroyed in September 1942 during bomb attacks on the city of Karlsruhe.[37]

A few years later, Bomberg achieved something else yet: Pope Leo X granted copyright to Bomberg in publishing the complete, largely uncensored Babylonian Talmud in 1520–1523! (fig. 3.10). Bomberg's edition of the Talmud comprises twelve volumes.[38] The papal printing privilege was explicitly mentioned in Bomberg's letter to Reuchlin of September 23, 1521.[39]

37. Posset 2015, 791.
38. Posset 2015, 790.
39. RBW 4: 387, 5 (no. 398).

Fig. 3.10. Pages from Bomberg's first Talmud print, 1520.

Conclusion

Johann Reuchlin's life and work is a prime example of the genial theory about church history, namely, that church history is the theological struggle over the proper interpretation of the Sacred Scriptures and its ramifications, provocatively formulated: church history is the history of the exposition of Scripture.[40] This is true for Reuchlin because Reuchlin was highly motivated by Christ's words "Search the scriptures" (John 5:39). He felt confirmed in pursuing this by Bishop Paul's book *Scrutinium scripturarum*. It is probably no exaggeration to assume that all aspects of Reuchlin's life and work have something to do with this biblical verse. He expressed his own self-understanding briefly already in his early work *The Wonder-Working Word* (1494) somewhat connected to this Johannine verse when

40. Ebeling 1968, 11–32.

he stated that he was an "inquisitive researcher of every school of thought."[41] Reuchlin was probably the first Christian to read Jewish texts without "polemical interests."[42] This Scripture verse inspired him to carefully read not only the Sacred Scriptures in the original languages but also the other scriptures of the Jews. In doing this he made not only church history, but made general history. Reuchlin in his interpretation of John 5:39 and, in acting upon his insights from it, developed a fondness for the sacred texts of the Jews and fiercely defended them during the famous controversy early in the sixteenth century of whether to confiscate, destroy, and burn all Jewish books. His response, based upon John 5:39, was an emphatic, *No*.

---

41. *Omnis sectae curiosus explorator*, SW 1-1: 58.25-26.
42. Price 2011 (in the conclusion of his book), 230.

4

God's Language, Catholic Praise of the Sacred Language of the Jews during the Early Reformation, with Georg Witzel's Speech in Praise of the Hebrew Language

Latin Original with English Translation

THIS TOPIC DEALS WITH several factors:

1. Catholic praise of the Hebrew language. The [three] Catholic eulogies with which we deal here are not very well known and are not mentioned, for example, in the recent book, *Christian Hebraism in the Reformation Era (1500–1660): Authors, Books, and the Transmission of Jewish Learning*.[1]

2. The speeches are delivered in Latin, i.e., the *lingua franca* of the time, occasionally with some Greek words in the original, but rarely any Hebrew words because the printers of these speeches were not equipped with Hebrew types.

3. The speeches grew from the milieu of biblical humanism.[2]

---

1. Burnett 2012.
2. On biblical humanism, see Augustijn 2003; Rummel 2008.

4. The speeches were delivered during the early years of Martin Luther's (1483–1546) Reformation, in the first half of the sixteenth century. Therefore, I first must say a few words on Luther and the Jews.

The spectacular celebrations of the five hundredth anniversary of the Reformation had culminated in 2017 after a decade of commemorative Luther studies worldwide. Many people commemorated the Lutheran Reformation, but did not celebrate it. Those who cherish Christian-Jewish dialogue probably have the least motivation to celebrate because the Reformation five hundred years ago was born with the "birth defect"[3] of antijudaism and/or antisemitism (whatever term you prefer), which is more than just the "tainting" of Luther's "greatness."[4] Both expressions (antijudaism and antisemitism) probably apply in his case, even though the expression "antisemitism" as a racially charged term first came into existence in the nineteenth century. This birth defect is noticeable most of all in Luther, whereas other reformers such as Ulrich Zwingli and John Calvin did not write books or pamphlets concerning the Jews.

The year 2017 should not have been only a year of the commemoration of the five hundredth anniversary of the Reformation, but also a celebration of the great Hebraist Johann Reuchlin. Unfortunately, this Catholic Hebraist does not have a "lobby" that would promote such a celebration today. Yet, a Florentine contemporary has already celebrated him as "the unique philosopher and theologian of our time who showed us a dialogue on the art of the Cabala," as Bartolomeo Cerretani reported in 1520 about his encounter with Reuchlin at the Frankfurt Book Fair.[5] Reuchlin was an older contemporary of the reformers in German-speaking lands.

1. The Context of the Praise of the Hebrew Language

With respect to the historical context (i.e., the Reformation) for the praise of Hebrew, a few introductory questions and observations are in order. Is Martin Luther really just a man of his times and can he, therefore, be exonerated of his outrageous agitation against the Jews? Luther could have swum against the current of his time as he did concerning so many other issues. Instead, Luther like a vacuum cleaner sucked up all the medieval

---

3. Wengst 2014.
4. Harrowitz 1994, 15–36 (on Luther).
5. Posset 2015, 14.

dirt that was thrown at the Jews and he more than willingly functioned as the megaphone par excellence of the late medieval and contemporaneous antijudaism. Luther, like the rulers of Portugal and Spain in 1492 and 1496, gave the Jews only one alternative: be baptized or get out.[6] Luther could have opted for an alternative, and he could have reminded himself and his followers that in recent history there was a different emperor, Frederick III (reigned 1440–1493), who was so fair to the Jews that he was ridiculed as "king of the Jews."[7] Fairness to Jews was not on Luther's agenda. Luther could have joined contemporaries like Reuchlin, the philosemitic scholar, who recommended dialogue with Jews in an Open Letter of 1505.[8] But Luther did not. Instead he opted to make use only of Reuchlin's expertise in Hebrew grammar, as he ignored Reuchlin's advocacy for the Jews as fellow citizens and for their religious philosophy, called Cabala.

In his book *The Wonder-Working Word* (Basel 1494) Reuchlin praised the Hebrew language as simple, unspoiled, holy, and concise. It is the language in which God communicated without a translator face to face.[9] Reuchlin saw in the Hebrew language the venue to God's mysteries and therefore a means of grace, a "*sacramentum*": "The Hebrew alphabet is the more sacred sacrament." There is nothing more enjoyable than this sacrament. Nothing is better than getting to "know God's foreseeing and to enter into God's secrets."[10] Reuchlin shared with his pen pal, Nicolaus Ellenbog (1481–1543), a Benedictine monk, his intimate thoughts about the Hebrew language and how through it he has a relationship with God:

> Thus may the best and greatest God love me since, after I have tried various other studies, nothing from among all other languages that I have learned connects me more to God than practicing the reading of the Sacred Scriptures in Hebrew. For whenever I read Hebrew it seems to me that God Himself is speaking with me as I think that this language is the means God and angels use in dealing with human beings. When I do that, I am shaken by some sort of shudder and terror, not, however, without ineffable joy that follows this awe or rather such numbness, a joy which I really would like to call wisdom of which the divine Hebrew verse says: "The

---

6. *An Admonition against the Jews* (1546); WA 51: 195, 9–17; LW 58:458.
7. Posset 2015, 108.
8. See chapter 6 of this volume.
9. SW 1-1: 162.36–39.
10. *De rudimentis*, preface 3, in RBW 2: 45.283 (no. 138); Posset 2015, 262–63.

fear of the Lord is the beginning of wisdom" [Ps 110:10 = 111:10; Prov 1:7].[11]

Father Ellenbog, after reading Reuchlin's works, was inspired to respond with a biblical quotation: "Salvation comes from the Jews," quoting John 4:22.[12]

In contrast, Luther chose to take a position concerning Jews which was much closer to, if not identical with, Reuchlin's formidable adversary Johann Pfefferkorn (ca. 1469–1521), an early ethnographer of Judaism, and self-appointed missionary to the Jews.[13] He, like Luther, was convinced that rabbinic Judaism is in theological discontinuity with the Hebrew Bible, and must be considered an aberration.[14] Both Pfefferkorn and Luther called for deportation and expulsion of Jews and for the destruction of their homes, houses of prayer, and even prayer books in order to prevent any blasphemies spreading in public. Luther "outpaced" him and all other contemporaries and their anti-Jewish writings, "both quantitatively and 'qualitatively.'"[15]

Luther's ferocious hatred of the Jews and their (in his mind, blasphemous) faith may not be generally known, neither the efforts of today's Lutheran Churches around the world to disassociate themselves from Luther's bad attitude toward the Jews. This happened, for example, at the international celebration of Luther's five hundredth birthday in 1983[16] and in 1994 with the *Declaration of the Evangelical Lutheran Church in America to the Jewish Community*.[17] Yet, to assume that Luther did not write against the "Jews as such," but only against "Jewish errors"[18] is a fallacy. First, because Jews at that time definitely felt in the words of their speaker, Josel of Rosheim (ca. 1478–1554), that Luther wanted "to annihilate all of Jewry in this world and in the world to come."[19] Second, Luther himself did not

---

11. RBW 2: 130.8–17 (no. 162).

12. RBW 3: 455.9 (no. 315, of 1516).

13. Adams and Heß 2017.

14. On Pfefferkorn's call to burn the Talmud (in *The Jews' Mirror* of 1507 and *Jewish Confession* of 1508), see Posset 2015, 300–302; for Luther, see Schramm and Stjerna 2012.

15. Schramm and Stjerna, 8.

16. *Statements from the International Jewish Committee on Interreligious Consultations (IJCIC) and the Lutheran World Federation (LWF) Consultation*, Stockholm, 1983.

17. Of April 18, 1994, http://www.jewishvirtuallibrary.org/jsource/anti-semitism/lutheran1.html.

18. Hagen 1999, 130–57, here 157 / Hagen 2016, 399–429.

19. Josel the Jew of Rosheim responds to Martin Luther's booklet against the Jews, July 11, 1543, in Schramm and Stjerna, 181–87, here 183. In his letter to Josel of June

make such a distinction (Jews as such and Jewish errors), but recommended "sharp mercy" in persecuting them and even refusing safe-conduct for them.[20] With his plan of action Luther was more in line with Pfefferkorn whose works he, however, never cited.

Pfefferkorn was so influential that in 1530 Antonius Margaritha (Margareta, Margalita, ca. 1490–1542) of Regensburg reused Pfefferkorn's illustrations in *The Jewish Confession* (1508) in his own book of 1530, *Der gantz Jüdisch glaub* (*The whole Jewish faith*),[21] a book which Luther highly recommended in 1543: "For further information you may read Anthonius Margaritha on their devilish practices [*Teufelswerck*]."[22] Luther also picked as a resource the book by the medieval Carthusian monk named Porchetus Salvaticus (d. ca. 1315) in the print from Paris 1520, in which Luther entered his marginalia.[23]

Clearly, Luther looked for and found primarily those secondary source materials, both medieval and contemporaneous, which matched his preconceptions against the Jews. Luther expressed those opinions about the Jews, for example, early on in a letter of 1514 in response to George Spalatin's (1484–1545) request to share his opinion about Reuchlin. True, Luther declared Reuchlin innocent, sound and pure of faith, and not at all a heretic as the men of Cologne (around Pfefferkorn and the inquisition) would have him. But Luther did not leave it at that. He continued with what he said was his "conclusion" (already in 1514!) about the Jews: "I have come to the conclusion that the Jews will always curse and blaspheme God and his King Christ, as all the prophets have predicted." "A hundred times worse blasphemies than this one [at Cologne] exists in the very streets of Jerusalem."[24] This early conviction of 1514 matches his late tirade of 1543 against the Jews which he uttered in his letter to the chief Lutheran pastor in Berlin, Georg Buchholzer (1503–1566), that with their blasphemies the

---

11, 1537, Luther addressed him as his "good friend" while simultaneously refusing to support him in his cause; WA.B 8: 89.1 (no. 3157).

20. WA 53: 417–552.

21. Rummel 2002, figs. 2–5; see above (introduction) with fig. 0.1.

22. WA 53: 152.29–30 (in 1543); see also WA.TR 5: 198.18–20 (no. 5504); Posset 2015, 291.

23. WA 60: 236.

24. WA.B 1: 23–24 (no. 7b).

Jews are personified devils: "For these Jews are not Jews, but devils incarnate who curse our Lord."²⁵ (fig. 4.1).

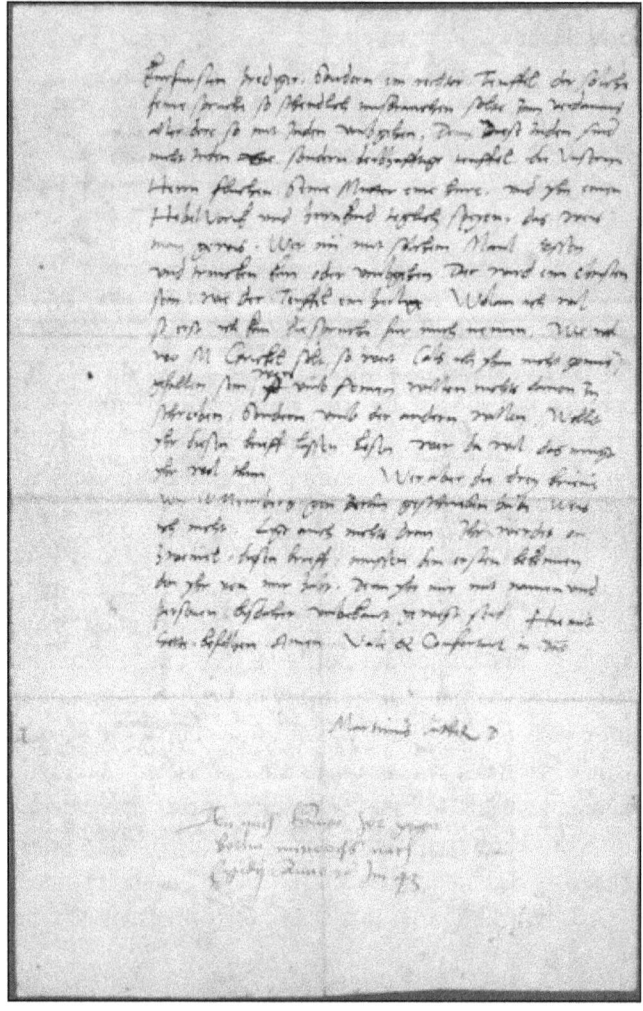

Fig. 4.1. Autograph letter from Martin Luther to Georg Buchholzer, provost of St Nikolai in Berlin. Written in Wittenberg, ca. September 1, 1543; backside, with Luther's signature; Luther's expression *leibhafftige teuffel* ("devils incarnate") is seen in line 4 (shown here).

25. "Denn diese Juden sind nicht Juden sondern leibhafftige teuffel, die Unserm Herrn fluchen." WA.B 10: 388–89 (no. 3909). Luther's letter to Buchholzer is already mentioned in a book of 1952 by Salo Wittmayer Baron, *A Social and Religious History of the Jews*, 431n30, https://books.google.com/books?id=BNKd2nSyxPAC&dq=Luther%2 7s+letter%2C+no.+3909&q=buchholzer#v=snippet&q=buchholzer&f=false.

Luther's attitude was consistent and also somewhat schizophrenic in his hatred/disrespect of the Jews and his simultaneous respect for their language. In his drive to better understand the holy Word of God in Sacred Scripture of both Testaments he needed to better understand the Bible in its original Hebrew in order to get to what then was called the "Hebrew Truth."[26] And with respect to the Greek New Testament, Luther wanted to explore its Hebraisms (see quote below). For him to be successful in such an exegetical enterprise he needed to study the Hebrew language and grammar as it was presented by Christian Hebraists such as Reuchlin. Luther made good use of Hebrew language studies, but rejected the Jewish (rabbinic) exegesis of the so-called Old Testament. He felt it to be an assault on Christianity. Thus, his aversion against Jews is biblically driven.[27] His aversion is connected to his "affective Christocentrism" which has been acknowledged by Catholic Luther scholarship of recent decades, but without condoning any anti-Jewish elements. Luther's doctrine of justification of the sinner by grace in faith is officially recognized, but—again—without including his antijudaism, in the *Joint Declaration* of 1999 between the Catholic Church and the Lutheran World Federation, which was signed by representatives of the Vatican and the Lutheran World Federation.

No other scholar in German-speaking lands on the eve of the Reformation was more dedicated than Johann Reuchlin to promoting the study of "sacred philology,"[28] i.e., Latin, Greek and Hebrew, but also the study of Jewish philosophy, the Cabala. It is often forgotten that Reuchlin wrote two books on Catholic Cabala: *The Wonder-Working Word of God* (1494) and *The Art of the Cabala* (1517), which was dedicated to Pope Leo X.[29] Reuchlin clearly pointed out his understanding and appreciation of Cabalistic sources and the importance of minute details, "that the divine word [is] to be taken allegorically, in the way of the Cabala. No word, no letter, however tiny, not even the accentuation, was without significance."[30]

Luther in particular ignored Reuchlin's benevolent statements about Jews as brothers and Reuchlin's love for the Cabala. Luther dismissed

---

26. Jerome, *Epistola* 57, in CSEL 54: 513, 23. In his *Epistola* 106 he used it seven times, CSEL 55: 247–70.

27. Schramm and Stjerna, 4 and 13.

28. Kristeller 1979, 72.

29. *De arte Cabalistica libri tres Leo X. dicati* (Hagenau: Thomas Anshelm, 1517); English version by Goodman 1983.

30. SW 2-1: 82.10–13.

Cabalistic speculations as "sorcery" which any proper interpretation of Scripture can unmask, and as the devil's feces (*Teufelsmist*).[31] Luther actually rejected Reuchlin's interpretation of the holy name of God, *Tetragrammaton*, without however any mention of Reuchlin's name. In regard to the latter issue, Reuchlin can in no way be regarded as a forerunner of the Reformer Martin Luther. The ideological concept that stands behind the *Luther Monument* of 1868 in Worms, Germany, had developed through the centuries under the spell of Philip Melanchthon (1497–1560).[32] Protestant Germany celebrated Reuchlin only as the Father of Christian Hebraism, and not as the promoter of the Cabala.

I am not convinced that there are major developments in Luther's attitude toward the Jews. Occasionally, Luther's treatise of 1523 *That Jesus Christ Was Born a Jew* is cited as proof that he had a changed attitude and an open mind toward Jews. This one pamphlet may sound a bit more positive, but it is not really a development to the better. In it Luther simply recommends what canon law recommended over the centuries: Be nice to the Jews if you want to convert them. This text of 1523 is "a sustained critique of Jewish exegesis of Christian proof texts."[33]

It is equally flawed to assume that in the sixteenth-century Lutherans (with their emphasis on Scripture) were the only ones who promoted the study of the biblical languages. Already in the second half of the fifteenth century Flavus Mithridates (ca. 1450–ca. 1490), who called himself a convert to the "evangelical truth,"[34] had no intention to refute the Jewish faith or to enlighten Jews in their "obstinacy." He did not want to speak "against the Jews" (*adversus Judaeos*), but instead make "our true credibility" much stronger on the basis of the various ancient languages, Aramaic, Hebrew, Arabic and Greek.[35]

Reuchlin was a fearless defender of the books of the Jews.[36] A Cistercian monk by the name Urbanus observed how Reuchlin stood up to the so-called theologians (*theologistas*) at Cologne in defense of the "ancient theology" and in defense of his "Hebrew clients,"[37] the Jews. Reuchlin

31. Hagen 2016, 420.
32. Posset 2015, 19–25.
33. Schramm and Stjerna, 77.
34. Wirszubski 1963, 90.
35. Wirszubski 1963, 80.
36. Price 2011; Lorenz and Mertens 2013; Shamir 2011; De Boer 2016.
37. RBW 2: 402.7 (no. 223).

was convinced that "the Jew is as worthy in the eyes of our Lord as am I"[38] and that "the Jewish faith is none of our business."[39] His adversaries were dismayed that he called the Jews "fellow citizens." To them he responded: "Now I would want them [Reuchlin's adversaries] to go berserk even more, their guts may burst open because I say that the Jews are our brothers."[40] No such words are known to have come from Luther's mouth or pen.

Reuchlin researched the Hebrew Bible because it originated from the "mouth of God." It was his conviction that from this divine font "all theology has gushed forth."[41] For that reason the language of the Jews "must be kissed tenderly and embraced with both arms" as one hugs little children.[42] And, one should remember that with his Hebrew grammar (*Rudimenta*) Reuchlin did not offer just a primer for the study of Hebrew. The knowledge of Hebrew is a necessary precondition also for the "arcane discipline of Pythagoras and the art of the Cabala" and for the oldest philosophy of the venerable ancient ones.[43]

Both Reuchlin and Luther liked the same adage (of obscure origin) that was generally known in their days. Reuchlin used it in 1512 in his letter to a physician: "We Latin people drink from the swamp, the Greeks from the rivers, the Jews from the springs." He immediately added: "For the prince of medicine is Raphael an angel of the Jews."[44] Although Reuchlin might not be the original author of the adage, he used it for his understanding of the origins of medicine coming from God through the archangel, not for the praise of the Hebrew language as such. Luther liked the adage, too, as he quoted it in the following wording in one of his numerous talks after dinner, dated August 9, 1532. Luther brought it up in the context of dealing with the study of Hebrew and of Hebraisms in the New Testament:

> If I were younger, I would want to learn this language better, because without it one can never understand Sacred Scripture. For the New Testament, even though it is written in Greek, is full of Hebraisms and of the Hebrew way of speaking. For that reason

---

38. SW 4-1: 59.20.
39. SW 4-1: 48.35.
40. SW 4-1: 344.19–22.
41. *A quo fonte omnis theologia scaturiuit*; Preface to *De rudimentis* (1506) in RBW 2: 35.13–22 (no. 138).
42. RBW 2: 35.26–28 (no. 138).
43. RBW 2: 37.105—38.115 (no. 138); Posset 2015, 257–63.
44. RBW 2: 250.69–70 (no. 192).

they are correct who say: "The Hebrews drink from the source, the Greeks from the rills that are flowing from the source, and the Latin people [drink] from the puddle."⁴⁵

Luther esteemed Hebrew so very much that he would have liked to study it more thoroughly. He moved within the tradition of "biblical humanism" with its emphasis on the Scriptures in the original languages.

Reuchlin always wanted to be a loyal son of the Catholic Church and was proud that in his struggles he had "almost all of Rome" on his side.⁴⁶ Luther could not care less. Apparently insiders like Ulrich von Hutten (1488–1523), an early Lutheran, began to realize that Reuchlin had no intention of going with Luther against Rome. An enraged Hutten wrote to Reuchlin on February 22, 1521 (about one and a half years before Reuchlin's death): "Go to Rome and kiss Lord Leo's feet. . . . You do not like Luther's cause, you disprove of it, you want to see it destroyed. . . . You will always find me in total disagreement with you, not so much when you fight against Luther's cause as when you submit to the Roman pontiff."⁴⁷

This much needed to be said for the historical context for what is to follow.

2. The Praise of Hebrew by Catholic Hebraists

First, it needs to be pointed out that neither Luther nor Reuchlin ever gave an entire speech in praise of the language of the Jews. Yet, in German-speaking lands, Reuchlin's love of and advocacy for the Hebrew language was widely known. He inspired younger scholars to compose speeches about this language. One outstanding and well-known example was his relative Philip Melanchthon in Wittenberg. On August 28, 1518, he delivered his inaugural address with the focus on a course correction in high education, titled *De corrigendis adolescentiae studii*. It was not an explicit eulogy of the Hebrew language, but a plea to learn the biblical languages. One wonders whether he had only theology students in mind when he declared: "Theology is partly Hebrew, partly Greek. We Latin people drink from their

---

45. WA.TR 1: 525.15–20 (no. 1040); two Latin versions: no. 3271a and no. 3271b; see chapter 5 in this volume.

46. Posset 2015, 713–809. In the end, Reuchlin, however, was fined by the Roman authority for his book *Eye Glasses*, but acquitted of heresy. It seems that he never paid the fine, though.

47. RBW 4: 376.19–42 (no. 395).

streams."[48] Melanchthon avoided the negative connotation about the dirty swamps from which the Latin people drink. Notably, he assigned the same rank to Greek and Hebrew, unlike Reuchlin. Melanchthon's later speech *Declamatio de lingua hebraica discenda*, given shortly before his death in 1560, was not a eulogy either.[49] It was an admonition to learn Hebrew and Greek. Melanchthon employed the metaphors of fonts and rills for the Hebrew sources and the runoffs into the Latin rivulets (*rivuli*) and ponds (*lacunae*). He framed his speech with the same Vulgate verse, Psalm 67:27 [Ps 68:27], reciting it at the beginning and at the end: "Bless the Lord [in the churches] about the fonts of Israel."[50] As a Reformer he was convinced that doctrinal clarity comes from the sources.[51]

2.1. The Spaniard Matthaeus Adrianus (ca. 1470–1521): Hebrew Holds the First Place

Matthaeus Adrianus was a well-known Hebraist of Spanish-Jewish descent. In 1512 Reuchlin had helped him get an instructor position for Hebrew at Tübingen. In Reuchlin's letter to his old friend Sebastian Brant, of January 4, 1513, one reads that he brought Adrianus "to our general study in Tübingen.[52] In 1513 Reuchlin recommended him also for a position with the printer Amerbach in Basel who needed help with the edition of the Jerome edition.[53] Adrianus knew Hebrew "like nobody else in Germany."[54] He may have been the author of a brief introduction to Hebrew[55] and he became known through the booklet in which he had translated central Christian prayers into Hebrew. This Latin-Hebrew booklet had been published by

---

48. CR 11: 22–23.
49. CR 12: 386–92 (no. 180).
50. *Benedicite Domino in Ecclesiis de fontibus Israel*; CR 12: 386 and 392.
51. CR 12: 389.
52. RBW 2: 366.13–14 (no. 214).
53. Posset 2015, 365.
54. Letter to Amerbach of January 4, 1513; RBW 2: 362, 3–7 (no. 213); see also 2: 366, 13–14 (no. 214); Posset 2015, 290; 305–7, 362–65.
55. *Introductio Utilissima Hebraice Discere Cupientibus*, which was printed first in Venice and reprinted in Erfurt in 1501 or 1502.

Reuchlin's printer, Thomas Anshelm, while at Tübingen early in 1513.[56] Adrianus did not like it in Tübingen and moved on,[57] probably to Louvain.

While Adrianus was still at Louvain, he gave a speech on the feast day of Saint Benedict (March 21, 1519), "*Oratio de linguarum laude*" (On the praise of the languages). The title page of the imprint does not reveal anything about any praise of the Hebrew language, but only something about the person to whom the print is dedicated, Father George Spalatin at the court of Elector Frederick the Wise, and about the author, who called himself a physician, a soldier of Christ, and a professor of sacred letters.[58] Why Adrianus did not last long at Wittenberg probably had something to do with disagreements with Luther's distinct theological positions. We know this for sure only of Adrianus's predecessor at Wittenberg, the Hebraist Johann Boeschenstain (1472–1540), a diocesan priest who had been hired for the university at the same time as Melanchthon. He quickly departed on January 20, 1520, to Melanchthon's great disappointment.[59] Luther and Boeschenstain had major differences over the theological function of teaching Hebrew. Luther suspected Boeschenstain to be a Jew at heart, called him an "arch-Jew," and Christian only by name.[60] Luther objected to the slightest traces of Judaizing among Christian Hebrew scholars.

---

56. *Libellus Hora faciendi pro Domino, scilicet filio Virginis Mariae, cuius mysterium in prologo legenti patebit* (Tübingen: Anshelm, 1513); Posset 2015, 306. See chapter 7 of this volume.

57. Posset 2015, 363.

58. Online: http://daten.digitale-sammlungen.de/~db/0002/bsb00024465/images/index.html?seite=00001&l=en; or: https://play.google.com/store/books/details/Matth%C3%A4us_Adriani_Oratio_quam_Lovanii_habuit_de_lin?id=imm7YbnXoBcC; also listed online as *Venerabili Sibi In Domino, Magistro Georgio Spalatino Illustris. Prin, Friderici & c̄. a sacris & Epistolis*.

59. Scheible 1993, 133; Posset 2015, 552.

60. Luther's letter to Friar Lang of April 13, 1519, WA.B 1: 368 (no. 167).

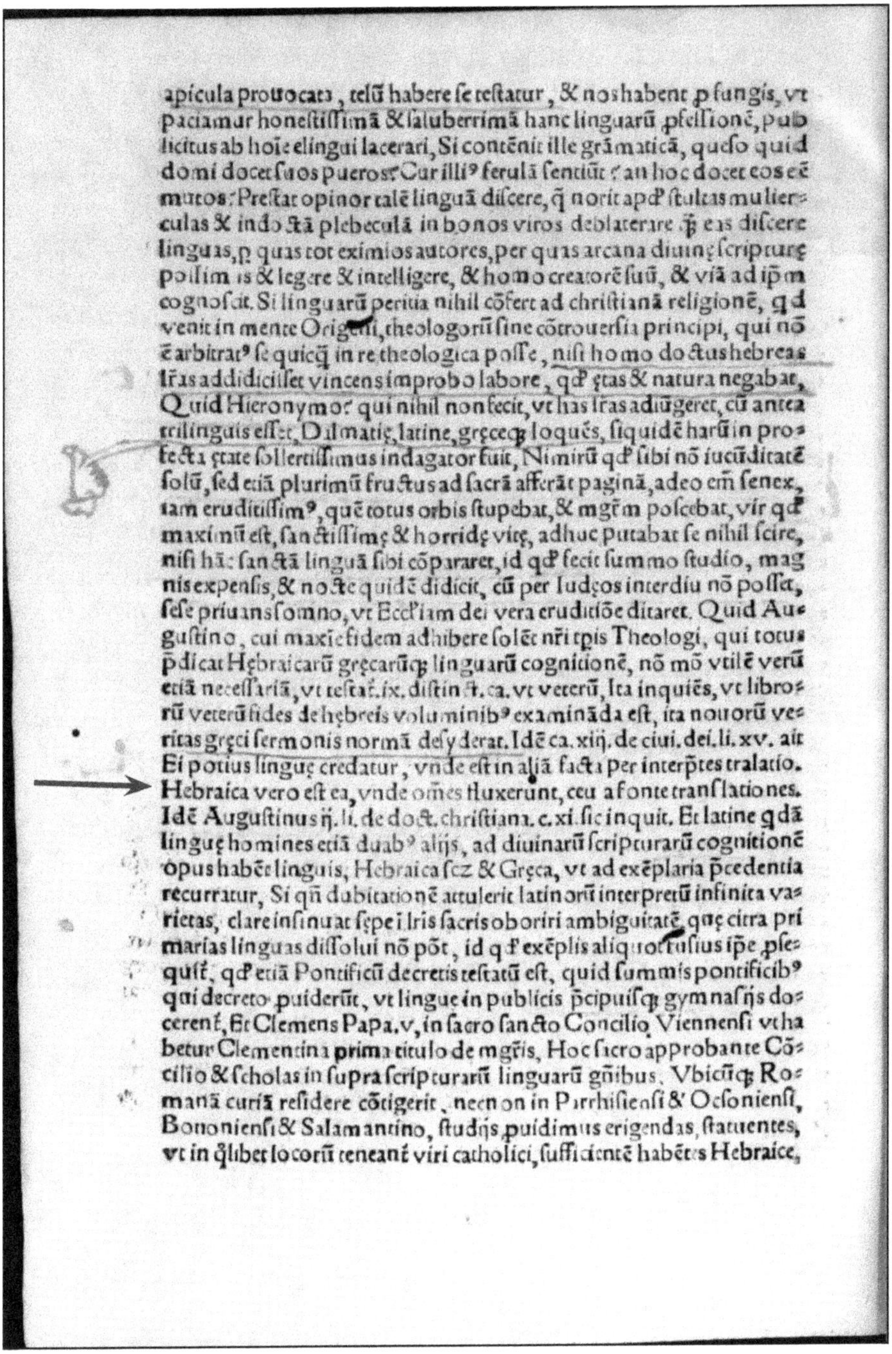

apicula prouocat?, telū habere se testatur, & nos habent p fungis, vt paciamur honestissimā & saluberrimā hanc linguarū pfessionē, pub licitus ab hoīe elingui lacerari, Si contēnit ille grāmaticā, queso quid domi docet suos pueros? Cur illi[9] ferulā sentiūt? an hoc docet eos eē mutos? Prestat opinor talē linguā discere, q̄ norit ap[d] stultas mulier- culas & indo ctā plebeculā in bonos viros deblaterare. ꝑ eas discere linguas, p quas tot eximios autores, per quas arcana diuinę scripturę possim is & legere & intelligere, & homo creatorē suū, & viā ad ipm cognoscit. Si linguarū peritia nihil cōfert ad christianā religionē, q d venit in mente Origeni, theologorū sine cōtrouersia principi, qui nō ē arbitrat[9] se quicq̄ in re theologica posse, nisi homo doctus hebreas lras addidicisset vincens improbo labore, q[d] ętas & natura negabat, Quid Hieronymo? qui nihil non fecit, vt has lras adiūgeret, cū antea trilinguis esset, Dalmatię, latine, grececq̄ loquēs, siquidē harū in pro- fectā ętate sollertissimus indagator fuit, Nimirū q[d] sibi nō iucūditatē solū, sed etiā plurimū fructus ad sacrā afferāt paginā, adeo eī senex, iam eruditissim[9], quē totus orbis stupebat, & mgīm poscebat, vir q[d] maximū est, sanctissimę & horridę vitę, adhuc putabat se nihil scire, nisi hā: sanctā linguā sibi cōpararet, id q[d] fecit summo studio, mag nis expensis, & nocte quid[e] didicit, cū per Iudęos interdiu nō posset, sese priuans somno, vt Eccliam dei vera eruditiōe ditaret. Quid Au- gustino, cui maxiē fidem adhibere solēt nr̄i tpis Theologi, qui totus p̄ dicat Hebraicarū grecarūq̄ linguarū cognitionē, nō mo vtilē verū etiā necessariā, vt testat. ix. distin ct. ca. vt veterū, Ita inquies, vt libro- rū veterū fides de hębreis voluminib[9] examināda est, ita nouorū ve- ritas gręci sermonis normā desyderat. Idē ca. xiij. de ciui. dei. li. xv. ait Ei potius linguę credatur, vnde est in alia facta per interp̄tes tralatio. Hebraica vero est ea, vnde omnes fluxerunt, ceu a fonte translationes. Idē Augustinus ij. li. de doct. christian. c. xi. sic inquit. Et latine q̄dā linguę homines etiā duab[9] alijs, ad diuinarū scripturarū cognitionē opus habēt linguis, Hebraica scz & Greca, vt ad exēplaria p̄cedentia recurratur, Si qn̄ dubitationē attulerit latinorū interpretū infinita va- rietas, clare insinuat sępe i lris sacris oboriri ambiguitatē, quę citra pri marias linguas dissolui nō pōt, id q f exēplis aliq̄uot fusius ip̄e p̄se- quit̄, q[d] etiā Pontificū decretis testatū est, quid summis pontificib[9] qui decreto puiderūt, vt linguę in publicis p̄cipuisq̄ gymnasijs do- cerent, Et Clemens Papa. v, in sacro sancto Concilio Viennensi vt ha betur Clementina prima titulo de mgr̄is, Hoc sacro approbante Cō- cilio & scholas in supra scripturarū linguarū gn̄ibus, Vbicūq̄ Ro- manā curiā residere cōtigerit, necnon in Parrhisiensi & Oesoniensi, Bononiensi & Salamantino, studijs puidimus erigendas, statuentes, vt in q̄libet locorū teneant viri catholici, sufficient[e] habētes Hebraice,

Fig. 4.2. Page from Adrianus's speech with reference to Hebrew as the font of all.

Adrianus had his eulogy, which he had delivered in Louvain, printed in early 1520, during his short stay at Wittenberg (from fall 1520 to February 1521). The print comprises only five and a half pages. From the title page of the print alone one could not expect anything about its content which is given on p. 2 in the opening sentence. With respect to the content, Adrianus had primarily the sacred letters of Greek and Hebrew in mind, which are the biblical languages to be praised. The interest was directed to the *veritas graeca* and *veritas hebraica*.

In his speech Adrianus declared that it is through the languages that we may understand the "arcane" things in divine Scripture. The central insight is that humans recognize their creator and that one's life is oriented toward God.[61] From his perspective in 1519/1520 Adrianus praised theologians who were skilled in Hebrew, including the scholars of old, Origen (185–243), Jerome (ca. 350–420), and to some degree also Augustine. He also mentioned Symmachus, Theodotion [of Ephesus], and Aquila [of Pontus] (translators of the Hebrew Bible into Greek). They were convinced that theologians can make a contribution in their field only if they know Hebrew, because when there are doubts or ambiguities in Latin, they can be cleared up from the insights into the original biblical wording. Similarly to Reuchlin, Adrianus added: "Hebrew, however, is the one from which all other translations have flowed as from a font."[62] Like Reuchlin he also recalled the request of the medieval Pope Clement V (in office from 1305–1314) that Hebrew, Greek, and Aramaic be taught in the universities. Adrianus pointed out that most recently Pope Leo X (in office 1513–1521) brought teachers of those languages to Rome, and the king of France, too, employed them at his university (Sorbonne). The Greek language is highly honored, he said. But how much more does one have to praise Hebrew as the original source? It was from the Hebrews that Greek authors ladled whenever they had something significant to say. If Greek philosophy, which is found in ponds (*lacunae*), is enjoying so much honor, how much more praise is then due to the Hebrew font?[63]

---

61. ... *per quas arcana divinae scripturae possimus et legere et intellegere, et homo creatorem suum et vitam ad ipsum cognoscit*; image no. 2.

62. *Hebraica vero est ea, unde omnes fluxerunt, ceu a fonte translationes*; image no. 2. See fig. 2, line 15 from below.

63. ... *quantum honoris debetur Hebreę linguę vnde hauserunt*...; image no. 3.

Theologians have the duty not only to study the Hebrew words, but also each letter of its alphabet and all its *apices*,[64] i.e., some sort of diacritics specific to Hebrew. With the mention of the linguistic details such as *apices*, Adrianus may have used the words of Matt 5:18, which in the Latin version speaks of *iota* and *apex*:[65] ("Amen I say to you, until heaven and earth pass away, not a *iota* or *apex* will pass from the law, until all things have taken place").

Adrianus included the detailed speculations about the Hebrew alphabet as they are practiced in the Jewish Cabala, which Reuchlin was promoting so forcefully for many years. If the old age of something is a criterion for its high esteem, then the Hebrew language qualifies most because it was used first by God at the creation of the world. Moses and the prophets have used this language and so had Christ. And, all three languages (Hebrew, Greek, and Latin) "were sanctified on the cross of our God Jesus Christ" ("and it was written in Hebrew, Latin, and Greek," John 19:20). "Among them it is Hebrew that holds the first place."[66]

2.2. *The Englishman Robert Wakefield (Wakfeldus, d. 1537)*

After Reuchlin's death in 1522, Wakefield became his successor at Tübingen on August 14, 1522, but only for a short period of time in 1522. After only one year Wakefield was called to Cambridge.[67] This Hebraist and Orientalist taught at Cambridge from 1524 to 1530. While there he composed a speech about the praises and usefulness of the tree languages Arabic, Chadaeic [Aramaic], and Hebrew and about the Hebrew idioms which are found in both Testaments: *Oratio de laudibus et utilitate trium linguarum: Arabicae, Chaldaicae et Hebraicae atque idiomatibus Hebraicis, quae in utroque testamento inveniuntur*, which was printed in London between 1524 and 1528 (fig. 4.3).[68]

---

64. *Theologi officium est, non verba solum, verumtamen apices omnes executere mysticae scripturae*; image no. 4.

65. *Amen quippe dico vobis, donec transeat caelum et terra, iota unum, aut unus apex nom praeteribit a lege, donec omnia fiant.*

66. *Tres lingae consecratae sunt in cruce dei nostri Ihesu Christi, inter has primum locum habet Hebraica*; image no. 4.

67. Posset 2015, 854–55.

68. Lloyd Jones 1983; Olszowy-Schlanger 2006, 61–87.

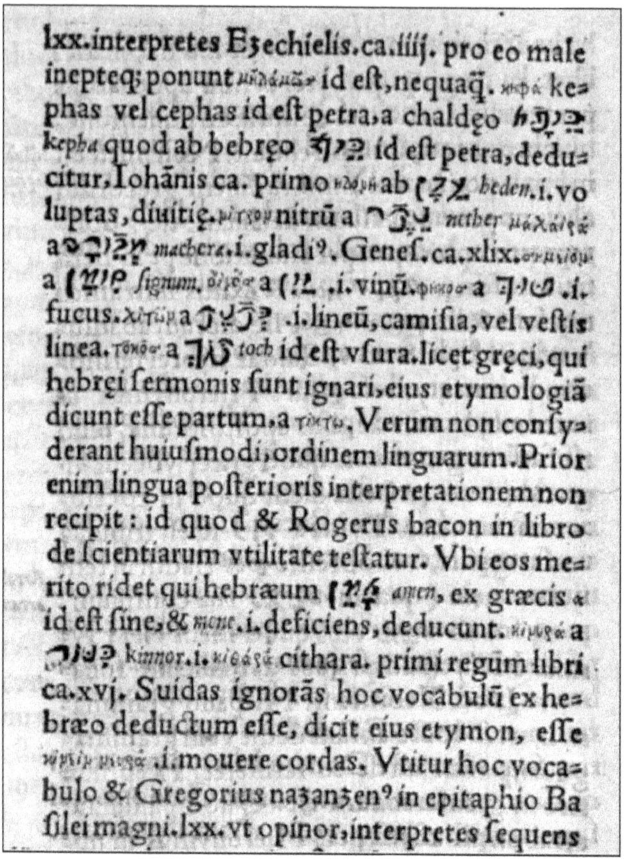

> lxx. interpretes E3echielis. ca. iiij. pro eo male
> inepteq; ponunt ⸺ id eſt, nequaq̃. ⸺ ke=
> phas vel cephas id eſt petra, a chaldęo הָכֵפָא
> kepha quod ab hebręo כֵּף id eſt petra, dedu=
> citur, Iohãnis ca. primo ⸺ ab עֶדֶן heden. i. vo
> luptas, diuitię. ⸺ nitrũ a נֶתֶר nether ⸺
> a ⸺ machera. i. gladiᵒ. Geneſ. ca. xlix. ⸺
> a ⸺ ſignum, ⸺ a ⸺ .i. vinũ. ⸺ a ⸺ .i.
> fucus. ⸺ a ⸺ .i. lineũ, camiſia, vel veſtis
> linea. ⸺ a ⸺ toch id eſt vſura. licet gręci, qui
> hebręi ſermonis ſunt ignari, eius etymologiã
> dicunt eſſe partum, a ⸺. Verum non conſy=
> derant huiuſmodi, ordinem linguarum. Prior
> enim lingua poſterioris interpretationem non
> recipit: id quod & Rogerus bacon in libro
> de ſcientiarum vtilitate teſtatur. Vbi eos me=
> rito ridet qui hebræum ⸺ amen, ex græcis &
> id eſt ſine, & ⸺. i. deficiens, deducunt. ⸺ a
> כִּנּוֹר kinnor. i. ⸺ cithara. primi regũm libri
> ca. xvj. Suidas ignorãs hoc vocabulũ ex he=
> bræo deductum eſſe, dicit eius etymon, eſſe
> ⸺ .i. mouere cordas. Vtitur hoc voca=
> bulo & Gregorius na3an3enᵒ in epitaphio Ba
> ſilei magni. lxx. vt opinor, interpretes ſequens

Fig. 4.3. Robert Wakefield. A page from his speech *Oratio de laudibus et utilitate trium linguarum*, 1524/1528.

Several times he came to speak of Reuchlin (Capnion) as "the light and teacher of the Germans." Completely immersed in Reuchlin's spirit this Englishman stated: "Once you have understood Hebrew, you will recognize the theft of the Greek and Latin people and you will despise the rills when you have begun to ladle from the sources."[69] Wakefield understood himself as a student also of the Augustinian friar and Hebraist Caspar Amman (ca. 1450–ca. 1524), of Lauingen on the Danube.[70]

69. *Certe cum hebraeum sermonem intellexeritis Graecorum Latinorumque furta cognoscetis, et contemnetis rivulos, cum coeperitis haurire de fontibus*; Posset 2015, 855 with n187.

70. Robert Wakefield: *On the Three Languages* (1524), ed. Lloyd Jones 1989, 4. On Amman, see Posset 2015c, 51–105.

2.3. *The Swiss Nicolaus Winmann (ca. 1500–ca. 1550): On the Holy, That Is Hebrew, Language*

Nicolaus Winmann (Nikolaus Wynmann, Vvinman) was a Swiss Catholic humanist. Not much is known about his life and career. For some reason he is known as the author of a dialogue on how to swim, written in Latin (1538). The book title explicitly mentions Winmann as the professor of languages in Ingolstadt.[71] It is the first instruction book in the world on swimming—written in Latin! He was one of the later successors of Johann Reuchlin in Ingolstadt in teaching biblical languages. He gave a lecture in 1536 with the title "Public Speech on the Holy, That Is Hebrew, Language, Held in Ingolstadt," which he published in Regensburg in 1538.[72] Since it was a public lecture, he evidently did not exclusively address students of theology. He dedicated it to Abbot Leonhard [Pfenningmann] of Saint Emmeram in Regensburg (who held this position from 1535 to 1540) who was knowledgeable in Latin, Greek, and Hebrew as the dedicatory preface tells.

Winmann saw it as his duty to praise the Hebrew language, the most holy language, as he says in the opening sentence, and not the Latin language of Cicero or the Greek of Demosthenes. Winmann mentions Mercurius (Roman God who was understood also to be the god of eloquence), Cadmus (son of the Phoenician king, the founder and first king of Thebes, who brought an alphabet of fifteen characters to Greece) and Simonides (a Greek poet and inventor of mnemotechnic). Like Adrianus, he mentions Aquila, Theodotion, and Symmachus.[73] But the important matter is that God has spoken in this language to his servant Moses, according to Eusebius, and to Abraham, according to Philo. Hebrew was spoken since the beginning of the world until the time of the construction of the tower of Babylon.[74] The other languages are inferior to Hebrew. The font is Hebrew and the rills are Greek and Latin. Therefore, Winmann asked the rhetorical question: "Why do we prefer the soiled rills over the immediate sources;

---

71. *Colymbetes, sive de arte natandi, dialogus & festiuus & iucundus lectu, per Nicolaum Wynman, Ingolstadii linguarum professorem publicum* (Augsburg: Steyner, 1538).

72. *Oracio Nicolai Vvinmann: In Sanctam hoc est hebraicam linguam, Ingolstadii habita publice*; online: MDZ, https://books.google.com/books/about/Oracio_Nicolai_Vvinmann.html?id=4a9RAAAAcAAJ.

73. MDZ, image no. 17.

74. MDZ, image nos. 10–12.

rills which end up in ponds and which degenerate, I would want to say, in some sort of sewer (*cloaca*)"?[75]

God has spoken in Hebrew to the holy men. Moses has handed down the Ten Commandments in this language. We should embrace this "most holy language," each word and *apix*.[76] In that way one may be able to penetrate to the Hebrew truth and "true theology." When fighting heretics, recourse is needed to the Hebrew Truth. Numerous Hebrew expressions are found in the New Testament; for example: *Eli eli lama sabactani* (Mark 15:34; Matt 27:46). And, the inscription on the cross of the Lord is trilingual (John 19:20).[77]

The study of Hebrew also allows an understanding of the rabbinic commentaries and medieval books such as those by medieval Jewish authorities such as David Kimhi.[78] Winmann lifted up among others the contemporary Hebraists: Elias Levita, Conrad Pellican, Caspar Ammonius (Amman), Sebastian Monsterus (Münster), and of course Johann Reuchlin (Capnio).[79] He reminded his audience that Reuchlin of blessed memory was the author of a book on Hebrew accents and orthography.[80] He was one of his predecessors in this "noble academy" (i.e., the university of Ingolstadt).[81] In conclusion, Winmann said, nothing is more useful than the study of the holy language, Hebrew.

2.4. Georg Witzel (1501–1573): Love and Admiration for the Most Holy Language

His "High Praise of the Holy Language" is to be featured here. The title page reads: *Encomium sanctae linguae. Georg[ius] Wic[el] Presbyt[er]*. He identifies himself as a presbyter (priest). Within the booklet itself his speech is titled: Speech in Praise of the Hebrew Language (*Oratio in Laudem*

---

75. MDZ, image no. 13.

76. MDZ, image no. 15; *apices*, see also no. 18.

77. *Eli eli lama sabactani* ... *titulus ille gloriosus trilinguis cruci domini impositus*, MDZ, image no. 21.

78. MDZ, image no. 22.

79. His list included one Rabbi David Calonymus (MDZ, image no. 23); Winmann may have meant Calman (living at the city of Ulm?) who was Reuchlin's teacher; on him, see Posset 2015, 72, 75–77.

80. MDZ, image no. 23.

81. MDZ, image no. 23.

Hebraicae Linguae). Witzel, too, praised Reuchlin, known by his humanist name, Capnion: "What shall I say about Capnion? To him the entire world looks up, adores and loves him as the strongest and most skilled protector of this oppressed language."[82]

Witzel is a relatively unknown German scholar of the Reformation time. He may be known to those who are familiar with the controversies in theology of the sixteenth century since Witzel became famous for his ecumenical efforts to reconcile Lutherans and Catholics in the 1530s. However, his eulogy of the Hebrew language is completely unknown. For example, in the entry on "Witzel" in the *Contemporaries of Erasmus*, Witzel's speech and Hebrew expertise find no mention.[83]

Fig. 4.4. Portrait of Georg Witzel, "The Bridge-Building Theologian," ca. 1595.

---

82. Böning 2004, 100.
83. For example, in the entry "Witzel" by Höss 2003.

Witzel was a special case among the early sympathizers of Luther.[84] He has changed sides twice (Catholic-Lutheran-Catholic). He had studied in Erfurt in 1516–1518 where he became familiar with the thinking of Erasmus of Rotterdam (ca. 1467–1536). As a very young man he was ordained to the priesthood and worked as a vicar and town clerk in his hometown Vacha. He studied for several months in Wittenberg, in 1521–1522, and followed Luther's thinking. While he was at Wittenberg, he learned Hebrew from two instructors of Jewish descent: (a) Bernhardus Hebraeus, who was a former rabbi by the name of Jacob Gipher from the south German city of Göppingen (no exact dates known). We know that Luther dedicated his pamphlet *That Jesus Christ Was Born a Jew* of 1523 to Bernardus.[85] (b) After Bernhard's departure, the already mentioned and the more qualified, Matthaeus Adrianus (ca. 1470–1521), was hired as the Hebrew instructor in April 1520.

Likely influenced by the Wittenberg reformers, Witzel as a young priest was one of the first to marry, in 1523/1524[86] (whereas Luther married later, in June 1525). For this violation of canon law Witzel lost his position in his hometown. In 1525 he became an evangelical pastor in Wenigen-Lüpnitz in Thuringia, and at the end of 1525 Luther recommended him for the pastorate in Niemegk, a town north of Wittenberg. Initially Luther praised Witzel for his excellent knowledge of Latin, Greek, and Hebrew.[87]

Witzel was suspected of anti-Trinitarian beliefs and was imprisoned in March 1530 at Belzig simply because he had provided temporary shelter for the anti-Trinitarian Belgian priest Johannes Campanus (ca. 1500–1575). This Belgian scholar had authored also an anti-Lutheran manuscript which was circulating in 1530.[88] On April 1, 1530, Luther sent a letter to Witzel in prison, informing him that he personally is trying to free him.[89] Witzel was rehabilitated and returned to his pastorate in Niemegk. Due to his studies of the church fathers, Witzel eventually returned to the Catholic Church and resigned from his (Lutheran) parish position in 1531.

84. Dolan 1996, 4: 287–88.

85. WA.B 3: 101–2 (no. 629). One may speculate whether Luther gave his pamphlet to the recently converted Bernhardus Hebraeus because he felt sorry for him that he had not found full employment at Wittenberg. The tone and content of Luther's letter point into that direction.

86. On this aspect in Witzel's life see Plummer 2012, 259–62.

87. WA.B 3, no. 945.

88. We know of it only from Johann Bugenhagen's notes.

89. WA.B 5: 270.

Luther soon perceived Witzel as a disciple of Erasmus of Rotterdam and as a defender of the value of good works. Witzel supposedly was falling away from the gospel as Luther understood it. Witzel's book *In Defense of Good Works against the New Evangelists* had been issued in 1532 under the pseudonym Agricola Phagus.[90] His polemic was directed against what he labeled *Lutheranismus*.[91] Witzel's pamphlet provoked vehement reactions from the Lutheran side such as from his acquaintance Balthasar Raida (1495-1565): *Response to Georg Witzel's Slanderous and Mendacious Book*, which was published with Luther's preface. In it Luther, however, did not address the issue, but merely condemned Witzel as an apostate. As his excuse Luther quoted the proverb: "An obvious lie is not worth answering."[92] Simultaneously Luther also viciously attacked his own former friend Crotus Rubeanus (1480-ca.1540), since "birds of a feather flock together." Crotus ("the Toad") "spat a good deal of his own venom" into Witzel's booklet.

Witzel had eight children. After Luther learned of Witzel's return to the Church, he in cooperation with Justus Jonas (1493-1555) prevented Witzel from becoming the professor of Hebrew at the University of Erfurt. On July 1, 1532, Luther urged the (Lutheran) preachers in Erfurt to work toward the rejection of Witzel's job application: "Grace and peace in Christ! A rumor has come to us, worthy men, that Georg Wicel [sic] is there in Erfurt to procure a position, at least, seeking a place to spew out his poison which consumes him, as he did when he was here with us."[93]

Witzel was denied the professorship, but he had already prepared his inaugural address, a eulogy of the Hebrew language. Witzel soon, in 1533, was appointed as Catholic preacher at St. Andrew Church in Eisleben, i.e., Luther's birthplace. Here he published his speech in 1534 (fig. 4.5), with a printer whose name is not given and whose press apparently was unable to print Hebrew letters.[94] Witzel had it reprinted with minor corrections in 1538 by Nicolaus Wolrab (ca. 1500-1560) at Leipzig, issued together with

---

90. Witzel, *Pro defensione bonorum operum adversus novos Evangelistas* (Leipzig: Michael Blum, 1532), MDZ, http://daten.digitale-sammlungen.de/~db/0001/bsb00010202/images/.

91. MDZ, image no. 12.

92. WA 38: 84.2-3.

93. Wilhelm Martin Leberecht De Wette, *Dr. Martin Luthers Briefe, Sendschreiben und Bedenken*, 4:385; online: https://archive.org/details/drmartinluthers09wettgoog.

94. [Anonymous], https://books.google.com/books?id=sFPM2ALsLioC&printsec=frontcover&source=gbs_ge_summary_r&cad=0#v=onepage&q&f=false.

two homilies (fig. 4.6).[95] No Hebrew characters were used for this edition either.

Eisleben was home to some Jews. Witzel recalled in 1544 that his Jewish dialogue partner and Hebrew teacher during his time there (1533–1538) was Nephtalim of Eisleben. When he conversed with him (and with other Jews), he always avoided controversial issues of faith, as he stated that he did not utter a single word about this. He did not want to repel them, who were genuinely literate, from the tasks of the liberal arts. He did not want to offend them. Their subject matter was strictly grammar, not theology.[96] This is how he practiced his respect for the Jews. Whereas Witzel as preacher at Saint Andrew Church (at Luther's birthplace!) had apparently close contacts with Jews, Luther never did.

Luther at the occasion of his last visit to Eisleben in January/February 1546 made no such efforts of contacts with Jews. To the contrary, Luther became upset when he learned that the town of Eisleben and its surroundings were now home to over fifty Jewish persons, as he wrote to his wife who had stayed back in Wittenberg.[97] He actually (sarcastically?) blamed the Jews of that region for his personal ailments which he suffered at the moment. Luther was irritated even more that "there are supposedly about four hundred Jews" in nearby Rissdorf, i.e., close to Eisleben. He promised that "if God grants it," he will help expel and outlaw them, and for that purpose "in my anger I had made up my mind to grease the carriage,"[98] in order to get them out as quickly as possible. During his stay at Eisleben Luther had preached four times from the same pulpit of Saint Andrew Church where Witzel as the Catholic preacher had delivered sermons a decade earlier. It turned out that Luther's sermons there were his last. For his sermon of February 7 he provided an afterword which is called *Admonition against the Jews* (1546). He claimed that the Jews "do great harm" to Christians. Yet, the Jews are to be invited to be baptized. If they refuse, "we will not tolerate them. . . . For if I tolerate in my midst someone who slanders, blasphemes, and curses

---

95. *Homiliae Duae de Ecclesiae Mysteriis, Baptismo & Eucharistia. Encomium sanctae linguae*, http://daten.digitale-sammlungen.de/~db/0003/bsb00035934/images/.

96. Böning 2004, 13–15.

97. Luther's two letters to his wife are dated February 1, 1546 (LW 50:290–92) and February 7 (LW 50:301–4).

98. Letter of February 7.

my Lord Christ, then I make myself a participant in the sins of another [*frembder Suenden*]. . . . They are our public enemies."[99]

Clearly, during the early Reformation years, church leaders and politicians had a choice, either with Luther to verbally abuse the Jews and physically abuse them by persecuting them, or, to dialogue with them in the manner of Reuchlin and Witzel.

Throughout his life, Witzel had conversations with learned Jews, as we know from his recollection in 1544. When he was in Prague in 1539/1540 he consulted in particular with Rabbi Abraham (ben Avigdor, who died in 1542). Witzel was especially interested in learning more about the Hebrew expression *caru iadai* in Ps 22:17b.[100] Christian exegetes interpreted this locus in terms of Christology. From 1553 on Witzel lived in Mainz where he died in 1573 and was buried next to the high altar of Saint Ignatius Church in Mainz.

---

99. WA 51: 195.9-29.

100. ". . . *Rabbi Abrahamum. qui cum de loco psalmi 'caru iadai' et cum paucis contuli*," image no. 29. His reference in Latin transliteration (*caru iadai*) meant the Hebrew expression כָּאֲרִי יָדַי in v. 17: "For dogs have encompassed me; a pack of evildoers closes in on me; like a lion, they are at my hands and my feet." Or, in the Vulgate-based rendering: "They have dug my hands and feet."

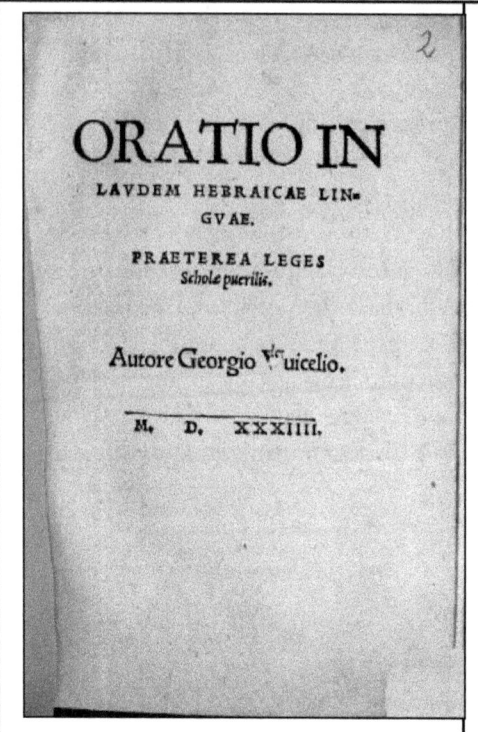

Fig. 4.5. Georg Witzel, *Oratio* of 1534.

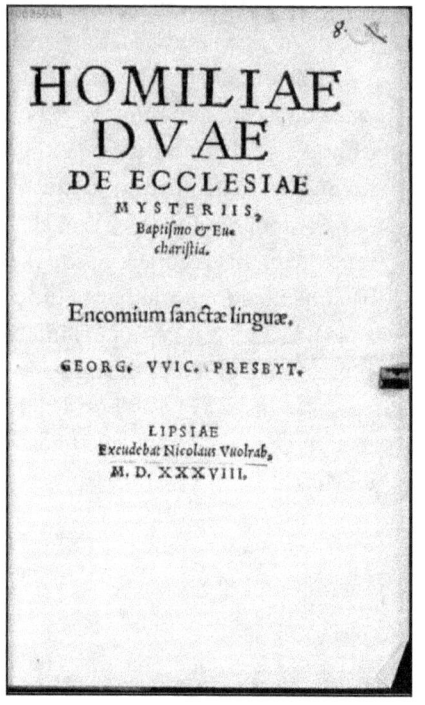

Fig. 4.6. Georg Witzel's *Encomium*, issued together with his *Homiliae Duae* (Two Homilies) of 1538.

There is no English translation of Witzel's speech *High Praise of the Holy Language by the Priest Georg Witzel*, printed by Nicolaus Vuolrab (Wolrab) in Leipzig in 1538 with the title: *Encomium sanctae linguae. Georg[ius] Wic[el] Presbyt[er]*; so says the book title, whereas within the booklet itself the speech is called: *Oratio in Laudem Hebraicae Linguae*. Witzel's speech is composed in highly sophisticated, humanistic Latin, interspersed with Greek notions.

The Latin speech is dedicated to a young man by the name Bernhard Walther in Leipzig who contrary to the trends of his time continues to study. Witzel encourages the student to carry on and pay attention to the study of antiquity. He has to labor now if he wants to harvest fruits later on. Witzel wants to foster in him and his fellow students the "love and admiration for the most holy language."

Conclusion

The necessity of Hebrew studies for Bible interpretation was advocated by the biblical humanists of the Renaissance and Reformation times. Luther and Melanchthon joined them. But only Catholic scholars gave exuberant praise of the sacred language during the first half of the sixteenth century. These Catholic scholars were Johann Reuchlin, Matthaeus Adrianus, Robert Wakefield, Nikolaus Winmann, and Georg Witzel. Their laudations in the lingua franca were the result of their insight that this language is God's and it has been God's means of communication with human beings since the beginning of creation. This language is divine and most ancient. The Bible in Hebrew originated from the "mouth of God." It was their conviction that from this divine font all theology gushes forth. Greeks drink from rills, the Latin people from the swamp. For that reason, in Reuchlin's words, the language of the Jews "must be kissed tenderly and embraced with both arms."

Georg Witzel
Speech in Praise of the Hebrew Language
Latin Original with English Translation on Facing Pages

ORATIO
IN LAVDEM LINGVAE
Hebraicæ.

I NVNC infantiæ iuxta ac inscitiæ meæ, auditores candidi, ratione habere ullam, profecto quiduis citius, q̃ in eum conscenderem locum, in quem uideo doctorum hominũ cum surrectas aures, tum conie⸗ ctos oculos. Quo fit, ut nisi inde expectationi omnium anxiæ satis fecero (ut non ignoro periculũ) & ronchos auferam minime iniu stos, & uobis horam, sumptum quippe preciosum, isto sermone sufturer. Verum cum considero, qua de re uerba facere statuerim, & animo meo contemplor, q̃ cu⸗ pide id uos audire gestiatis, non equidem

[Georg Witzel, Presbyter]
   Speech in Praise of the Hebrew Language
   Esteemed listeners, if now I would take into any consideration my lack of eloquence and inexperience, I would rather do something else than coming here where I see in front of me learned persons not only with pricked up ears but also with critical eyes. It could happen if I would not satisfy the anxious expectations of everybody here (for I know the risk very well), that on the one side I will deserve the by no means unjustified hissing and on the other side the accusation that I have wasted your precious time with my words. However, when I take into consideration the subject matter before me and when I contemplate how eagerly you want to hear something about it,

ENCOMIVM HEB. LINGVAE.

equidem possum nõ audere, atcp quod uolebam in medium proferre, confidens uestrum fauorem magna ex parte paruitatem dicentis adiuturum. Res ea, crede mihi, dignissima est, ad quam prædicandam atcp ornandam eloquentissimorum quorumcp ora certatim exerceantur, idcp non rei per se satis laudatæ, sed studioforum ad amorem adcp admiratione huius rapiendorum gratia. Dicturus enim sum de linguæ Hebrææ maiestate ac eminentia. Hanc cũ maiores haud abs re sanctam dixerunt, & eandem ad religionem pertinere certum est, non paulo decentius professioni meæ fuerit, in eius uersari laudibus, q̃ si aut fictum aliquod pro scholæ more

I could very well dare to make my presentation, confident that your goodwill will assist me in my weakness of eloquent speaking. Believe you me that this is a most worthy subject for whose praise the most eloquent speakers should compete. The reason for it is not that the subject as such is praised sufficiently, but that the students are to be drawn to the love and admiration of it.

I want to speak about the majesty and eminence of the Hebrew language. The ancestors called this language the holy one and as such it certainly pertains to religion. It may be more fitting, therefore, for my profession [of theology] to praise it than to present some fable in the way schools do,

ENCOMIVM

declamarem, aut aliquem Heroa assentandi studio celebrarem, aut euentum hesternum lucri spe defenderem, aut in hostem odij dictamine intonarem. Vos, quæso, rem benigne diligenterq3 audite, cuius deprædicandæ gratia huc accessi. Et quoniam de lingua dicendũ est mihi, uotis cõprecamini omnibus, ut a superis lingua detur, quæ expediundis coeptis par sit. Solet uero cum primis de rerũ, si quas tractandas suscipimus, inuentione quęri, ut uidelicet tanto in maiore precio id sit, q̃d attollimus, quo plura retro sæcula numeret. Equidem si uetustas rei dignitatem adauget, nihil dignius lingua Hebrea sit oportet, utpote, quæ neq3 a Mercurio, neque a Cadmo

or to eagerly celebrate some hero, or to defend an event of yesterday in the hope of some gain, or to make some hateful noise against an enemy. I ask that you listen benevolently and diligently to the matter which I have come here to praise. And since I have to talk about this language, your fervent prayers are needed so that the right words are being sent from above in order to accomplish this. When we undertake something like that, we usually ask first about the origin of such matters. What is being lifted up here is considered of higher value because of its age. Indeed, if the age of something augments its value, then nothing is more valuable than the Hebrew language. Hebrew does not have its origin with Mercury,[101] nor with

---

101. Mercury, identical with the Greek Hermes, messenger of the gods; god of oratory.

HEBRAICAE LINGVAE,
Cadmo, neq; a Phœnicibus, neq;
Palamede, neq; a Simonide, neq;
ab Euandri matre, sed uel a Mose, quod tradit Eusebius, uel ab
Abrahamo, sicuti uisum est Phi-
loni, uel (ut ad orbis initium re-
cta regrediar) a liberis Sethi, si qd
Iosepho credimus, originem du-
cit (ut uideas fide carere, çp quidam dicunt, Esram inuenisse Hebræas literas) Nec ab hac senten-
tia longe abest Plinius, literas Syris repertoribus uēdicans. Quan-
tillū uero dissonet, si quis Syriace loquat̄ & Iudaice, neminē puto uel semidoctorum fugit. Ferūt
Enochum scriptum opus reliqsse
ante cataclysmum, & ea opinio
firmatur Thaddęi atq; Tertullia-
ni graui elogio. Si scripsit igitur

E ij   Enoch

Cadmus,[102] nor with the Phoenicians, nor with Palamedes,[103] nor with Simonides,[104] nor with the mother of Evander,[105] but either with Moses, as Eusebius wants it,[106] or with Abraham, as Philo has seen it,[107] or by going straight back to the beginning of the world, it was with Seth's children,[108] if we can believe Josephus. Thus, it is not very credible to maintain as some do, that Esra would have been the inventor of the Hebrew characters. Not far removed from such a position was Pliny[109] with his opinion that the Syriacs invented the letters.[110] The difference between Syriac and Jewish is minor which is being noted even by half-educated folks. Before the Flood, Enoch supposedly left behind some writing, an opinion which Thaddeus[111] and Tertullian[112] confirm.

---

102. Cadmus was credited with the introduction of writing into Greece by means of an alphabet of fifteen characters.

103. Palamedes, like Cadmus, was credited with the invention of the four Greek letters Theta, Xi, Phi, Chi (Θ, Ξ, Φ, Χ).

104. Simonides (ca. 556–468 BC), a Greek poet.

105. Mother of Evander invented the Latin alphabet.

106. Eusebius of Caesarea (ca. AD 260–339) in his *Preparation for the Gospel*.

107. Also called Philo Judaeus, was a Hellenistic Jewish philosopher who lived in Alexandria, ca. 20 BC–ca. AD 50.

108. According to Gen 4:25.

109. Pliny (AD 23–79) was a Roman scholar.

110. In antiquity, Syria extended from the Euphrates to the Mediterranean.

111. I.e., Letter of Jude 14–15, quoting the *Book of Enoch*.

112. Noah supposedly had taken the writing with him into the ark.

ENCOMIVM

Enoch, his pfecto literis scripsit, quas postea ab Heber filio Sem Hebræas appellauere. Eat nunc qui uolet, & Græcas literas Hebræis antiqtatis prærogatiua anteferat, ut sunt multi impij nugones, qui non uerentur eas ceu barbaras irridere, idq; ut ipsi sibi nõ uident ineruditi, Græcitatis cæco quodam amore, malentes Herodotum aut Euripidem, q̃ Esaiam aut Ezechielem legere. Certe Iosephus, quẽ haud immerito Græcum Liuiũ appellant, negat Græcas literas ante Homeri ætatẽ extitisse. Quod si extitere, uix tamen uerisimile est, eas ante Lini Orphei & Musæi extitisse tempora. At quid horum ętas est, ad Sethi, Enochi & Abrahę ætatem collatą?

Therefore, if Enoch did some writing, he surely made use of those characters which later were called "Hebrew," naming them after Heber[113] who was the son of Shem.[114] There may be someone who, [supposedly] because of the age issue, prefers the Greek characters over the Hebrew characters since there are many faithless nonsense-talkers who will not shy away from ridiculing the Hebrew characters as barbaric. Since they do not want to appear uneducated, they—in their blind love for everything that is Greek[115]—prefer to read Herodotus and Euripides[116] over the Prophets Isaiah and Ezekiel. Josephus, who is called with some right the Livy of the Greeks, firmly denies that the Greek characters existed prior to Homer's time. Whenever they came into existence, it is not very likely that it was before the time of Linus, Orpheus and Musaeus.[117] But does their age matter in comparison to that of Seth, Enoch and Abraham?

---

113. As spelled in the Vulgate; *Eber* in the Hebrew Bible.

114. Gen 10:21, 25–26.

115. *Graecitatis caeco quodam amore.*

116. Herodotus (fifth century BC), father of historiography. Euripides (fifth century BC), author of tragedies.

117. Three mythological musicians.

HEBRAICAE LINGVAE.

ta? Iam quo antiquior est lingua
Hebrę́a, hoc & diuiniorem et au-
gustiorem quoqʒ eam esse cõstat.
Vox Dei Opt. Max. huius linguæ adminiculo ad humanas au-
res pu̯asit, atqʒ hoc eo etiam tempore, quando ne Graiũ neqʒ Latium nomen in orbe esset. Is deus
se a Mose huius linguæ notulis,
Ero qui Ero, nominari uoluit,
Qua nimirum origine descendit
sacrosanctum illud & ter adoran
dum ADONAI, quod ob reueren
tiam ἄφρασον habent. Atque adeo
deus Hebræorum & dici & esse
gaudet. Quonã dialecto egressæ
sunt ex ore dei Hebręorũ dulciss.
‚pmissiones, blandissima solatia,
iustissimæ minę, deniqʒ potentiss.
quæqʒ uerba ad patres Hebręos,
    E iij nisi

Since the Hebrew language is the older one, it must also be the one that is more divine and more august. The voice of God Most High and Almighty has reached human ears with the support of exactly this language, and this happened at a time when the name Greece or Latium did not exist yet in this world. It was this God who wanted to be talked about by Moses in this language [speaking to Moses in Hebrew]: "I will be who I will be" ["I am who I am"].[118] From the same origin stems undoubtedly also the word ADONAI [Lord], which is sacrosanct and three-times worthy of adoration, and which [the Jews] take to be ineffable.[119] And the God of the Hebrews enjoys both to be spoken of in this way and to be [to exist] in this way.[120] In which language were these so very sweet promises issued from the mouth of the God of the Hebrews,[121] these most kind consolations, the most righteous threats, and thus the most powerful words spoken to the Hebrew fathers,

---

118. *Is deus se a Mose huius linguae notulis, Ero qui Ero, nominari voluit* [Exod 3:14]. Witzel uses the future tense here as does Luther in quoting Exod 3:14.

119. ’άφρασον; here, for the first time, Witzel entered a Greek word in the original spelling, but without translating it, within his Latin text: *Qua nimirum origine descendit sacrosanctum illud et ter adorandum ADONAI, quod ob reverentiam* ’άφρασον *habent*.

120. *Atque adeo deus Hebraeorum et dici et esse gaudet.*

121. . . . *ex ore dei Hebraeorum.*

ENCOMIVM

nisi Hebrçco? Quo sermone cecinit tam suauiter Dauid, Heman & Iedithun? Quo sermone multifariam locutus est nobis deus in prophetis sanctis? Quo sermone tradidere nobis Israëlitici historiographi tot Adonai nostri prodigia, tot uirtutes, tot edicta, & ipsas adeo populi Iudaici res gestas, nisi Hebrœo? Arca sacra in tanta religione apud istam gentē habita, continebat uerborum decada. At cuius erat linguæ decas illa? an nō Hebrçæ? Iesus dei summi unigenitus, seruator mundi, non solum apud Hebrœos nasci uiuerecq̃ uoluit, sed etiā Hebræis Hebraice loq. Vnde quanta gloria linguæ huic nostræ accedat, quis nō uidet? O linguam omniũ longe

if not in Hebrew? In which language did David,[122] Heman[123] and Jeduthun[124] sing so sweetly? In which language did God speak to us through the holy prophets in so many different ways? In which language did the Israelitic historiographers[125] hand down to us so many signs of our Adonai, so many [manifestations of] power, so many edicts and altogether the acts of the Jewish people, if not in Hebrew? The sacred ark which is held by this people in so great esteem[126] contained the Ten Commandments. And in which language were they given? Not in Hebrew?

Jesus, the Son of the highest God, the savior of the world,[127] not only wanted to be born and live among the Hebrews, but he also wanted to speak in Hebrew to the Hebrews. Who does not see that from these facts the glory of this language stems? O what a language

---

122. The psalmist.

123. A chanter and musician according to 1 Chr 15:16–17. In Ps 88:1 Heman is called the author of this psalm.

124. Vulgate: Idithun; Jeduthun was a temple musician according to 1 Chr 25:1–3.

125. *Israelitici historiographi.* Here is the first locus where Witzel employed the word "Israelitic."

126. *Arca sacra in tanta religione.*

127. *Iesus dei summi unigenitus, servator mundi.* Note that *servator mundi* is the humanistic Latin for the biblical Latin *salvator mundi* of 1 John 4:14. Witzel as an Erasmian adopted Erasmus's expression of *servator*; so did Luther.

HEBRAICAE LINGVAE.
longe præcellentissimam, o pri∕
mā, o nunquam pro merito necʒ
laudatam, necʒ laudandam. Quis
piorum nõ ammiretur, imo quis
non supplex adoret characteres,
syllabas, apices, quos sanctissimo
atcʒ diuiniss. ore egregie insigni∕
uit sacrosanctoscʒ mire reddidit
coelestis doctor? Paulus Euange∕
lij buccina incomparabilis non so
lum Hebræum se esse gloriatur,
uerū idem etiam disserere ad po∕
pulum Hebręo idiomate amauit,
præbens argumentum, quantæ
curæ Euangelicis hominibus il∕
lud esse debeat. Quid de uno Pau
lo dico? An nõ doctrina noui Te
stamenti tota ab Apostolis omni
bus primum sparsa, atque huius
p̄sidio Ecclesia fundata est? Quor
         E iiij   sum

which excels all other languages by far, O first language, O language which never has been praised enough and cannot be praised enough! Must not any pious person admire and humbly adore the [Hebrew] characters, syllables and diacritical marks[128] to which the heavenly teacher gave such special honor through his most holy, divine mouth and thus wonderfully made it most holy?

[Saint] Paul, the incomparable trumpet of the Gospel, not only gloried himself to be a Hebrew, but also truly loved to speak to the people in the Hebrew idiom; thus proving how much this language meant to the evangelical people [the people of the time of the gospel].[129] But why speak only of Paul? Was not the entire teaching of the New Testament spread first by all the apostles, and was not the Church founded on the trust in this doctrine?

---

128. *Apices*; seethe expression *iota* and *apex* in Matt 5:18.
129. ... *quantae curae Evangelicis hominibus illud esse debeat.*

ENCOMIVM

sum attinebat, ut Ioannes Euan-
gelista toties mentionem linguæ
Hebraicæ in sacro scripto faceret,
nisi ad laudum eius cumulum immensum? Ais, Christus Chaldaice, non Hebraice locutus fertur.
Atq ego utranq; linguam id tem
poris adeo unam eandemq; fuisse
autumo, ut utra locutus fuerit,
Hebraice tamen locutus legatur,
non Chaldaice. Scio gentem Iudaicam e Babylone paululū mu-
tata lingua reducem Hierosoly-
mam uenisse. Scio toto post tempore usam Babylonica seu Chaldaica, cui assueuerant. Necq; tamē
hoc exprimunt scripturæ, opinor
propter summam linguarum affi
nitatem, aut ne gloria gentis inde
minueretur, Nam quur prophanos

What was the purpose that the Evangelist John so often made mention of the Hebrew language, if not in order to increase the praise of this language?[130] You may object that Christ actually had spoken Chaldean [Aramaic], not Hebrew. To this I respond that at that time both languages were one and the same to a degree that whatever he may have spoken, he has spoken in Hebrew, as one may read occasionally, not in Chaldean [Aramaic]. I know that the Jewish people[131] returned from Babylon to Jerusalem with a somewhat changed language. I know that after that entire time the people used Babylonian or Chaldean to which they had become accustomed. However, the writings do not say this explicitly; in my opinion this is so because of the fact of the closest affinity of the [two] languages, or, that the glory of the people not be diminished. For why should they honor the undeserving

---

130. It is noteworthy that Witzel does not mention John 19:20 ("it was written in Hebrew, Latin, and Greek").

131. *Scio gentem Iudaicam* . . .

HEBRAICAE LINGVAE.

nos Chaldæos titulis immeritis honestent? Quur dominū ac apostolos Syriace locutos esse affirment, ob pauculas atq; leuiculas finalium quarundam syllabarum discrepantias? An non Hebræa lingua, Chaldaicæ (quam et Aramicam, Syriacam, Assyriacam cognomines licet) matrix una solaq; est? Vtra uetustior? Num Chaldaica? Minime. Ea enim post cataclysmum primum exorta scribitur, & exorta a uicinia Hebraicę. Rectissime itaq; legitur Hebraice locutus Dominus una cum Apostolis, non tam q̃ essent Hebræi ex Hebræis, q̃ q̃ conuersarentur in Hebręorum terris, ut non addam de origine ac primatu Hebraismi. Fateor, sunt uoculæ ali

E v   quot

heathen Chaldeans?[132] Why should they maintain that the Lord and the apostles would have spoken Syriac, only because of very few and only slight discrepancies in the ending syllables? Is not the Hebrew language the one and only matrix of Chaldean (which one may also call Aramaic, Syriac, or Assyrian)? Which one is older? The Chaldean one? By no means. That one, as is written, came into existence only after the Flood and that language came from the one related to it, i.e., the Hebrew language. One therefore reads, and it is very true, that the Lord spoke Hebrew with the apostles, but not because they were Hebrews from Hebrews, but because they lived in Hebrew territories. Thus I do not add anything about the origin and primacy of Hebrew [*Hebraismi*]. I admit that there are a few small

132. *Nam quur prophanos Chaldaeos titulis immeritis honestent?*

ENCOMIVM

quot in Euangelio Chaldaismū spirantes, quas est effatus Dominus. At una atcp altera duntaxat in causa est, cur minus Hebraicissimæ sint. Igitur ne propter illas uariatiūculas perexiguas, suppresso Hebræo nomine, Chaldęa appellatione rem totam censebo? Nisi uererer immodicā orationis prolixitatem, exemplis collatis declararem uobis auditores, quanta sit utriusc̨ sermonis similitudo, unde plane intelligeretis, scripturas non abs re Hebraice, non Chaldaice, locutum dominum ac Apostolos attestari, quamuis constet, uocabula quædam Syris q̃ Iudęis uiciniora esse. Necp tamē asseuero, dominum ac Apostolos semper ea lingua locutos, quam Hebraicam

Chaldean words in the Gospel, which the Lord has spoken.[133] But only rarely is there a case of a less authentic Hebrew wording. Should I—because of so minor differences—not call it Hebrew, and call the whole thing Chaldean? If I would not fear an undue expansion of my speech, I would give you, my audience, some examples of how great the similarities are between the two languages. You would then understand quite well that the Scriptures testify that the Lord and the apostles spoke Hebrew and not Chaldean, although it is obvious that certain words are related more to the language of the Syriacs [Aramaean] than of the Jews. But nevertheless I do not claim that the Lord and the apostles always spoke in the language which we call Hebrew.

---

133. *Abba*, Mark 14:36; *ephphatha*, Mark 7:34; *talitha koum*, Mark 5:41; *sabachtani*, which is an Aramaic rendering in Mark 15:34 of the Hebrew *asabthani* of Ps 22:2.

HEBRAICAE LINGVAE.

braicam uocamus. Populari sermone sæpe eos locutos etiam, nemini non uerisimile est. Dicunt extare Matthęum in Hebraica literatura, & is certe dominū Chaldaizantem coram audierat, Cur igitur non Chaldæus Matthæus extare dicitur? Paulus ad Hebræos Hebraice quoq; scripsisse narrat, Chaldaice non audiui, ut maxime illa sæcula Chaldæā amuricam resipuerint. Sed autoritatem atq; dignitatem sanctissimæ linguæ uix disertissimus rhetor uerbis assequatur. Cōpendio dicam, quantū uestra poscit pietas. Hæc lingua a nullo homine repta, nec inuecta, sed a diuino spiritu procedens, in homines eius capaces demissa est, Et ea ipsa usus est dominus

It is evident to everybody that they often spoke in the vernacular.[134] Some say that [the Gospel of] Matthew existed in Hebrew and it was exactly him who had heard the Lord speak Chaldean in public. Why then does nobody speak of a Chaldean Matthew? Some say that Paul, too, had written to the Hebrews in Hebrew, but I did not hear anybody say he wrote in Chaldean, although those times smelled very much like a Chaldean olive tree.[135]

But hardly any orator is able to adequately grasp the authority and the dignity of the most holy language. This language was not discovered or introduced by a human being, but comes forth from the divine Spirit to the people who have the capacity for it. And from all the languages the Lord

---

134. *Populari sermone saepe eos locutos etiam, nemini verisimile est.*
135. *... ut maxime illa saecula Chaldaeam amurcam resipuerint.*

ENCOMIVM

minus omnium, quando aperiret mysteria coeli reuerēda, Ea deniq; salutis humanæ primū instrumen tū. Vos pro uestra sapientia au﹖ ditores singula in animis uestris copiosius accuratiusq;, q̃ a me in p̄sentiarū dicuntur, reputetis. Cę﹖ terum fortasse erunt, qui eius lin﹖ guæ sanctitatē cum maiestate exi﹖ mia coniunctam, ut debent, reue﹖ reantur, illiq; palmam inter reli﹖ quas attribuant: sed abhorreāt ab ea addiscenda, partim, ut quæ nō ita multum utilitatis afferat, par﹖ tim, quæ habeat plurimum diffi﹖ cultatis, nihil uoluptatis aut gra﹖ tiæ. Erras homo tota uia, qui tale existimes. Et quid est per Deum immortalē, ut tanto nisu tantoq; conamine feramur ad non inuti﹖
les

employed exactly this one when he disclosed the awesome mysteries of heaven. This language thus is the prime instrument of salvation.

You, [dear] listeners, according to your interests, may want to think about some of the details more extensively and more accurately than what I can provide momentarily. There may be some people who feel compelled to appreciate the sanctity and with it the extraordinary majesty of this language, and to award the palm of victory to this language. But they shy away from learning it, partly because they perceive it as useless, partly because they find it very difficult and have no fun or benefit from it. [But] you, my man, when you think like that, are wrong all the way. And, by God immortal, what is the reason that we spend so much energy not only on useless subjects

HEBRAICAE LINGVAE.

les modo disciplinas, uerũetiam cultoribus suis sæpe perniciosas, atq3 hoc facimus inani decepti gloria, qua iam omnia metiuntur stolidi homines, de futura gloria parum soliciti? Equidem autor ego nulli fuerim, ut a disciplinis humanioribus resiliat, imo harum suasor semp ab amicis habitus. Illud modo queror, q̃ tã turpiter nauseent quidam ad ea studia, quę sola diuina, cœlestia, angelica, sacrosancta sunt, amplectentes interim nescio quæ sæculo huic conformia, terrena, prophana, ob sordidum quæstum & popularem auram. Dicite mortales, quæ uos habet spes? Num mundum hunc cũ Xenophane & Aristotele æternum somniatis? Fortasse mortales

uos

but also on subjects that are often pernicious to those who pursue them?[136] Are we doing those things, deceived by vainglory, which dumb people use as a measuring stick for just about everything, and forget about the future glory? As for me, I do not want to give anyone reason to give up the study of the humanities. To the contrary, my friends know that I recommend them. There is only one thing I deplore, namely that some people are so shamefully disgusted with those studies which alone are divine, heavenly, angelic, and most holy, as they embrace the studies that conform to this time and age and that are worldly and heathen and for dirty profit and popularity. Tell me, you mortal beings, what do you place your hope in? Do you dream like Xenophanes and Aristotle that the world would last forever?

---

136. Witzel may have had astrology in mind.

ENCOMIVM

uos dici patimini, at esse non creditis? Fortasse cum Epicuro deū non curare hæc infima opinamini? Fortasse animam immortalem non sentitis, id quod sensit & M. Tullius? Aut auerni poenas pro fabula ducitis, quas tamen credidit apud Platonem Socrates, Maro, Lucianus? Aut anastasim generalē cum Sadducæis & Valentinianis, & Carpocratianis & Cerdonianis & Plinio diffitemini? Quo uos nomine appellē? Christianos? Atq huiusmodi in Christianos haudquaq̄ cadūt. Dicam doctos? Ii si essetis, melius profecto deligentes, uilius abijceretis omitteretisq̃. Dicā homines physicos? At fuere olim homines naturæ ductu uiuentes longe alij,
quippe

You allow perhaps being called mortal, but you do not really believe it? Perhaps you opine like Epicurus that God does not care about the lowest things? Perhaps you do not think that the soul is immortal, something even M. Tullius [Cicero] thinks? Or, do you believe that punishment in hell is fable-talk whereas Plato, Socrates, Maro and Lucian believe [in hell]? Or do you deny the general resurrection[137] like the Saducees,[138] Valentinians,[139] Carpocratians,[140] Cerdonians[141] and Pliny? By which name should I call you? Christians? Yet views like that are not Christian. Should I call you "learned"? If you were, you would actually choose what is better, and throw away and give up what has no value. Should I call you men of nature? Moreover, once upon a time there were people who lived their lives of nature

---

137. *Anastasim generalem.*
138. See Matt 22:23, etc.
139. After Valentinus, a Gnostic, 2nd century.
140. After Karpokrates's teaching about the migration of souls.
141. After Kerdon, a Gnostic, 2nd century.

HEBRAICAE LINGVAE.

quippe qui liquido intelligebant, prestare futura praesentibus, qui excellentiora studio indefesso uestigabant, qui contemnenda atque defugienda ea docebant, quae tu ἄλογον ζῶον tā enixe sectaris. Necque tamē illi nisi homines erāt, humana sanaque ratione praediti. Iterum testificor, me neminem ab ulla retrahere disciplina. Hoc unū ago, ut id quod est excellentissimum, praedicem, predicando suadeam, suadendo ad salutarē eius rei fructum attraham, qbus libeat. Humanis diuina praefero, & terrenis coelestia. Video maximope opus esse urgentibus atque uehementibus monitis, quibus permoueantur studiosi huius tempestatis. Irrumpunt nūc ad eas modo artes,
quas

and they clearly understood, of course, that the future surpasses the present; they indefatigably searched for the higher things; they taught that you should despise and flee from exactly what you, like an irrational animal,[142] so eagerly pursue. Yet they still were human beings gifted with human and healthy understanding. I want to state again that I do not keep anybody away from any [other] science [*disciplina*]. All I am doing is to praise what is most excellent [and] by praising to recommend, [and] by recommending to attract you who like it to this salutary fruit. I prefer the divine to what is human, what is heavenly to what is terrestrial. I see that urgent and vehement admonitions are very much needed by which students of our time are to be stirred up. Right now they rush only to those arts

---

142. ἄλογον ζῷον, quoting in original Greek letters, but in the singular form from 2 Pet 2:12, ἄλογα ζῷα (But these people, like irrational animals born by nature for capture and destruction, revile things that they do not understand).

ENCOMIVM

quas homo reperit, & quæ uel corpori, uel hæreditati conseruandæ conducunt. Hic desudant, hic unicam nauant operam, hic exercent ingenia. Omnē substantiam in has prodigunt, omnem ætatē in his conterunt, lactati spe caducorum commodorum. Theologiæ sola friget schola, uacua mœret, spreta iacet, posteaquam huc uenit, ut omnes fieri Hippocrates, Iustiniani, Cicerones ambiāt: nemo Paulus, nemo Hieronymus. Adeoq; apud quosdā prodigiose elegantes in eum contemptu abijt Theologia, ut uituperij uice, si quādo stomachus illis motus est, obijciant Theologiam huius candidatis. Alij rusticam et triuialē eam iudicant, uidelicet quæ cuiuis

which man finds [useful] and which help one's body or inheritance.[143] This they sweat over, this alone they energetically work on, this they put their mind to. They waste their entire possession on them, they spend their entire time with them, enticed by the hope of transitory advantages. The school of theology alone leaves people cold, stays empty, dejected,[144] after it has come to this that everybody wants to become a Hippocrates, a Justinian, or a Cicero,[145] but not a Paul, and not a Jerome. And some of those strangely elegant people despise theology so much that they, when they are angered, do not [just] criticize it, but object altogether to any representative of theology. Others take theology to be boorish and trivial, as if it [theology] were

---

143. The speaker has the disciplines of medicine and jurisprudence in mind.
144. *Theologiae sola friget schola, vacua moeret, spreta iacet.*
145. That is, everybody wants to become a physician, lawyer, or orator.

HEBRAICAE LINGVAE.

cuiuis aurigæ, lanio, tonsori, fosso ri obuia notaq; sit. Sunt q̃s si ad theologiā extimules, Monachis, inqunt desertoribus Theologiā iniūgito, Cito fit theologus: unus sexternio Germanicorum scripto rum ex Mimo facit Theologum. Eiusmodi haurire inuitis auribus cogimur. Eadem impudentia dicam an impietate repellit, linguæ sanctæ propagatio, siquidem ex eadem schola est Theologia & Hebraismus. Obijciunt, ad Iudęos spectare eam literaturam, non ad Christianos, ipsi neque Iudæi, neq; Christiani, neque homines, sed grylli. Alij causantur superuacuum esse, ut plures hebraicentur q̃ interpretes Bibliorum. Alij ob notularum deformitatem, punF ctorum

obvious and known to every driver, butcher, barber, or digger. Some say that if you want to stimulate them to do theology, you should attach them to monks who have deserted theology. A theologian is quickly made: Just one sesternio[146] of a German writing makes a theologian out of an actor. We are forced to listen to such stuff. With the same shamelessness, or should I say godlessness, the propagation of the holy language is repelled if indeed theology and Hebrew studies are from the same school. They object by saying that [Hebrew] literature is not meant for Christians, but for Jews, and they themselves are neither Jews nor Christians, nor human persons, but piglets. Others caution that it is super-useless to have numerous people study Hebrew[147] beyond those who are Bible translators. Still others despise this most noble matter because they think the Hebrew characters are ugly

---

146. Sesternio, a set of 12 pages.
147. *Hebraicentur.*

ENCOMIVM

ctorum insolentiam, præposté
rum legendi morem, oris accoḿ
modatam uarietatē, & nescio ob
quæ alia minuta rem nobilissimā
respuunt. Alij non ob aliud Hebræa uitant studia, nisi quia alios
eadem uitare cernant, nolētes ad
id applicare animū, quod in nulla
esse celebritate intelligant. Isthæc
scilicet gratitudo nostra erga dá
torem bonorum? Nihil addam
amplius. Neque uero tanti mali
caussam inuenire possim, nisi ita
solere semp infimo haberi loco,
quicquid a Deo est singulare dó
num. Quo minus mirandum, cp
uulgus Christianorū, uelut ab́
dicato Christo seruatore, ter ma-
ledicto zabulo in tenebrarum factis ex animo seruiat, quandoqui
dem

and because they are not used to employ points [Hebrew punctuation] and because this language is to be read from right to left and because it sounds strange to their ears and I know not for what other petty details. Others shy away from Hebrew studies only because they see others stay away, since they do not want to apply themselves to something that has no prestige. Is this then our gratitude toward the giver of all that is good? I do not want to say more. But I might not find any other reason for so much evil, except that people always hold in low esteem what [actually] is a unique gift of God. It is no wonder that the Christian people seem to reject Christ the Savior and wholeheartedly serve the three-times cursed devil in deeds done in darkness.

HEBRAICAE LINGVAE.
dem doctorum ordo ac sal uulgi
tam præpostere iudicans diuina
fastidiat,& se totum terræ affiget
consecretque. Sed satis longe di-
gressum. Querelæ nunquam gra
tæ sunt,ne tum quidem,cum forsan necessariæ erunt,quemadmo-
dū uerissime scripsit Liuius. Non
uideo,quid uspiam aliud agant et
docti et indocti,q̃ q̃d postea,seri-
us licet,deplorent. Si debetur satis malum, age procedat, dum licet. Foelicem uero qui ab hoc pu-
rum semet seruarit. Vos adolescentes hortor, ut rei magnitudi-
ne,maiestate, prestantia,diuinita-
te,utilitate atq̃ necessitate expen-
sa,animos uestros ad hoc studio-
rum genus confirmetis, ut ij qui
se dei cultores esse norint,et ij qui
F ij   non

This is so because the learned ones with vulgar taste think that way and feel distaste for the divine things, and they are totally attached to the earth and devote themselves to it. But enough already with such digressions.

Quarrels are never pleasant; not even when they might be necessary, as Livy has written. I do not see the learned and the unlearned acting in different ways which they later, perhaps when it is too late, regret. When by fate evil is going to happen, let it be as long as it may last. Happy is the one, however, who remained pure.

I encourage you, young people, to dedicate your studies to what is divine—due to the obvious greatness, majesty, excellence, godliness, usefulness, and necessity of the subject—and to live in the awareness of being worshipers of God

ENCOMIVM

non dubitent, de factis olim red
dendam rationem, non Rhada
manto, non Cædicio, sed Chri
sto. Cogita etiam atque etiam,
quanto amore id cuiuis pio prose
quendum sit, quod dei est. Qua
re te Theologiæ emancipa, regi
næ uni atq; heroinę artium quot
quot sunt. Hęc tibi æternas para
bit sedes, & thronum altitonan
tis tecum ex æquo diuidet. Hæc
demū philosophia est, quam diu
quæsitam nō inuenit docta Græ
cia. Vmbellam huius uiderunt so
phi, ipsam nō uiderunt. Ad hanc
enisi sunt, sed uires recusarunt. At
nobis, nobis, inquam, cōtigit huc
penetrare, uidere, frui. O fortuna
tos, si serio norimus oblatum ine
narrabilium bonorum mare. Por
ro in

and to have no doubts that one day you will have to give an account of your doings, not before Rhadamantys[148] or before Caedicius,[149] but before Christ. Be mindful, time and again, with how much love every pious person must attend to what is God's. Therefore, you should dedicate yourself completely to theology, the only queen and heroine of the arts—how many of the arts there ever might be. Theology will prepare eternal seats for you[150] and will adorn the throne of the Thundering One on High,[151] sharing it with you. Theology is that philosophy which the learned Greece has sought for such a long time, but never found. The wise [Greeks] have seen her shadow, but have not seen her herself. To her they tried to work their way up, but they did not have enough force. But we, we were granted to reach her, see and enjoy her. O how happy are we, if we really get to know the sea of indescribable goods that are offered us.

148. A judge in the netherworld.
149. Someone of a Roman family.
150. See John 14:2.
151. *Thronum altitonantis.*

HEBRAICAE LINGVAE.

ro in Theologico studio non satis commode uersabere citra linguæ huius cognitionem, quemadmodum in bello citra armorum præsidia uix salua cute diu durabit miles. Persuade tibi, nihil esse utilius, nihil iucundius, nihil expetitius huius linguæ studio. Non libet hic oratorijs uti collationibus ad exaggerandam utilitatem Hebraismi, rem ipsam consideremus. Primum ne scientia quidem ulla est, si utilitatem tollas. Quid enim scientia sine utilitate ac fructu? Iam constat, eam non scientiam modo eximiam atq; singularem raramq; esse, uerūetiam e cœlo descendisse, id quod in supioribus p certo affirmauimus. Tun' loqui linguis inutile putas? Quasi

F iij   non

However, you cannot sufficiently study theology without the knowledge of this language [Hebrew], just as a soldier in battle cannot last long without proper gear. Be persuaded that nothing is more useful, nothing more beautiful, nothing worth striving for more than the study of this language. We do not want to make rhetorical comparisons in order to point out the usefulness of Hebrew studies, but let us consider the subject matter itself. First, something is not science when it has no use. What would science/knowledge be without usefulness and any results. It is certain that this knowledge [of Hebrew] is not only exceptional and unique and rare, but also has descended from heaven, as we have affirmed for sure before. Do you think it is useless to speak other languages?

ENCOMIVM

non ea ratione fuerit impressa pe﹐
ctoribus mortalium doctrina re﹐
gni. Tolle linguarum usum, &
Euangeliū omne sustuleris. Mi﹐
rum si quis de hoc ambigat. Ve﹐
rū hoc cōmodi peculiariter ex lin
gua Hebræa capies, ut tutus ob﹐
ambulare p interp̄tationes omni﹐
um possis, id quod alioqui nullus
feceris. Quotidie exoriuntur no﹐
ui scripturæ interpretes, quorum
quisq; pro suæ partis commodo
sacras literas transfert, in quibus
lustrandis nisi catus fueris, ilico
in errorem præceps eas oportet.
Si munitus sis huius linguæ sci﹐
entia, pergrassari uales absq; ullo
insidiosi serpentis periculo. Ma﹐
gnum est, mihi crede, interpretem
lectoris iudicium metuere, & ue﹐
rua for﹐

It is as if that through it [Hebrew] the teaching of the reign [of God] was impressed into the hearts of the mortals. Do away with the use of the languages and you have taken away the entire Gospel.[152] It would be strange if someone would doubt this. Truly, you will draw special benefits from the Hebrew language. Truly, the immediate advantage gained from learning the Hebrew language is this:

You can safely navigate through all the translations which otherwise you would not be able to do. New interpreters of Scripture emerge daily who each translates according to his own taste. If you are not skilled enough to examine them, you may easily fall into error. If you have a solid knowledge of this language, you can get started without any danger coming from the insidious serpent. Believe me, it is a big thing that a translator fears the reader's

---

152. *Tolle linguarum usum, et Evangelium omne sustuleris.* See the same conviction in Martin Luther, *To the Councilmen: Das[s] wyr das Evangelion nicht wol werden erhalten on [ohne] die Sprachen*, WA 15: 38.

HEBRAICAE LINGVAE.

rua formidare doctarũ manuum. Continet illum hoc in officio, facit diligentiorem, facit percontatiorem, cohibet præmaturas editiones, & admonet sæpius retractandum, nonumq; in annũ premendum(quemadmodũ & Flaccus, & in Epistolis Plinius etiam consulunt) quod alioqui uix natum protinus publicandum existimabat scriptor interpres. Hinc suspicor fieri, cp ŋs qui Biblia Germanis donant, nõ admodum arrideat adolescentum in discendis linguis sedulitas, siquidem uerentur magistros. Sed qualis fides isthęc, qualis candor, aliŋ dixerint. Præterea afferet hoc q̃q; emolumēti linguę Hebraicę cognitio, cp te de fidei Christiaęn ueritate cer-

F iiŋ   tissimum

judgment and that he dreads his manicula.[153] They keep him true to his task, make him more diligent; they make him more inquisitive; they prevent premature editions. [In being mindful of a critical reader] one is led to the reworking of a text which may take nine years (something which both Flaccus [Horace] and Pliny in his Letters take into consideration). Otherwise a translator assumes that a text must be published as soon as it comes into existence. Because of that, I suspect, it can happen that the zeal of the young people to learn languages makes those not smile all too much who are giving the Bible to the Germans, if indeed those students are afraid of their masters. But of what sort this trust is, what sort of clarity, others may decide.

Furthermore, the knowledge of the Hebrew language will help to make you very certain about the truth of the Christian faith;[154]

---

153. ... *et verua formidare doctarum manuum*. A critical reader often entered "little hands" (*manicula*) in the margins.

154. The Latin print has the printing mistake of "Christiaęn" instead of *Christianę* [= *Christianae*].

ENCOMIVM

tissimum reddit. Exhibet enim il﹈
la tuæ religiosę curiositati fontem
ipsum & fundamentum ueritatis
scripturarum mysticarum, omni
excluso dubio. Nam eum qui du
bitaturus erat de certitudine rerū
diuinarum, eo pacto fulciendum
iudicauerim, si illi ostendatur sca﹈
turigo scripturæ sanctissima, ut
est primum a deo per seruos suos
prophetas disposita. Qualecunq;
hoc alijs, mihi certe maximum ui﹈
detur, & eo ppemodum ceu mi﹈
raculo dei singulari, si quid diffi﹈
derem, ad Christianismi fidem al﹈
licerer. Dubitare poteram de sa﹈
cris literis, deq; harum authorita﹈
te, nisi me certum & securum esse
iuberet fons ille lympidissimus a
tot sæculis scatens. Affert lingua
hæc

and it helps to show you in your religious curiosity the font and the foundation of the truth of the mysteries of the Scriptures—without any doubt. Whoever has doubts about the certitude in divine things will, in my judgment, gain it if he is shown the most holy bubbling spring of Scripture.[155] Its waters were distributed at first by God through his servants, the prophets. Whatever other people may say about all this, to me it certainly appears to be the greatest. And if I had any doubts in any regards, the study of the Hebrew Scriptures, as if by a unique divine miracle, would entice me to come to the faith of Christianity. I could have doubts about the Scriptures and their authority, but they are dispersed and I am made certain by the most limpid font which bubbles now for so many centuries.

---

155. ... *scaturigo scripturae sanctissima*. Witzel's Latin notion of "bubbling spring" echoes Reuchlin's saying that all theology has bubbled up, or gushed forth (*scaturivit*), from God's mouth.

HEBRAICAE LINGVAE,
hæc concioni qꝗ fulcra ac bases
robustiss. addit concionatori uehementiam constantiamcꝗ. Nam
quo est de scripturarum ueritate
certior, hoc solidius, uirilius atcꝗ
potentius docet & urget. Eidem
subministrat materiã, de themate
copiosius disserendi, dum aperit
uim contextus ipsissimam. Transeo quantum conducat ad literariam pugnam, maxime ubi de religione & huius articulis disputatio incidit. Non unquam uidisti
Hebræum ænei muri instar inuictum stare in cõflictu, quoties ad
huius linguæ præsidium cucurrerit? Qui posset homo Christianus
de Iudęo uictoriam reportare, nisi præsidijs sanctę linguæ? Transeo, q̃ ualde conferat linguæ He
   F v   bręæ

The Hebrew language provides a preacher with the most robust basis, but also provides strength and firmness. The more certain a preacher is about the truth of the Scriptures, the more solid, forceful and powerful he will teach and motivate. [The command of Hebrew] allows him to discuss a theme in an exhaustive way while at the same time the full meaning of the context can be disclosed. I leave aside that such knowledge contributes to the literary struggle, especially concerning a disputation about religion and its [individual] articles.

Perhaps you have seen once a [Christian] Hebrew expert.[156] He stands firm like an iron wall in any conflict whenever he takes refuge with this language. How could a Christian win victory over a Jew without the help from the holy language?

---

156. *Hebraeus*; i.e., a Hebraist.

ENCOMIVM

breæ scientia ad legitime intelli∕
gendum enarrandumq; libros ue
teris instrumēti. Nodosa loca ex∕
plicat, obscura elucidat, intricata
extricat, dubia certificat, breuiter
est magistra exponendæ scriptu∕
ræ certissima. Transeo quantum
fœcūditatis afferant doctis Theo
logis fonticuli isti ͵ppriorum no∕
minum Hebræorum. Innumeras
͵pfecto allegorias, pulcherrimos
lusus, & seueriores etiam doctri∕
nas plurimas peperit ͵ppriorum
etymologica interpretatio, quam
orbi donauit post Philonem Hie
ronymus : sed ita, ut aliquid tibi
quoq; agendū reliquerit. Trans∕
eo cætera commoda, quę confer∕
tim sui studiosis ceu amplissima
præmia largietur. Nonne uides
contra

I leave aside how much the knowledge of the Hebrew language helps to better understand and proclaim the books of the Old Testament. Such expertise can explain any knotty verses, shed light on what is obscure, extricate the intricate and make the ambiguous verses certain. In short, Hebrew is the most reliable teacher in expounding Scripture.

I leave aside how much help the learned theologians receive from these sources with respect to the meaning of Hebrew names. Indeed, the etymological interpretation of proper names has brought forth countless allegories, most beautiful wordplays, and very many more serious teachings, [an interpretation] which after [the time of] Philo was given by Jerome to the world; but it was given in a way that there is still something left also for you to do.

I leave aside the other advantages which such interpretation will award with great benefits to those who study it.

HEBRAICAE LINGVAE.

cõtra, quanta sit miseria istorum, qui linguas nesciunt: Pendere illi de interpretũ nutu cogũtur, quibus cũ aut bene sentiunt, aut male. Credere coguntur, quæcunq; obtruduntur illorum manibus. In concionibus frigent, in disputatione languent, in enarrandis locis ancipites huc atq; illuc feruntur, & ut quidã uerissime inquit, alienis ingrediuntur pedibus, alienis cernunt oculis. Sed nolim in foelicitatẽ istorum traducere, quorum quidam partim ætatis uitio, partim præceptorũ penuria, partim laboris sustinendi diffidentia a schola Hebræorum abacti esse uidẽtur. Colligere hinc quiuis poterit linguæ huius necessitatẽ, nedum utilitatem, salubritatem, precium

Don't you see how great in contrast the misery is of those who do not know the languages? They are forced to remain dependent upon the work of the translators with whom they may either agree or disagree. They are compelled to believe whatever the translators throw at them. Their sermons leave you cold, their discussions leave you weary; when they recite [Bible] verses they remain ambiguous, as someone very correctly says: They walk with other people's feet and see with other people's eyes.[157] But I do not want to expose to ridicule the misfortune of those who seem to be frightened away from the school of the Hebrews,[158] be it because of their [old] age, be it because of the lack of teachers, or be it because they have no self-confidence to endure hard work. Hence everybody will be able to understand that this language has to be learned, and even more so that it is useful, healthful and precious.

---

157. Paraphrasing Pliny, who talks about the slaves who carry their lords and who are looking ahead in order to tell them who is coming.

158. *Schola Hebraeorum*.

ENCOMIVM

cium. Verum de ea disserere festi-
nanti longius equo fuerit. Videa-
mus nunc, an aliquid ea lingua iu-
cūdius sit. Qui uoluptatem quæ-
runt in momentaneis illis, quæ
hoc sæculum admiratur atq; con
cupiscit, nę illi uel philosophorū
gentilium iudicio fatui sunt. Qui
delectātur in ingenuis artibus, eis
id solatij concedo. Nulla tamē est
solida ac uera uoluptas pijs animis, nisi in re pietatis. Iam uero nihil magis spectat ad pietatem, q̄
piæ literę. Qua igitur in re sese ob
lectet dei cultor, nisi in tam augu-
stis, tam antiqs, tam sacratis, tam
diuinis deniq; literis? Amœnissi-
mum, sic me Christus bene amet,
& perpetuo uernantissimum pra
tum est scriptura in suo idiomate,
& tot

Enough of these deliberations! Now let us see whether there is anything more enjoyable than this language. Those who seek pleasure in the fleeting things which are admired and coveted in the present time, are fools even in the judgment of the philosophers of the pagan people.

I concede some solace to those who delight in the liberal arts. Nowhere is there, however, any solid and true enjoyment for pious souls except in matters of piety. Nothing pertains more to piety than pious writings. What, therefore, would bring joy to a worshiper of God, if not the august, ancient, consecrated and divine writings? By the love of Christ, the loveliest and in the long run most verdant pasture is Scripture in its original wording,

HEBRAICAE LINGVAE.
& tot habet flores, quot uoces, unde decerpere cuicꝗ liceat, quod sibi usui esse putet ad iustitiæ culturam. Est hortus delitiosus, Balsami diues, & omnis pomorū generis, semper suaue olens, semper ridens, semper formosus. Deest nobis sermo in delectamento Hebraici studij attollendo. An non uolupe est pietati hominis, eas uidere literas, quas ipsa Maiestas summa inuenit? Quid putas deesse dulcedinis illi, cui eo loq ore obtigit, quo locutus est Christus, ꝓphetæ & Apostoli? Quid mellitius, quid gratius, quid desideratius, q̄ nosse etiam, quibus uerbis orbi secreta sua retexerit Dominus, quandoquidem præsentem audire non cōtigit? O immensum
quiddā

which has as many flowers as words. Everybody may pick from it what is deemed best for one's cultivation of righteousness. It is a garden of delight, rich with balsam, with all kinds of fruits, always sweet smelling, always pleasing and always beautiful. There are no words to describe the delight in studying Hebrew. Is it not joyful for a person of piety to see those letters which the highest Majesty has invented? What do you think is lacking in sweetness to someone who has learned to speak in the language of Christ, the prophets and the apostles? What is sweeter, more pleasing and more desirable than to know the words with which the Lord has uncovered his secrets to the world, now that it is no longer possible to hear him in person? O how immense it is

ENCOMIVM

quiddam, nempe hominem mor
talem callere linguam Dei. Non
hic commemorabo, quantopere
adficiat legentis animum intelle=
cta lingua. Vnicum dei nomen in
suo isto originali fortius figit se=
dem in credētis pectore. Mirum
dictu est, quanto uehementius so
letur atq; serenetur precans He=
braice, q̄ si quis Græce aut Latine
precetur. Vim uiuidam addunt ti
bi uoces sacratissimæ, adeoq; so=
nus ille. Rapiunt te alio, et res per
gūt occultis quibusdam gaudijs,
ut alacrior a psalmodia discedas,
& promptior redeas. Summatim
animus in nulla lingua tam con=
quiescit & pacificatur, ut in He=
bræa. Vt taceam per se delectare
quamlibet scientiam, hanc uero
co ma

that a mortal being understands the language of God.[159] I will not think here about the degree to which the language that is [well] understood may affect the mind of that reader. The unique name of God in its original does more likely find a place in the believer's breast. It is wonderful to be able to say how much more somebody is being consoled and cheered up when praying in Hebrew than in Greek or Latin. The most holy Hebrew words convey a lively power to your voice in addition to the way they sound. By the Hebrew words you are rapt and you experience hidden joys so that, after singing the psalms in Hebrew, you walk away refreshed and more than ready to return. In sum, [your] spirit quiets down so much and is at peace through no other language than Hebrew.

---

159. *O immensum quiddam, nempe hominem mortalem callere linguam Dei.*

HEBRAICAE LINGVAE.

eo magis delectare, quo est diuinior. Etenim non uulgare gaudiū est, linguas alias iuxta hanc nostram conferre, et ad hanc ceu Lydiā regulā omnia exigere, omnia dijudicare trutinareue. Ipse Hieronymus sæpe miratur eius linguæ dulcedinem, non dubium, quin eam iterum atq; iterum expertus. Hæc atq; huiusmodi uos quoq; experiundo potius discite uiri Christiani, si mihi minus fidei datis. Porro qui causantur difficultatem linguæ huius immodicam, uehementer errant. Fortasse reris te eam una diecula, & citra laboris molestiam cōsecuturum. An est sine labore uirtus? Adeoque qd sine labore dulce aut honestū; Dic mihi, quot annos Romanæ

I do not even want to mention that any insight as such brings joy, but the Hebrew language brings it even more because it is holier. For, indeed, it is no ordinary joy to place other languages next to ours [for comparison] and to use Hebrew quasi as Lydia's ruler in order to measure everything and weigh everything.[160] Jerome himself often admires the sweetness of this language which, no doubt, he himself experienced time and again. You too, Christian men, should learn this and similar things from your own experience, if you do not believe me. Furthermore, very wrong are those who argue that this language would be excessively difficult. Perhaps you think you can learn it in a short period of time and without much trouble. Does any expertise come without work? And furthermore, what would be sweet and honorable if gained without labor? Tell me, how many years did you spend learning the Roman language [Latin]?

---

160. ... *et ad hunc ceu Lydia regula omnia exigere, omnia diiudicare trutinareve.* "Lydia regula" is a perfectly straight stick.

ENCOMIVM

manæ linguæ addiscendę dedistis
Horum dimidium imperti He-
bręæ. Nec refert, si non cōscendas
ad summum, Satis esto, si in me-
dio consistas. Est aliquid, pauca
posse intelligere. Non exigo a te
Epistolas Hebraicas, marte tuo
scriptas, non colloquia Hebraica, nec aliorum omnium scripto-
rū dictorumue intelligentiam, sed
illud uolo, ut Biblijs adsuescas
Hebraicis, ut phrasin & idiomata
imbibas, ut uocabulorum ratio-
nes rimeris, ut ex his translationes iudices. Breuiter, ut animum
tuum his literis obfirmes, ceu uere Hieroglyphicis, uere Sibyllinis
uere Delphicis. Illud forsan quosdam remoretur, quo minus animos ad sancta ista studia adiun-
gant

Spend just half of it on Hebrew! And it does not matter if you do not reach the highest level [of expertise]. It is enough if you remain mediocre. It is already an achievement to be able to understand a little bit. I do not expect you to read and write letters in Hebrew and have conversations in Hebrew, or that you understand all the other writings and sayings. However, this I expect: that you familiarize yourself with the Hebrew Bible; that you appropriate its idiosyncrasies; that you research the meaning of the words so that you can evaluate any translations. In short: Be determined to study the Hebrew characters as if they were really hieroglyphs, Sibyllinian or Delphian sayings.[161]

There might be some issues that would prevent people from attaching themselves to these holy studies:

---

161. I.e., mysterious Egyptian pictographs, sayings of the prophetess Sibyl, and the oracles of Delphi.

HEBRAICAE LINGVAE.

gant, Nimirū ꝗ audiunt uix pau‑
cissimos scriptorum Ecclesiastico
rum Hebraice doctos fuisse, un‑
de consequi, non adeo fructuo‑
sam, nec tam ad res Theologicas
necessariā esse linguam istā. Hic si
patienter me audire dignabimini,
expediam uobis isthuc obiectum
q̃ potero breuissime. Ab Aposto
lorum & aliorum ex circumcisio‑
ne obitu, nacta est Ecclesia uiros
antesignanos ex gentilitate, idꝗ
tam in oriente, q̃ occidente, quo‑
rum alij Græci nati erant, alij La‑
tini. Quos autem tum ex Iudæis
acceperit, obscuri nobis sunt &
incelebres. Nolo enim hic commi
nisci eos, qui ex ijs accepti in Eccle
siam, postea Iudaizantes, hæreses
inuexerunt. Quoniā igitur Chri‑
G   stia‑

They hear, and this is no surprise, that only very few ecclesiastical writers were skilled in Hebrew. Therefore, this language would not be that fruit-bearing and not that necessary in matters of theology. Allow me to disarm this argument in all brevity: After the death of the apostles and of the others who were circumcised [i.e., Jews], the Church brought forth standard-bearers from the pagan nations in the east and in the west; they were born Greeks, others were Latins. But those who had been accepted from among the Jews are not known to us and are not celebrated [*incelebres*]. For I do not want to recall here those who from among them have been accepted into the Church, but who later became judaizers and brought in heresies.

ENCOMIVM

ſtianiſmus ad Græcas & Latinas gentes reciderat, & ſacræ ſcriptuᷓ ræ Biblia iam Gręca Latinaue habebantur, factum eſt, ut ‚pgreſſu temporis inter pleroſcᷤ obſoleuerit Hebrææ linguæ exiſtimatio. Enimuero notum eſt ex Irenæo, et Auguſtino, quo deſiderio Ptolomęus rex Lagi filius apud Aleᷓ xandriam Eleazari pōtificis Hieᷓ roſolymitani opera Hebræos arᷓ canarum literarum codices, per ſeptuaginta ſeniores in Græcaniᷓ cum ſermonem uertendos curaᷓ uerit, ut tantus theſaurus, ad quē ſolis Iudæis aditus patebat, alloᷓ phylis etiam euulgaretur, nec hoc ſine Dei conſilio ac prouidentia. Pręterea nemo neſcit, alios poſtea ſenioribus hiſce ſucceſſiſſe interᷓ
pretes

When then Christianity came to the Greek and Latin nations, and when the Sacred Scriptures became available in a Greek and Latin Bible, it so happened that in the course of time many people lost the appreciation of the Hebrew language. To be sure, we know from Irenaeus and Augustine how much King Ptolemy, son of Lagus, at Alexandria—with the help of the high priest Eleazar in Jerusalem—wanted the Hebrew codices with its secret mysteries to be translated into Greek by seventy elders. Thus, the great treasure to which only Jews had access is now accessible also to others [*allophylis*]. This happened not without God's plan and providence. It is generally known that after the completion [of the Septuagint translation] by these elders, other Greek translators followed who were Jewish proselytes,

HEBRAICAE LINGVAE.

pretes Græcos, uidelicet Symmachum, Aqlam Pontium, et Theodotionem Ephesium, Iudęos proselytos. Istorum igitur laboribus contenti scriptores Ecclesiæ ueteres, Hebræorum fontes neglexerunt, non cõtempserunt, atq; hoc præceptorũ magis, sicut ego quidem opinor, inopia, q̃ rei ipsius fastidio. Sed heus, igitur non uis e fonte dulcissimo bibere, posteaquam in gustũ dati tibi sunt Gręci riuuli? Eliges ne amēs pro ,ptotypo deuterotypon, aut etiã tritotypon? Nõ obluctor, quo minus deames ac usurpes septuaginta interpretes una cum successoribus, sed ea lege, ut primas Mosi ac Prophetarum primario stylo tribuas. Scio amice scio, quantum

G ij   autoris

namely Symmachus, Aquila of Pontus, and Theodotion of Ephesus.[162] Since at that time then the old writers of the Church were content with the fruits of their [elders'] labors, they neglected the sources of the Hebrews, without despising them; this happened, as I believe, more so because there was a lack of teachers than because of any low opinion about the matter. But don't you want to drink now from the sweetest font after you have had a taste from the Greek rills? You would not be so stupid as to prefer secondary and third-class versions to the original?[163]

I do not object to the high esteem you have for the seventy translators [Septuagint] and that you use them along with their successors, but only as long as you attribute any primacy to the language of Moses and the prophets. My friend, I know very well

---

162. Other Christian Hebraists such as Adrianus and Winmann had mentioned them, too.

163. *Sed heus, igitur non vis e fonte dulcissimo bibere, posteaquam in gustum dati tibi sunt Graeci rivuli? Eliges ne amens pro prototypo deuterotypon, aut etiam tritotypon?* Witzel follows Reuchlin in this.

ENCOMIVM

autoritatis isti uiri apud uetustissi
mos quoscp obtineant, presertim
apud Irenæum, Hilariũ, Ambro
sium & Augustinum, qui acriter
dimicant pro illorum maiestate
minime omniũ uiolanda. Atqui
non deserenda, ppterea Hebrço
rum autoritas, quæ tanto maior
est, quanto antiquior, et hoc emi
nentior, quo diuinior. Cõdonan
dum aliqd Aurelio arbitror, qui
mordere nõ dubitauit Hierony
mianas ad Hebræum uersiones,
præ immodica quippe septuagin
ta admiratione. Satis ulti eũ sunt
errores quidam ex Hebrçæ lin
guæ ignorantia ab ipso exorti.
Equidem non ualde non placere
mihi possunt Latini scriptores,
qui quum hebraicari non liceret,
saltem

what high authority those men obtained among the oldest [writers], particularly Irenaeus, Hilary, Ambrose, and Augustine. They [the church fathers] fought heavily for the prestige of these [elders] that it not be violated in any way. Nevertheless, the authority of the Hebrews must not be abandoned which after all is greater, older, and more eminent because of its divinity. I think one must forgive Aurelius [Augustinus] for not hesitating to criticize Jerome's translations from the Hebrew because of his [Augustine's] exaggerated admiration for the Septuagint. He [Augustine] made enough errors due to his ignorance of the Hebrew language. For my part, I do like the Latin authors who, since they were unable to study Hebrew,[164]

---

164. *Hebraicari*.

HEBRAICAE LINGVAE.
saltem ad Gręca se tanto contule﹖
runt studio. Nam da mihi unum
ex uetustissimis Latinis Theolo﹖
gum, qui Græce nescierit, & qui
non proprias ferme uersiones ex
Græco in suis scriptis usurparit.
Quo magis excusandi nobis sunt
de Hebraismi imperitia, & hoc
magis tu incusandus uidere, qui
Latinus duntaxat theologus esse
uis, originales & genuinas literas
nõ ita magnipēdens, quæ nisi exi﹖
sterent, ne Latina quidem habe﹖
res. Diuus Hieronymus esto exē﹖
plar colēdi id genus studij. Hunc
ob oculos pone, hunc imitare. Is
patefecit uiam ad Hebręorũ ady﹖
ta, dignus profecto, non dico, qui
in Olympia aureus stet, & Argi﹖
uum gestet clypeum, sed quē cun﹖

G iij   ctæ

at least turned to the study of Greek with so much eagerness. Name me one of the oldest Latin theologians who would not have known Greek and who usually would not have made use of his own Greek translations in his own writings. All the more do we have to excuse their ignorance of Hebrew, and all the more you [dear student] would have to be faulted, you who want to be no less a Latin theologian, but who does not appreciate the original and genuine works. These works survived because they were preserved also in Latin.

For the learning of Hebrew, Saint Jerome should be the model to be emulated. Keep him in front of your eyes; imitate him. He has opened the path to the sanctuary of the Hebrews. He is, indeed, worthy—I am not saying that he should stand gilded in Olympia holding a Greek round shield—to be made the patron of all the schools.[165]

---

165. ... *et Argivum* [=Greek]; *clypeum* [= *clipeum*, a round shield].

ENCOMIVM

ctæ scholæ ceu patrem suum te﹖
rant. Aquila is in nubibus est, &
talis, ut plures habeat qui inuide﹖
ant, q̃ qui ipsum exęquent. Is e ma
tre lingua quæsiuit ueritatem con
textus, diues in rerũ scientia, alijs
interim mendicantibus. Quin tu
itaq; ipse ipse potius tibi para fa﹖
cultatē, dũ licet, ne quando opus
est, cogaris uel ad Iudæorum per﹖
fidiam cõfugere, uel incerta alio﹖
rum consulere interpretamenta.
Vir ille in Paulæ Epitaphio cum
uellet sanctę huic linguæ tribuere
laudem maximam, sic inquit: He﹖
bræam linguam non desero, ne
ipse ab ea deserar. Testatur ibi﹖
dem Paulam hanc consequutam
esse eam linguam, ita ut Psalmos
Hebraice caneret, &c̃. Exemplar
item

to be made the patron of all the schools. He is an eagle in the clouds and he has more men who envy him than are equal to him. He is the one who sought from the mother tongue the truth of the context; he was rich in the knowledge of the subject matter when others were poor. Come, therefore, and prepare your own capacity as long as it is possible, so that, if it should become necessary you are not forced either to get help from the perfidy of the Jews or to consult other people's uncertain explanations.

When this man [Jerome] wanted to express his highest praise of this holy language on Paula's epitaph,[166] he said this: I do not turn away from the Hebrew language so that it does not turn away from me. He gives witness there that Paula was so proficient in this language that she sang the psalms in Hebrew etc [*sic*].

---

166. Paula was Jerome's disciple.

HEBRAICAE LINGVAE.

item esto Origenes, qui, Eusebio teste, addidicit Hebreæ linguæ uirtutem, ut uel agnosceret qua‑ lia essent, quæ a Iudæis Hebraicis literis leguntur, uel quæ esset Grę‑ corum interpretum diuersitas cer‑ neret. Nam exapla columnatim composuerat non minus fœlici‑ ter q̃ mirabiliter. Propone tibi Nicolaum Lyranum in ijs literis exercitatum, adeo, ut Iudæorum proles esse credatur. Propone ti‑ bi Paulum Episcopum Burgen‑ sem, et Galatinum. De Capnione quid attinet referre, quem totus orbis, ut linguæ huius oppressæ uindicem fortissimum iuxta ac pe ritiss. suspicit, colit, amat? Adeoq; si nulla esset causa, cur hebraicari in animũ induceres, sat, puto, cau‑

G iiij   sæ

Origen should be [a similar] model to you. He, according to Eusebius, appropriated the power of the Hebrew language in order either to find out exactly what the Jews are reading in their writings, or to discern the difference in the translation of the Greeks. For he had arranged the *Hexapla* in six columns[167] no less felicitously than admirably.

Think also Nicholas de Lyra[168] who was so skilled [in Hebrew] that he was thought to be of Jewish descent. Think also of Bishop Paul of Burgos[169] and of Galatinus.[170] What else is there to report? There was Capnio [Reuchlin].[171] The whole world looks up, honors and loves him since he is the most courageous and most skilled protector of this oppressed language?[172] Even if there were no other reason to delve into the study of Hebrew,

---

167. A word-for-word comparison of Greek translations of the Old Testament with the Hebrew original, arranged in six columns (this work is lost). The Greek versions comprise Aquila's, Symmachus's, Theodotion's, and the Septuagint.

168. Franciscan Bible scholar (ca. 1270–ca. 1349).

169. Paulus Burgensis (ca. 1351–1435), Jewish Bible scholar who converted to the Christian faith, living in Burgos, Spain.

170. Franciscan Bible scholar Petrus Galatinus (ca. 1460–1540).

171. Johann Reuchlin (1455–1522); see Posset 2015.

172. . . . *ut linguae huius oppressae vindicem fortissimum iuxta ac peritissimum suscipit, colit, amat?*

ENCOMIVM

se foret, q tot modis pugnant in­
ter sese Græci interpretes septua­
ginta et posteriores illi tres. Quid
igitur cosultius, q ad certam illam
atque natiuam scripturam se ad­
plicare, quæ sola sibi constat, sola
non errat, sola rata, firma, pbacz
est, citra quam in ambiguo relin­
quere miser & miserandus? Non
detraho interpretibus, sed hoc qd
interpretati sunt, undecz nomen
interpretum sortiti sunt, prędico.
Eos ppemodum inuidiosos fece­
rat Hieronymo Augustinus sua
ista improba laudatione, quæ cu
iniuria sanctæ linguæ coniuncta
erat. Habes hac tempestate in ui­
uis uiros egregios atcz summos,
quibus uti magistris cius linguæ
queas: quorum si unum atcz alte­
rum

it is reason enough, I believe, [to explore] the places where the seventy Greek translators and those three later ones differ. Is there anything better than to turn to the certain and original Scripture[173] which alone remains consistent, which alone does not err, which alone is settled, firm, and fine? Is not the one who is without it [the Hebrew Bible] left with ambiguities, miserable and to be pitied? I do not despise the translators. I do praise what they have translated. Augustine almost made Jerome hate them with his [Augustine's] mean laudation which was connected to an injustice committed against the holy language.

You have among our contemporaries excellent and very good men whom you may seek as your masters of this language:

---

173. *Nativa scriptura.*

HEBRAICAE LINGVAE.

rum habuissent Græci Latinique ueteres, mirū ni omnē nauassent operam in addiscēdis Hebraicis. Quin & librorum Hebraicorum copia caruerunt, nondum uideli= cet reperta Chalcographica arte, qua leui negocio plurimi libri cir= cumquaq; diffunduntur. Cunra= dus Pellicanus emeruit doctorū candida suffragia. Huius discipu= lus Sebastianus Munsterus, bo= ne Deus, qualis ac quantus uir? Quid ille rerū Hebraicarum non exquisiuit excussitq;? An uicturū speras, qui melius de Hebrçorum studijs mereri queat? Sacrarium quoddam eius linguæ is mihi esse uidetur, & scientiæ exoticæ pela= gus. Hunc rogo uos amore singu lari complectamini, hunc admi=

G v   remini

If the old Greek and Latin people would have had one or the other of them, they surely would have made extra efforts to learn Hebrew. But they did not even have many Hebrew books since obviously the art of printing[174] was not invented yet by which very many books are easily being distributed everywhere. Conrad Pellican[175] has earned brilliant reviews. His disciple, Sebastian Münster,[176] O dear God, is he not a great man? What did he not research and shake out in matters of Hebrew? Or do you hope a better man would come earning merits in Hebrew studies? He appears to me somewhat of a shrine of this language and a sea of outlandish [*exotica*] knowledge. I ask that you embrace him with singular love and admire him,

---

174. *Chalcographica.*
175. Pellican (1478–1556), with whom Witzel corresponded.
176. (1489–1552); became a Protestant in Basel.

ENCOMIVM

remini, huic linguis animisq̃ fa‑
ueatis, ceu uni, qui in humeros su‑
os totum sanctiss. literaturæ ne‑
gociũ susceperit. Volphgangus
Capito æterna quoque memoria
dignissimus iudicatur, ob labores
maximos, quibus id studij com‑
plusculis iam annis fideliter adiu‑
tat. Horum illustrium catalogo
quid uetat attexere Matthæum
Aurogallum, Antonium Mar‑
garetam, Ioannem Buchsenstei‑
num, & eos, qui nobis Biblia &
nuper Prophetas in supiore Ger‑
mania Germanice reddiderunt,
licet notæ illis infames inurantur?
Maxime celebrandos existimo,
quamuis mihi ignotos, q̃s Mun‑
sterus in p̃fatione triplicis Lexi‑
ci commemorat. Tales uiros no‑
bis

favor him with tongue and heart as a person who loaded the entire most holy task of this literature onto his shoulders.

Wolfgang Capito,[177] too, will be held most worthy of eternal memory because of the so great labors with which he is faithfully of service to these studies for so many years. Nothing prevents us from adding to the catalogue [the names of] Matthaeus Aurogallus,[178] Anthonius Margaritha,[179] and Johannes Buchsenstein[180] and those who have given us in Upper Germany the Bible and recently the Prophets in German,[181] although they are being denigrated? Highly to be celebrated, in my estimation, are those whom Münster mentions in the preface of his triple [trilingual] lexicon, although I am not familiar with them.

---

177. (1478–1541). Reformer in Strasbourg.
178. Goldhahn (ca. 1490–1543), Hebraist at Wittenberg.
179. (ca. 1490–1542), former Jew who became an antijudaist.
180. I.e., Johann Boeschenstain (1472–1540); priest and Hebraist.
181. He meant Ludwig Hetzer (ca. 1500–1529) and Hans Denck (ca. 1500–1527).

HEBRAICAE LINGVAE.

bis offert Germania nostra, o adolescentes, Nec putandum est, Galliæ ac Italiæ deesse similes, Inter quos sine controuersia Santes Pagninus arcem summæ laudis iure obtinet. Hos itaq; quotquot passim uiuunt, uobis ceu stimulos quosdam cœlitus esse datos existimate, quorū recordatione fiat, ut euigiletis ad tam diuinas, necessarias, salubres literas. Auditis magistrorum esse copiam, uidetis codicū optimorū referta omnia, cognostis rei commoda multiplicia, Quare huc animos cōuertite, Absit pudor, inscitiæ alendæ autor, Procul exigite diffidentiam, & difficultatis opinionē. Is cuius est peculiare munus lingua isthęc, audenti aderit. Persuasum habete uobis

O young people, our Germany offers us men of this caliber. But do not assume that France and Italy would not have any. Among them is undisputedly Santes Pagninus who rightly receives the highest praise.[182] You certainly should assume that they all, wherever they may live, are given to you as a stimulus from heaven. When you remember these [scholars], may it happen that you now get to work hard on such divine, necessary, and salvific writings. You hear of the large number of teachers, you see so many of very good books, you know the multiple usefulness of this matter. Therefore put your mind to it. Do not be shy which would be a reason [*autor*] to remain ignorant. Chase diffidence far away and also the opinion that all this is difficult. The one [i.e., God], whose special gift this language is, will stand by [to help] the one who dares. Be convinced

---

182. A Dominican friar (1470–1541).

ENCOMIVM HEB. LINGVAE.

uobis præclarissimũ esse, dici Hebrẹum. Quid enim est Hebræus, nisi περώτης, hoc est, transitor? Quicunq; ita ad futurã uitam transire festinant, merito Hebræos uocari conueniet. In eadem schola, cui te addices, sedent prophetæ, & cẹteri Bibliographi, socij tui laboris & exercitatores. Hos Rabinos hodegosq; amplectere, nec, si obtemperes, dubito, quin ad bonã frugem breui euadas.

DIXI.

that it is a great honor when you are called a Hebrew/Hebraist.[183] For what else is a Hebrew/Hebraist if not a περώτης.[184] All who so hasten to pass over to the future life merit to be called Hebrews/Hebraists. In that school, which you will attend, also sit the prophets and the other biblical writers;[185] they are fellows in your laboring and they are experienced practitioners. Embrace them as rabbis and guides;[186] I have no doubts that if you comply with them you will soon be rather successful yourself.

I am done speaking.

---

183. ... *dici Hebraeum*.
184. *Perotes* means *transitor* in Latin (one who goes over).
185. *Bibliographi*.
186. *Rabinos hodegosque*.

5

"The Hebrews Drink from the Source, the Greeks from the Rills, and the Latin People from the Puddle"

Some Observations on a Lutheran Table Talk

THE ADAGE-LIKE SAYING "THE Hebrews drink from the source, the Greeks from the rills . . . , and the Latin people from the puddle" is taken from one of the numerous talks after dinner in the Luther household, dated August 9, 1532. It had become a proverbial saying already by Luther's time and it has been handed down through the centuries. Its authorship is assigned to various people. Its origins remain obscure.

The idea that Johann Reuchlin (1455–1522), the Christian Hebraist, was the original author of the proverb was promoted in the early seventeenth century by the Lutheran church father Johann Gerhard (1582–1637), who in his *Theological Commonplaces*[1] connected the proverb to Reuchlin as moving in the footsteps of Saint Jerome: *Reuchlinus Hieronymi vestigia premens dicit: hebrei fontes, greci rivos, latini paludes bibunt* (Reuchlin says,

---

1. Johann Gerhard, *Loci theologici: Cum pro adstruenda veritate tum pro destruenda quorumvis contradicentium falsitate per theses nervose solide et copiose explicati. Praefationem, indicibus generalibus post G. H. Mullerum adauctos ac vitam Io. Gerhardi*, vol. 1:135 (*De Scriptura Sacra*) (Preuss edition; Internet); Gerhard 2006, 278. In 1811 the English bishop Robert Gray repeated Gerhard's wording in his *A Key to the Old Testament and Apocrypha* (1811), but assigned it to Pico della Mirandola as its author (without proof).

in following in Jerome's footsteps: The Hebrews drink from the sources [plural], the Greeks from the rivers [no diminutive form] and the Latin people from the swamps ["swamp" being used by Reuchlin, but not by Luther]).

Fig. 5.1. Luther's Table Talk. Johannes Aurifaber, *COLLOQVIA Oder Tischreden Doctor Martini Lutheri so er in vielen jaren die Zeyt seines Lebens gegen Gelehrten Leuthen auch hin vnd wider bey frembden Gesten vnd seinen Tischgesellen gefuehret*. Frankfurt am Main: Peter Schmidt, 1567.

1. Problems with Table Talk

This particular table talk was never translated into English. We focus on it here, fully aware of the pitfalls Luther's *Table Talk* presents as historical source material since none of the participants' original notes that were recorded at table are extant.[2] Talks at table were an important feature of many evening meals in Luther's household.[3] Originally the talks were not

---

2. In the Weimar edition of Luther's works, the texts of the following copyists are accepted: Dietrich, Medler, Schlaginhaufen, Lauterbach, Weller, Mathesius, Heydenreich, and Besold. The products of these copyists were gathered in the following collections: Dietrich, Medler, Rabe, Cordatus, and Khummer, according to Junghans 2001, 154–76.

3. Markwald and Morris Markwald 2002, 127.

intended for publication. The collection of anecdotes and sayings was at times later revised by the writers themselves and edited from hindsight and altered by copyists.[4] *Table Talk* has been used uncritically at times as if it were original source material. Occasionally *Table Talk* contains misinformation that may come from mistakes the speaker made, and/or incorrect note-taking by students, and/or by rewriting of the notes. Many Luther scholars, past and present, display at times a naïve trust in them and misuse them as if they were clean, primary sources for biographies of the historical Luther. Recently, though, even Lutheran Luther scholars accuse the collector Johannes Aurifaber (ca. 1519–1575) of incorporating some fabricated talks in his first edition of 1566, two decades after Luther's death. He was dependent for his collection on the notes that others had taken in earlier years. He was not yet present in Wittenberg when the talk under consideration here took place in 1532. Aurifaber began his studies there five years later, in 1537.[5]

Aurifaber is accused of "correcting" Luther's offensive, all too coarse and boorish language, and of transforming the sayings into "pious platitudes."[6] Aurifaber's edition circulated some so-called "Luther quotations" which at times have no basis in Luther (Helmar Junghans).[7] And, one must note that Aurifaber's edition was entirely in his own German translation which he had provided under the title "Table Talk or *Colloquia* of Doctor Martin Luther, which over many years he held with learned people, including foreign guests and his table fellows, collected according to the main articles of our Christian teaching." Aurifaber's book title indicates that he himself arranged the material according to the main articles of "our Christian teaching." The entire edition is placed under the Word of John 6:12: "Gather the fragments left over, so that nothing will be wasted."

For the following reason we nevertheless focus on this Table Talk with the peculiar proverb contained in it: When a reported talk or conversation is so unusual as is the case under consideration here, as if it were a more difficult reading (*lectio difficilior*) in biblical exegesis, one may have a good chance that one actually deals with an authentic recording of what was said.

---

4. LW 54:xxiii.

5. Junghans 1979, 752–55.

6. Posset 2011, 30. On recent research about Table Talk, see Bärenfänger et al., *Martin Luthers Tischreden: Neuansätze der Forschung* (Tübingen: Mohr Siebeck, 2013); Klitzsch 2016, 147–99.

7. Junghans 2001, 163.

We are fortunate to have two almost identical Latin versions of it in Talk no. 3271a and b from the collection of Conradus Cordatus (1476–1546), which was gathered in 1532–1533, composed of pieces which were not necessarily recorded by him personally.[8]

Aurifaber's edition was modernized in 1743 by Johann Georg Walch for his German edition in vol. 22 of *Luther's Works*.[9] That German version (of Talk no. 3271) is not quite identical with the one transmitted in Talk no. 1040 which is taken from the original (Latin?) collection of Veit Dietrich (1506–1549) and Nikolaus Medler (1502–1551) which Georg Rörer (1492–1557) copied. But we may safely assume that we deal with a doublet here of one original conversation at Luther's table. It remains undecided whether Luther spoke in German or in Latin. Often the recorders wrote in Latin shorthand what was spoken in German.

2. The Latin and German Versions of the Table Talk

Hebraeos bibere ex fontibus, Graecos ex rivulis et Latinos ex lacunis (no. 3271a).

Ebreos ex fontibus bibere, Graecos ex rivulis, Latinos autem ex lacunis (no. 3271b).[10]

The German version reads:

Die Ebräer trinken aus der Bornquelle; die Griechen aber aus den Wässerlin, die aus der Quelle fließen; die Lateinischen aber aus der Pfützen (no. 1040).[11]

"The Hebrews drink from the sources, the Greeks from the rills [that flow from the source], but the Latin people [drink] from the puddles."

---

8. LW 54:169. Cordatus revised all the notes in his possession. Unfortunately this removed them further from what was actually said. For this reason, only a small sampling was selected for LW; see LW 54:170.

9. *Ohne diese Sprache [Hebraisch] kann keine Erkenntniß der Schrift da sein, denn auch das Neue Testament, wiewohl es griechisch geschrieben ist, ist es doch voll von hebräischer Redeweise [hebraismis]. Darum hat man recht gesagt: die Hebräer trinken aus den Quellen, die Griechen aus Bächlein, die Lateiner aber aus Pfützen;* Dr. Martin Luthers *Colloquia oder Tischreden*, ed. Joh. Georg Walch (Saint Louis: Concordia, 1887), XXII:1543.

10. WA.TR 3: 243.9–10 (no. 3271a) and 244.10–12 (no. 3271b).

11. WA.TR 1: 525.18–20 (no. 1040).

The differences between the German and the Latin rendering in alternating from singular to plural are minor and insignificant: German singular: *Bornquelle*; Latin plural: *ex fontibus*. The translation of German *aus der Pfützen* (from the puddle) and Latin *ex lacunis* (from the puddles) have virtually the same meaning. The addition, *die aus der Quelle fließen* (which flow from the spring), is simply a flourish.

3. The Context of the Sophisticated Conversation in the Summer of 1532

During the talks of August 9, 1532, Luther had carried on by saying: the Hebrew language suffered corruption after the Babylonian captivity and turned into the commonly used Chaldean language, to a degree that if Moses and the prophets were revived today they could not understand it.[12] He added that biblical linguistics alone does not make a theologian. Knowledge of these languages is helpful. But before people discuss something, they should know their subject matter well enough—before they open their mouths.

As to its historical setting (*Sitz im Leben*) we learn that the talk actually took place in the yard after the evening meal, not at the dinner table. Apparently the weather was so pleasant that they could converse outside, on the eve of Saint Lawrence Day, which is August 9.[13] The German version of Table Talk no. 1040 is introduced with a passage in Latin which provides the general topic of the conversation, namely remarks on the comparative study of religion. Luther said: the "wisdom of the Greeks" aims at "virtue" and is a worldly wisdom, literally, "a wisdom of the world," whereas Jewish wisdom aims at the belief and trust in God and at the fear of God.[14] The German text that follows the Latin introduction gives the similar theme of their conversation, namely: "the Greek, Hebrew, and Latin languages." The German text duplicates the entire Latin introduction, but adds the devastating judgment about the (pagan) Greek wisdom that it is beast-like or animal-like (German *viehisch*) because true wisdom cannot be had without God. The Greek language as such, however, has nice lovely words, but is not very rich in proverbial sayings (*nicht reich von Sprüchen*). The Hebrew

12. WA.TR 1: 524.33–35 and 525.29–32. WA.TR 3: 244.
13. *Am Abend S. Lorenzen, im Garten*; WA.TR 1: 525.5.
14. *Finis sapientiae Graecorum est virtus. Iudaicae vero credere Deo et timere Deum. Est autem sapientia mundi Graecorum sapientia*; WA.TR 1: 524.6–7.

language may be comparatively simple in expression, but it is majestic and glorious. This language may use few words, but they run deep unlike those of any other language. Luther praises Hebrew as the best and richest of all languages, and Hebrew is pure, and it does not borrow (*bettelt nicht*) expressions from other languages (by introducing alien words), and so the language keeps its "own color." The Greek, the Latin, and also the German people borrow words from other languages and they use many composites, quite unlike Hebrew.[15] The borrowing and, consequently, the mixing of languages is explained by their proximities to other foreign language areas.

Luther digresses and makes some observations about the language of the Bohemians neighboring Saxony. "Bohemian" was the mother tongue of one of the men who supposedly were conversing with Luther, namely Aurogallus (Goldhahn, ca. 1490–1543), who was born in Komotau (Sudetenland). His name is mentioned only in the Latin version, but with the incorrect first name Matthias (it should be Matthaeus Aurogallus). In the talk at hand, strangely, not one but two Hebrew professors for Wittenberg are introduced, for [Johannes] Forstemius (Forster, Forsterus, 1496–1556) is said to have been present in addition to Aurogallus.[16] This must be a mistake, because there were never two simultaneous Hebrew teaching positions there. In 1532, only Aurogallus was teaching Hebrew, as he had been since 1521; Forstemius did not teach at the time of the talk of 1532. Such inconsistencies demonstrate once more that the information given in Table Talk is to be used with caution.

Part of the wider context of this particular talk is the contemporaneous issue of Ciceronian Latin. By Ciceronianism one means the deliberate imitation of the style of Cicero as it was practiced by some writers and orators before and during Luther's time. In Luther's view the Latin language became so corrupted in the course of time, especially because of the impact of the barbarian Goths of the Middle Ages, that a classical orator like Cicero and his contemporaries, if they came to life again today, would not be able to understand their own mother tongue.[17] Renaissance scholars at the papal

---

15. WA.TR 1: 524.10–20.

16. *In vigilia Laurentii vesperi in horto Martinus Lutherus cum Matthia Aurogallo et Forstemio Hebraeae linguae professoribus*; WA.TR 3: 243.35–36 (no. 3271b).

17. *Also ist die lateinische Sprache von den Gothen so verderbet, daß auch Cicero und Andere, so zu ihrer Zeit gelebt haben, jetzt ihre eigene Muttersprache nicht verstünden, wenn sie wieder lebendig sollten werden*; WA.TR 1: 525.33–35. The Latin rendering in no. 3271b also speaks of the Goths as corrupters of the Latin language so that Cicero would not recognize it.

curia began to translate the church fathers into elegant classical Latin. As papal secretaries they wrote Latin letters in the Ciceronian style. They even tinkered with the Church's traditional Latin liturgy, trying to make prayers and hymns attractive through a classical Latin rendering. Even Erasmus of Rotterdam (ca. 1466–1536) thought the curia tried too hard to be classical and in 1528 he wrote a satire of the Roman followers of Cicero: *Ciceronianus* ("The Ciceronian"). Although Luther was not part of this trend of Ciceronianism, he nevertheless was well aware of it and he kept his very high opinion of Cicero's eloquence.[18] No Latin puddles or swamps here!

Nevertheless, what is so unusual about this proverb is its simultaneous devaluation of the Latin waters, people drinking from a puddle, pond, or swamp. The imagery of the unclean Latin waters is fairly well explained as far as Luther is concerned by his own reference within the talk: his characterization of the polluted Latin language of post-classical times, due to the Goths' corrupting influence, may have something to do with the humanistic *Zeitgeist* of contemporaries who promoted the return to Ciceronian Latin, the so-called Ciceronianism of the Renaissance. Luther once said: "I am able to write letters, but not in Ciceronian style."[19] Luther as a preacher felt a strong affinity to Cicero whom he called "the wisest man" who "wrote more than all the philosophers and also read all the books of the Greeks. I marvel at this man."[20] Luther hinted at the idea (touched upon in the proverb under discussion) that a Latin orator like Cicero gained his knowledge from having read "all the books of the Greeks." The Latin Cicero thus drank from the Greek creeks. Elsewhere: "[Cicero] collected every good thing that he found in all the Greek writers."[21] All in all, Luther's primary talking point when citing the proverb could not simply have been the degradation of Latin. In agreement with the proverb Luther declared that the Latin people (like Cicero) drink from the Greek rills. Relying on Latin alone would be like drinking from the puddles.

Cardinal Pietro Bembo (1470–1547) at the papal court strove for Ciceronian Latinity and even advocated refraining from reading the Epistles of

---

18. The WA Index shows over 300 references to Cicero and his works.

19. *Literas scribere possum, sed non Ciceronianas*; WA.TR 4: 595.7-8 (no. 4967).

20. *Cicero sapientissimus fuit et plus scripsit omnibus philosophis; omnium Graecorum libros perlegit. Miror hunc hominem*; WATR 3: 4.22-24 (no. 2808b); English translation in LW 54:171. Springer 2007, 23–50.

21. Talk no. 5440; LW 54:423.

Saint Paul because of their stylistic failings.[22] Some Reformers were affected by this trend of employing good classical Latin; for instance, when Philip Melanchthon (1497–1560) called the Christian church buildings "temples."

4. The Immediate Context of Luther's Use of the Proverbial Saying during the Conversation with Johannes Forstemius, the "Hebrew Theologian" at Wittenberg

With the mention of Johannes Forstemius, a former student of Reuchlin (in 1521), in the records of the talk, one could build a bridge between the Hebraist Reuchlin in Ingolstadt and the Wittenberg Reformers so as to the transfer of the content of the proverbial saying from Reuchlin's circles to Luther via Forstemius. Indeed, if there had been an indirect transfer from Reuchlin to Wittenberg, the better option would be via Forstemius, not via Melanchthon.[23] Besides that, Melanchthon is not named at all as a dialog partner in the talk at hand. Forstemius as a potential source for the content of the proverb remains a speculation since the proverb is not found in his works. In addition, the report about the talk does not show Forstemius as quoting the proverb. Unrecorded oral transmission would be the way in which it may have been communicated. Be that as it may, one may still ask: what did Luther mean when he mentioned it in his talk and in what context did it occur?

Not unusual at all is the high appreciation of Hebrew; it can be expected from any biblical humanist of that time.[24] During the conversation Master Johannes Forstemius is reported to have spoken much and very highly of the Hebrew language, although in their days other people despise

---

22. For a biography of Bembo, see Kidwell 2004.

23. Someone could suspect Melanchthon to be the source for the adage that Luther used. There is, indeed, a similarity of thought in Melanchthon's inaugural address of August 29, 1518, but it does not qualify as the origin of the saying found in the talk of 1532. Melanchthon, the new teacher of Greek at Wittenberg, only states that because theology is partly Hebrew, partly Greek, one must learn these languages for the better understanding of the meaning of the Bible; otherwise "we Latin people drink only from their streams." For Melanchthon the two sources are Hebrew and Greek: *Itaque cum theologia partim Hebraica, partim Graeca sit, nam Latini rivos illorum bibimus*; in *De corrigendis adolescentiae studiis*, CR 11: 22–23. See also Bauch 1904, 151 (Internet). The metaphor which Melanchthon uses does not fit at all with the proverb Luther quotes because Melanchthon combines Hebrew and Greek as equal sources vis-à-vis the Latin run-offs. Melanchthon cannot be the source for the quotation.

24. On biblical humanism, see Augustijn 2003.

this language, perhaps because of their lack of piety or because the language is so difficult to learn.[25]

During the conversation with Luther, Forstemius ventured the opinion that the best way to learn Hebrew is by means of a Hebrew Grammar. "Then spoke Doctor Martin Luther," presumably in order to qualify the statement by Forstemius:

> As to the phrases and manner of speaking, and as to the construction of how one should connect and express the words—all of this one cannot render nor teach, for the construction often changes the meaning of the words.[26]

Luther again talks about his own insufficient knowledge of Hebrew. Earlier in their conversation he had made the statement: "I can do neither Hebrew nor Greek ..."[27] But those words must be held against his other comments within this talk which appear somewhat contradictory, namely that he has learned more Hebrew whenever he, while reading the Bible, held one saying against another, than whenever he would have followed only the *Grammatica*.[28]

After further remarks by Forstemius and by Luther, Luther turns their conversation to the proverb which is quoted in the following context: One must know Hebrew well so that one may recognize the Semitisms/Hebraisms that are contained in the Greek New Testament, which is full of them. Thus, the context of our proverb is the discussion of Semitisms in the New Testament. The talk has turned away from the initial comparison of the religions, of the pagan Greeks and of the Hebrews.

Luther's focus with respect to this proverbial saying is very narrow and is quoted in connection with the hermeneutical issue of interpreting the Greek New Testament from its matrix, the Hebrew Bible. Luther was well aware of the issue of the "Hebrew way of speaking" (*unnd ist die hebreisch weyß alßo tzu reden*) in the New Testament which he observed for instance in his Christmas Postil of 1522 on Heb 1:1–12.[29]

25. WA.TR 1: 525.5–8.
26. WA.TR 1: 525.8–10.
27. *Ich ... kann weder Griechisch noch Ebräisch*; WA.TR 1: 524.37.
28. *Ich habe mehr Ebräisch gelernt, wenn ich im Lesen einen Ort und Spruch gegen dem andern gehalten habe, denn wenn ichs nur gegen der Grammatica gerichtet habe*; WA.TR 1: 525.14–15.
29. WA 10-1: 157.1–2; similarly in a sermon on Eph 3 of 1 October [?] 1525: *das ist auff Ebreische weyse soviel geredet: das[s] wir erfullet werden auff alle weise ... da[s] wir*

Luther struggled with this issue already a few years earlier, in 1527, when he lectured on the *First Letter of John*. Lecturing on 1 John 1:10 ("If we say, 'We have not sinned,' we make him a liar, and his word is not in us"), Luther declared:

> For the Hebrew manner of speaking explains a verb in the past tense through a verb in the present tense. Indeed it is my understanding that [the Evangelist] John himself often Hebraizes [uses Hebraisms].[30]

During the same lectures on 1 John in 1527, Luther pointed out Hebraisms in several other places, as in 1 John 2:21, "from the truth does not come any lie," is a Semitism; he says: *Hebraismus "Ex veritate nullum venit mendacium."*[31] On 1 John 3:15, "and you know that no murderer has eternal life remaining in him," the notetaker Georg Rörer has in his manuscript a marginal note saying that the expression *vitam manentem* is a Hebraism.[32] On 1 John 3:17, "Yet he closes his heart to his brother," Luther commented that "*viscera*, i.e., to close up mercy, [is] a Hebraism."[33]

The topic of Hebraisms in the New Testament apparently was still on Luther's mind during the talk of 1532 that is under consideration here. Luther confessed:

> If I were younger, I would want to learn this language better, because without it one can never understand Sacred Scripture. For the New Testament, even though it is written in Greek, is full of Hebraisms and of the Hebrew way of speaking. For that reason they are correct who say: "The Hebrews drink from the source, the Greeks from the rills that are flowing from the source, and the Latin people [drink] from the puddle."[34]

---

vergottet werden; WA 17-1: 438.14–21.

30. ... *imo Ioannem saepe hebraizantem intelligo*; WA 20: 629.30–33.

31. WA 20: 680.10.

32. See n. to line 15 of WA 20: 710.15. The Vulgate verse 1 John 3:15 reads: *Et scitis quoniam omnis homicida non habet vitam aeternam in semetipso manentem*.

33. "*Viscera*," i.e. *misericordiam prohibere, Ebraismus*; WA 20: 714.5. Posset 1988, 78–81 (reprint, Wipf and Stock, 2018).

34. *Wenn ich jünger wäre, so wollte ich diese Sprache lernen, denn ohne sie kann man die h[eilige] Schrift nimmermehr recht verstehen. Denn das neue Testament, obs wol griechisch geschrieben ist, doch ist es voll von Ebraismis und ebräischer Art zu reden. Darum haben sie recht gesagt: Die Ebräer trinken aus der Bornquelle; die Griechen aber aus den Wässerlin, die aus der Quelle fließen; die Lateinischen aber aus der Pfützen*; WA.TR 1: 525.15–20.

Luther approvingly quotes the proverb. He clearly refers to the saying as something that others have said before him: "For that reason they are correct who say this." He stands in the tradition of "biblical humanism" with its emphasis on trying to understand the Scriptures in the original languages. And perhaps Luther is still more specifically to be located within the tradition of the Augustinian order to which he belonged, with its openness to Renaissance humanism in general and its concerns for the classical and biblical languages in particular.[35] Luther's saying is misunderstood, however, if applied to the three versions of the Bible as such—that is, the Hebrew Bible as the source, the Greek Septuagint as the stream, and the Latin Bible, the Vulgate, as the puddle. This misinterpretation is maintained, for instance, in the nineteenth-century edition of Luther's *Table Talk* (Berlin, 1848).[36]

Five years after Luther's Johannine lectures, he stresses in the talk of 1532 the study of Hebrew and the awesome task of translating, which he calls a "special grace and gift of God." This statement (in Talk no. 3271a) was so important to the students who recorded it that they preserved it in the German original within their Latin recording.[37] As to the seventy Greek translators (that is, of the Septuagint), Luther opined that they were not skilled translators at all. They were so bad at what they were doing that Saint Jerome's Vulgate is preferable and, when it comes to translating, he (Jerome) is the altogether better translator. This statement openly contradicts the nineteenth-century interpretation of this table talk.

In the conclusion of Talk no. 1040 a digression is found on the late medieval Bible scholar of the Franciscan order, Nicholas of Lyra (ca. 1270–1349). Luther esteemed him highly. Lyra's postils were world-famous. The impact which Lyra had on Luther is captured in the famous observation: "If Lyra had not lyred, Luther would not have danced." Yet Luther finishes the conversation with the thought of not remaining with a translator, even if he were as good as Lyra. He preferred the original wording.

Luther, in taking up Forstemius's reference to Hebrew grammar books, says the following about his (Luther's) preference for one specific Hebrew

35. Vonschott 1915 (Vaduz: Kraus Reprint, 1965).

36. Internet edition: Karl Eduard Förstemann and Heinrich Ernst Bindseil, eds., *D. Martin Luther's Sämmtliche Schriften XXII. Band, Die Colloquia oder Tischreden (nach Aurifabers erster Ausgabe)* (Berlin: Gebauer'sche Buchhandlung, 1848), 568–70, here 570n10.

37. *Ists ein sunderliche Gotts gaben*; WA.TR 3: 243.14 (no. 3271a); *Das ist ein sonderliche Gottes gabe*; 244.15–16 (no. 3271b).

grammar book: "When I would want to study the Hebrew language once more, I would use the purest and best textbook authors (*Grammaticos*) such as David Kimhi (or, Kimchi) and Moses Kimhi who are the purest."[38] Luther meant the two medieval Jews whose Hebrew textbooks were printed in Germany earlier in the sixteenth century. When still an Augustinian friar, Luther had become aware of the work of the two rabbis, and on April 13, 1519, that is, as soon as he had been able to obtain a copy, he had sent the *Introductorium grammaticae Hebraicae* (listed usually under Moses Kimhi's name) to Friar Lang in Erfurt. The grammar had been printed first in January 1519 by Thomas Anshelm in Hagenau.[39] By explicitly referring to these two rabbis as the best textbook authors for Hebrew, Luther (intentionally or not) may have offended his colleague and collaborator Matthaeus Aurogallus who was present at the after-dinner conversation on August 9. He had issued his own Hebrew textbook the previous year (1531).[40]

However, Luther would have made a wise choice (if he had started anew to study Hebrew) since already the elder Reuchlin as a professor of Hebrew in Ingolstadt in 1519/1521 had used Rabbi Moses Kimhi's Hebrew grammar book. After Luther's mentioning of the two medieval rabbis with whose works he would have mastered Hebrew, he added that he would then be able to enjoy reading the Bible in the original Hebrew, starting with Moses and ending with the Prophets, who are more difficult to read because of their flourishes:

> Then I would have wanted to read Moses . . . , then the Psalter and Solomon's Proverbs, and finally the Prophets who employ many figurative words and speeches.[41]

In conclusion: An analysis of the Talk with the proverb under consideration shows that Luther cites the proverb within the wider context of his views on the comparative study of religions (somewhat similar to Johann Reuchlin's philosophy of religion and the sciences)[42] and of the histori-

---

38. WA.TR 1: 525.36–39.

39. *Rabi Mose Kimhi In Introdvctorio Grammaticae* (Hagenau 1519), MDZ, urn:nbn:de:bvb:12-bsb00013770-7.

40. *Grammatica hebraeae chaldaeaeque linguæ a Mattheo Aurogallo in luce ædita Vitebergæ* (Vitebergæ: in ædibus Iosephi Clugi, anno salutis 1531).

41. *Darnach wollte ich Mosen lesen, . . . nach dem wollte ich den Psalter und die Spruche Salomonis lesen, und zuletzt die Propheten, die brauchen viel verblumt Wort und Rede*; WA.TR 1: 525.39–41.

42. As to Reuchlin, see Posset 2015.

cal development of ancient religions from the Hebrews to the wisdom of the pagan Greeks to the Latin people, and also in the context of the issues surrounding Ciceronianism. But the citation of the proverb as such was provoked in the more immediate context of Luther explaining the phenomenon of Hebraisms in the Greek New Testament. To Luther the classics, when only Greek and Latin classics are meant, are of less importance than Hebrew because the Greek New Testament can only be properly expounded from the matrix of the Hebrew Bible.

While the derogatory part of the proverb with respect to Latin may be obvious (since Latin was no longer considered a pure language like Hebrew), the origins of the exact wording for the glorification of Hebrew and of Judaism as given in the cited proverb remains an unexplained mystery. What is truly remarkable is the fact that Luther's Latin wording is very similar to the version that is reported to have been inscribed on a wall of the Augustinian friary at Lauingen on the Danube, near Augsburg: *Hebraei fontem, Graeci rivulos, Latini paludem bibunt*. "The Hebrews drink from the source, the Greeks from the rills, the Latin people from the swamp."[43]

---

43. Vonschott 1915, 103 (the inscription is not dated; the building no longer exists).

6

Hebrew Translations of Christian Prayers on the Eve of the Reformation

CATHOLIC PRAYERS IN THE language of the Jews are not really common knowledge. One may occasionally read that in German-speaking lands of the Late Middle Ages and the Renaissance times the interest in *Hebraica* was spawned by the Lutheran Reformation, specifically by the Lutheran scholar of Jewish descent Anthonius Margaritha (ca. 1490–1542) with his book of 1530, *Der gantz Jüdisch glaub* (The entire Jewish faith). Margaritha was born in Regensburg, where his father, Jacob Margolioth, was a rabbi. The renowned Hebraist Johann Reuchlin had corresponded with his father Jacob in 1495.

Martin Luther (1483–1546) utilized Margaritha's book for his attacks on the Jews, as he recommended it for further reading. Margaritha's illustrated book was based upon that of Johann Pfefferkorn (1469–1521) whose illustrations in *The Jewish Confession* of 1508 (and later editions) were reused by Margaritha.[1] Interest in *Hebraica* is older than Margaritha. The pivotal role of the Reformation as assumed in the introductory statement is an exaggeration. One can demonstrate the far more nuanced thesis that several pre-reformation authors from ca. 1500 to 1514 reveal great interest in *Hebraica*.

From within that subject area, we concentrate here specifically on Hebrew translations of traditional Christian prayers in the Latin language

1. First edition at Cologne 1508, Danish translation 1516.

which several scholars included in, of all places, their Hebrew grammar books. Their labors emerged and spread from Venice, such as on the Our Father, Hail Mary, and the Creed of the Church. They are extant in rare prints in which one would not expect to find them, namely in grammar books that are designed to familiarize non-Jews with the Hebrew alphabet and grammar. However, there are others who for other reasons worked with Hebrew translations of central Christian prayers during the given time period.

We restrict ourselves primarily to the Hebrew versions of the Our Father, although some authors included numerous other prayers. Other aspects of this phenomenon within the field of *Hebraica* would deserve discussion in greater detail. We shall see that the thesis is mistaken that the Our Father was first translated into Hebrew in the nineteenth century (see internet, German). First though three examples of grammar books are to be considered.

HEBREW TRANSLATIONS OF CHRISTIAN PRAYERS

1. Aldus Manutius, 1500

Fig. 6.1. Four pages with the entire Our Father (and the Holy Holy Holy) in Manutius's grammar book of 1500. Folios 11v–12r and 12v–13r.

The first such grammar book with the inclusion of Christian prayers in Hebrew translation for the study of the Hebrew language became available in 1500 in Venice when Aldus Manutius (ca. 1450–1515) published a brief introduction to the Hebrew language (comprising sixteen folios), titled *Introductio utilissima hebraice discere cupientibus* (Most useful introduction for those who wish to learn Hebrew).[2] Manutius provides the preface. However, from the given title we today could not imagine or expect to find Christian prayers in Hebrew in it.

Manutius's layout of the prayer text in his large print requires more than three pages. He uses red ink for the Latin title of the prayer (*Oratio dominica*), and for the Latin words for which he used numerous abbreviations for the familiar Latin passages of the prayer. For some reason he opts on a few occasions for his own peculiar Latin wording (deviating from the standard Latin liturgical version). For his transliteration in Roman letters of the Hebrew words, he also uses red print. Printed in black are the vocalized Hebrew words. Manutius struggled evidently with the traditional Latin wording of the second half of the petition for forgiveness ("as we forgive those who trespass against us"), as he daringly replaces the Latin words [*dimittimus*] *debitoribus nostris* with his idiosyncratic suggestion of [*dimittimus*] *qui iis debent nobis* (folio 12v; see fig. 6.1).

He presents the prayer line by line in reasonable, small units (such as on folio 11v): *Pater noster q[ui] es i[n] caelis—Sa[n]ctificetur nom[en] tuu[m]—Adueniat regnu[m] tuu[m]* (Our Father who art in heaven—Hallowed be thy name—Thy kingdom come).

---

2. Manutius's booklet of 1500 is bound to the *Sefer Tehillim*. Basel, 1516; extant at Württembergische Landesbibliothek, Stuttgart, Signatur: B hebr.1516 01.

2. Nicolaus Marschalk, 1502

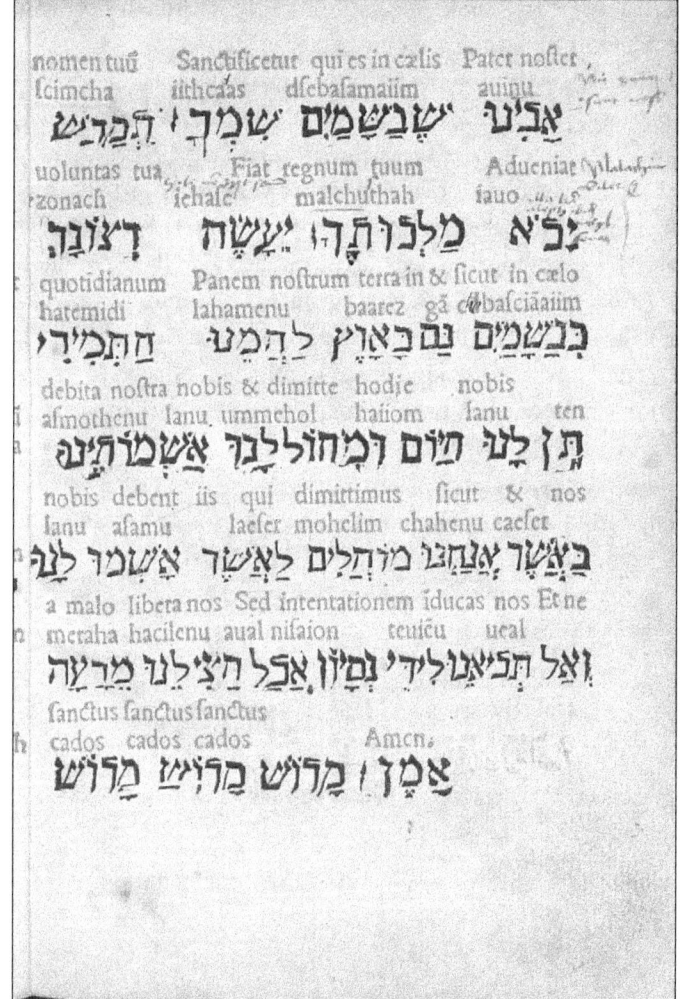

Fig. 6.2. The Our Father, in Marschalk's reprint of Manutius's grammar book, *Introductio ad litteras hebraicas Vtilissima Alphabetum*. Erfurt: Marschalk, 1502.

The earliest such grammar book in German lands appears to be virtually unknown among researchers today. It was edited by Nicolaus Marschalk (Thurius or Thuringius, i.e., from Thuringia, ca. 1470–1525) in Erfurt in 1502. He pioneered in German lands with his reprint of Manutius's Venetian model in Germany. He was a printer, chief administrator of the city of Erfurt, and member of the local humanistic sodality.³ In contrast to his Venetian model, Marschalk's book title clearly tells of the content of the booklet, including a hint at the Our Father in Hebrew.⁴

Marschalk's execution of the cuts of the individual Hebrew letters is somewhat crude (fig. 6.2), as he was trying as best as he could to imitate the clean Venetian letters of the Hebrew. Marschalk's reprint (though in a different page lay-out) includes Manutius's very short preface in which is stated that for the knowledge of the Sacred Scripture the study of Hebrew is necessary.⁵ He offers together with an introduction to the Hebrew alphabet, the *Our Father* in Latin and in Hebrew. Just like Manutius he includes the biblical, trilingual inscription that was posted over the cross of Christ (John 19:20, "... and it was written in Hebrew, Latin, and Greek." Marschalk's Erfurt edition shows one of the early versions in Germany of Hebrew letters in print. As an aside, this trilingual inscription (*titulus*) appears at about the same time in Conrad Pellican's (1478–1556) booklet written in 1501 and printed in 1504,⁶ as found in its second part, where he also includes the Hebrew numerals and the various names for God.⁷

Marschalk in following his Venetian model gives the *Our Father* also line by line in the same sequence:

1. The same slightly emended liturgical Latin version of the *Pater noster*; Marschalk copied from Manutius the same deviation with respect to the Latin wording of the second half of the petition for forgiveness, as he, too, replaces the Latin words *debitoribus nostris* with *qui iis debent nobis*.
2. the similar Hebrew transliteration in Roman letters, and
3. the same vocalized Hebrew.

---

3. Stievermann 2002, 122–26.

4. *Introductio ad litteras hebraicas* || *Vtilissima* || *Alphabetum hebraicum & eius lectura* || *Vocalium hebraicarum characteres* || *Vocalium cū consonantibus cōbinationes* || *Oratio dominica hebraice: & iuxta latine* || *Emendata quaedam quae leguntur deprauate.*|| *Et alia Titulus saluatoris nostri* || *graece latine & he*||*braice.*

5. http://digital.staatsbibliothek-berlin.de/werkansicht/?PPN=PPN815418078&LOGID=LOG_0007, image no. 6.

6. On this, see Nestle 1877.

7. Posset 2015, 232. Further research is needed to determine any dependency upon Manutius's edition.

Marschalk also imitates the Venetian's presentation of each Latin line and of each line of Hebrew transliteration in red; and like his Venetian model he shows the vocalized Hebrew words in black. However, Marschalk differs in the layout of his pages from that of Manutius in order to accommodate the complete prayer text on one page (fig. 6.2). Marschalk's reprint of the Hebrew transliteration in Roman letters is flawed, as he has, for instance, the spelling mistake *iithcaas* (for the Latin equivalent of *sanctificetur*) in the opening line where Manutius has the correct one, *iithcadas*. Not being very skilled in the Hebrew language, Marschalk mistakenly switches the third and fourth Hebrew words of the opening of the prayer. Manutius has the proper sequence: שְׁמָךְ יִתְקַדַשׁ. Marschalk prints them in the wrong way, whereby he in addition has the letter iota disconnected from the word and he lets it float between the two words, which makes no sense at all. Marschalk apparently was not skilled enough to match the two vocalized Hebrew words with the transliteration which he, however correctly, had copied from Manutius's pattern. The mistakes and flaws in Marschalk's edition of the bilingual Our Father alone would have made his booklet unfit for the proper study of the Hebrew language.

3. Franciscus Tissardus, 1508

ORATIO DOMINICA.

Pater noster	אָבִינוּ	Auinu
qui es in cœlis.	שֶׁבַּשָּׁמַיִם	Schebasamaim
sanctificetur	יִתְקַדַּשׁ	Iithcadasch
nomen tuum,	שְׁמֶךָ	Schimcha
Adueniat	יָבֹא	Iauo
regnum tuum,	מַלְכוּתְךָ	Malcçuthacç
Fiat	יֵעָשֶׂה	Ieçasche
voluntas tua	רְצוֹנֶךָ	Resonacç
sicut in cœlo	כַּשָּׁמַיִם	Chebasamaim
et in terra,	וּבָאָרֶץ	Gambaares
Panem nostrum	לַחְמֵנוּ	Lacçamenu
quotidianum	הַתָּמִיד	Hatemidi
da	תֵּן	Ten
nobis, al. ad nos	לָנוּ	Lanu

hodie;	הַיּוֹם	Haiom
Et dimitte	וּמְחֹל	Vmcçol
nobis, al. ad nos	לָנוּ	Lanu
debita nostra	אַשְׁמוֹתֵינוּ	Aschmothenu
sicut	כַּאֲשֶׁר	Caascher
et nos	אֲנַחְנוּ	Anacçnu
dimittimus	מוֹחֲלִים	Mocçulim
Iis qui	לַאֲשֶׁר	Laaser
debent	אָשְׁמוּ	Aosemu
nobis, al. ad nos	לָנוּ	Lanu
Et ne	וְאַל	Veal
nos	אוֹתָנוּ	Othanu
inducas	תָּבִיא	Tauij
in tentationem	לְנִסָּיוֹן	Lenisaion

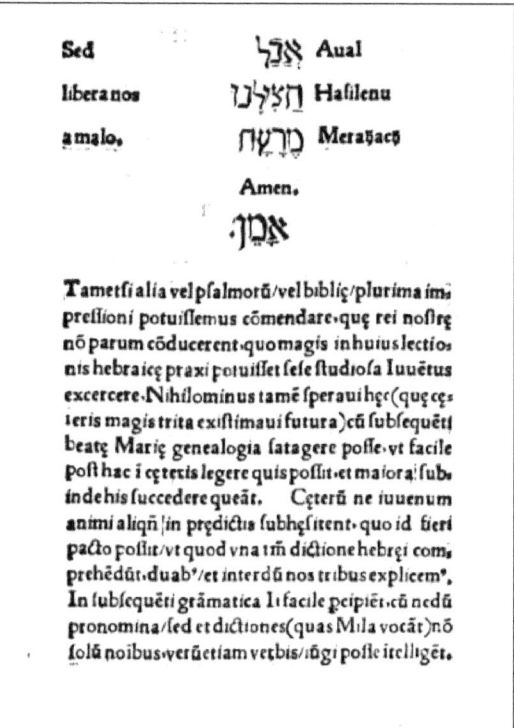

Fig. 6.3. The Our Father in Tissardus's presentation in the rare column format.

Needless to say that the shapes of the Hebrew letters in Tissardus's book of 1508 are still as crude as Marschalk's of 1502 (fig. 6.3). The French jurist and humanist Franciscus Tissardus (François Tissart, ca. 1460–1508), apparently without knowing Reuchlin's work of 1504 (*Rudimenta Hebraica*), published his own, very detailed Hebrew Grammar (*Grammatica Hebraica*)[8] in Paris in 1508, in which he included Christian texts, mainly prayers, in Hebrew. Although his book title only shows "Hebrew Grammar," he also included a Greek grammar. Tissardus's book represents an early and influential work on Greek and Hebrew linguistics, containing the alphabet, numerals, Hebraic declensions and conjugations, the *Pater noster* (Our Father) and other short devotional texts. A celebrated aspect of his work is the first appearance in print of the Hippocratic Oath, in Greek with

---

8. Tissardus's book is accessible at MDZ, http://www.mdz-nbn-resolving.de/urn/resolver.pl?urn=urn:nbn:de:bvb:12-bsb10163789-9.

a Latin translation (*Hippocratis Iusiurandum Pro Medicis*), arranged line by line.[9] Tissardus earned the reputation of being the "Reuchlin in France."[10]

Tissardus, too, in following the Venetian edition of 1500 (see folio 13r) includes (after the presentation of the Our Father) the Holy Holy Holy acclamation of the Roman liturgy, also arranged in three columns (MDZ, image no. 75) and the inscription over the cross (John 19:20) the wording of which Tissardus gives only in Latin and Hebrew (not in Greek). A unique feature is Tissardus's incorporation of the bilingual "genealogy of the blessed and immaculate Mary, mother of God" (MDZ, image nos. 77–81), from Adam on to Mary's father Ioachim.

Tissardus with his layout of the Our Father on two and a half pages employs his own unique way of presenting the bilingual text, namely in three columns (see fig. 6.3), thus, not at all in the way other earlier editors/translators have it with their line-by-line approach: His arrangement of the columns from left to right looks like this:

1. His *Pater noster* version differs from the standard liturgical wording and in this he follows the Venetian wording which also Marschalk in Germany has adopted.
2. The middle column contains Tissardus's vocalized Hebrew.
3. The right column has the transliteration of the Hebrew in Roman letters.

His deviation (in conformity with that of Manutius) from the Latin standard version of the prayer shows up in these instances: For Latin *nobis* (which occurs three times in the Latin version of the prayer) he suggests *ad nos* as for the line "give us," in Latin *da nobis*, and for "and forgive us" (in Latin *dimitte nobis*), and finally for the second part of the petition of forgiveness, which in the Latin liturgical version says [*sicut et nos dimittimus*] *debitoribus nostris*, Tissardus has *iisqui debent nobis*. With respect to the latter, Tissardus apparently must have taken Manutius's Latin version into close consideration, or actually copied and adapted it to the convention of the French pronunciation of that time. Tissardus's Hebrew version is an exact copy of the Venetian one, with only a minor mistake which crept in during the copying process: Tissardus (or, his printer/cutter of Hebrew types) mistook the shape of Manutius's Hebrew letter מ for a combination

---

9. MDZ, image no. 177.
10. Kirn 1989, 21 and 160.

of two Hebrew letters, י (*iota*) and מ (*mêm*), as in מי (in the word *lahamenu*, for the Latin *panem nostrum*, "our bread"). With a scholar less skilled in the Hebrew language, such a mistake could easily creep in. Due to this observation, one may be inclined to question Tissardus's reputation as the "Reuchlin in France." Or, one may solely have to blame the carver of the Hebrew letters for a less than perfect execution. Or, Tissardus overlooked this flaw when and if he was proofreading. The comparison of the prayer editions of Tissardus and of Manutius results in this: the Frenchman is totally dependent upon the Venetian.

4. Johann Pfefferkorn, 1508

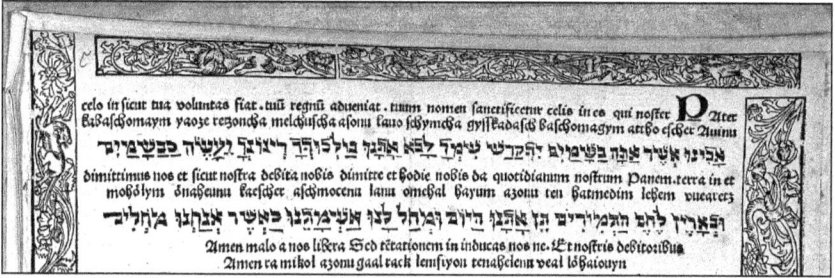

Fig. 6.4. The Our Father; upper detail of Pfefferkorn's broadsheet. Cologne: Landen, 1508 (entire page is shown in chapter 8 below).

Johann Pfefferkorn, a Catholic of Jewish descent, often vilified and defamed as an ignoramus and "butcher," was actually, next to Victor von Carben, one of the first ethnographers of Jewish life and rituals.[11] Pfefferkorn was a hospital administrator in Cologne.[12] He was a lay missionary to the Jews. For that purpose he utilized classical catechetical material (the Our Father and the Apostles' Creed) which he translated into Hebrew, together with the Hail Mary. In 1508 he designed a broadsheet with those three standard Christian prayers on it and used it most likely for his training of future missionaries to the Jews. Only one exemplar is extant[13] (see fig. 6.4 with

11. Deutsch 2012. MDZ offers most of Pfefferkorn's booklets in digital form. For an overview of the "books of the Jews" in Pfefferkorn's polemics, see Leicht 2010, 45–68. A biographical sketch of Pfefferkorn in English is offered in *The Jews' Mirror (Der Juden Spiegel) by Johannes Pfefferkorn*, Cape 2011, 11–27.

12. Jütte 2012, 153–57.

13. This single leaf print is available in digital form from Niedersächsische Staats- und Universitätsbibliothek Göttingen: 2 TH POLEM 564 / 81 RARA: Titel: Pater noster

the detail of the upper part of the broadsheet, i.e., with the *Pater noster*). Pfefferkorn squarely fits into "convert culture" of his time. Reuchlin and the humanistic Reuchlinists during the second and third decade of the sixteenth century and beyond became Pfefferkorn's chief detractors during the great controversy over the use of Jeish books.[14]

With respect to the Our Father, Pfefferkorn uses the line-by-line approach as did Manutius and Marschalk (thus, not the layout in three columns which Tissardus employs in his edition of the same year 1508. However, Pfefferkorn does not imitate the layouts employed by Manutius or Tissardus (since he most likely was not aware of them), nor does he make use of red ink in the way the predecessors did. Unlike Manutius and Marschalk, he does not dare to alter the traditional Latin liturgical wording of the Our Father—neither will Matthaeus Adrianus a few years later. Pfefferkorn employs the line-by-line format, but does not arrange the prayers in an easy to survey way (which we see at work in the Venetian edition). For example, he crams the words of the Our Father into three major segments, disregarding any reasonable subdivisions. In the following description we observe how he handles the text of the *Pater noster*, exemplified here only for the beginning of the prayer:

1. The first line on his broadsheet gives the beginning of the *Pater noster* in the standard Latin liturgical wording, arranged from right to left—in the way Hebrew texts are being read. The first letter (P) of the first Latin word (*Pater*) is given in an enlarged font size, with which the printer marks the beginning of the prayer. The enlargement of the first letter indicates the beginnings also of the other two prayers on his broadsheet. The opening of *Pater noster* reads from right to left as follows:

    celo in sicut tua voluntas fiat, tuu[m] regnu[m] adueniat, tuum nomen sanctificetur celis in es qui noster Pater

    [as in heaven thy will be done, thy kingdom come, thy name be hallowed, in heaven art who our Father].

2. The second line in his design consists of the transliteration of the Hebrew words in Roman letters similar to Manutius and Marschalk.

[und] Credo; Lateinisch u. hebräisch transkribiert. Verfasser: Pfefferkorn, Johann. The entire broadsheet is reprinted in chapter 8 below, with fig. 8.4.

14. Recent scholarship has concentrated on this issue, see Rummel 2002; Price 2011; Shamir 2011); O'Callaghan 2012; De Boer 2016.

Pfefferkorn's transliteration resonates the somewhat odd pronunciation practices which apparently were predominant in his former community of the Jewry of Cologne. Pfefferkorn's pronunciation of the Hebrew goes like this (for the beginning of the prayer, to be read, as said, from right to left):

kabaschomaym yaoze retzoncha melchuscha asonu lauo schymcha gysskadasch' baschomagym attho escher Auinu.

His transliteration shows only one printing mistake; the print has "l" instead of "I" in the word *lauo* which should be *iauo*.

3. With the third line of his layout Pfefferkorn offers his very own translation into Hebrew with the complete Hebrew punctation (vocalization) as follows:

אָבִינוּ אֲשֶׁר אַתָּה בַשָּׁמַיִם יִתְקַדַּשׁ שְׁמָךְ לָבֹא אָתָנוּ מַלְכוּתָךְ רְצוֹנְךָ יַעֲשֶׂה כְּבַשָּׁמַיִם

The use of the two words given here in extra-large print (אֲשֶׁר אַתָּה = *qui es* in Latin, "who art" in English) is unique to Pfefferkorn's Hebrew translation as he renders it here word by word from the original Latin: *Pater noster qui es in celis* = "Our Father who art in heaven." No other contemporaneous translator into Hebrew includes those two words of the *Pater noster*. They always only have the rendering אָבִינוּ בַשָּׁמַיִם = "Our Father in heaven" (see above for Manutius and Marschalk, and below for Tissardus, Adrianus, and Boeschenstain). This means that Pfefferkorn's Hebrew translation is completely independent from others, not at all dependent upon any other contemporaneous versions, especially not upon the Venetian and Erfurt version. His transliterations, too, of the Hebrew words are idiosyncratic and thus they, too, demonstrate his independence from any other potential influence.

One must keep in mind that his broadsheet of 1508 has nothing to do with Hebrew grammar books of that time since his Hebrew translations of the traditional chief prayers of the Latin Church are put at the exclusive service of his mission to converting the Jews.

5. Matthaeus Adrianus, 1512/1513

Sequitur oratio dominica
adueniat nomē tuū fanctificet qui es in cœlis   Pater nr̄
אָבִינוּ שֶׁבַּשָּׁמַיִם יִתְקַדֵּשׁ שִׁמְךָ יָבֹא
iabo   fimcha   itkadas   febafamaim   Abinu
& in terra   ficut in cœlo   uolūtas tua   fiat   regnū tuū
מַלְכוּתָךְ יְהִי רְצוֹנָךְ כְּבַשָּׁמַיִם וּבָאָרֶץ
ubaarez   kebafamaim   rezoncha   iehi   malchutcha
& dimitte   hodie   nobis   da quotidianū panē nostrū
לְהַמִּיצֵנוּ תָּמִידִי תֵּן לָגוּ הַיּוֹם וְהַנַּח
uehanach   haiom   lanu   ten   temidi   lachmenu
dimittimus   & nos   ficut   debita nostra   nobis
לָגוּ חוֹבוֹתֵינוּ כְּמוֹ שֶׁאָנוּ מַנִּיחִים
manichim   feanu   kemo   choboteuu   lanu
fed   in tentationem nos inducas & ne debitoribus nr̄is
הוֹבִיאֵנוּ וְאַל תְּבִיאֵנוּ בְּנִיסָיוֹן אֶלָּא
ella   benistaion   tebienu   ueal   chobenu   B

Fig. 6.5. The Our Father in Adrianus's *Libellus Hora faciendi pro Domino, scilicet filio Virginis Mariae, cuius mysterium in prologo legenti patebit.* Tübingen: Anshelm, 1513, MDZ, image no. 16 (Beginning of the Lord's Peayer, *Oratio dominica*).

Fig. 6.6. Virgin Mother and Child. Illustration, used twice in Adrianus's book.

Fig. 6.7. Portrait of Adrianus praying the rosary, and also as an itinerant with stick and spur.

Matthaeus Adrianus (ca. 1470–1521), a somewhat itinerant scholar coming from Spain to Germany, was a convert from Judaism as was Pfefferkorn in Cologne. Adrianus found favorable mention in Reuchlin's letter to the dean and the theological faculty of Paris of June 19, 1514, whereas Pfefferkorn did not, because Reuchlin probably judged the language skills of his archenemy, if compared to Adrianus's, as flawed.[15] Reuchlin had recommended Adrianus already in a letter of January 4, 1513, for the Hebrew teaching position at Tübingen, probably because of Adrianus's Hebrew translations Christian prayers, produced at about that time. According to his *peroratio*, he finished his book two days after the Feast of the Immaculate Conception of Mary (December 8) in 1512, opting for a Latin title[16] which gives no clue as to his incorporation of Christian prayers in Latin and Hebrew. Only in his preface does he mentions the basic reasons for his translations, namely to translate "into true Hebrew" (*in veram linguam hebraicam*) in honor and in gratitude to the Virgin Mary for rescuing him from great danger (MDZ,

15. Posset 2015, 290.

16. *Libellus Hora faciendi pro Domino, scilicet filio Virginis Mariae, cuius mysterium in prologo legenti patebit.*

image no. 2). It may not have been intended as a grammar book, yet the fact that he included the guide to pronunciation (i.e., transliterations in Roman letters) in his line-by-line approach suggests that it was meant to study Hebrew or to be able to pray the Christian prayers aloud in Hebrew.

With his booklet (of 34 pages), this Spanish Catholic of Jewish descent displays a distinct Marian devotion. He is probably the only Christian Hebraist on the eve of the Reformation who labored on those Hebrew translations in order to offer them as the token of his gratitude to Mary as his protectress. Other Hebraists, such as Reuchlin, were devotees of the Virgin, too, being a member of the Salve Regina Confraternity in Stuttgart and author of Marian poems,[17] but Adrianus with his collection of Hebrew translations of Marian prayers (along with others, such as the Our Father) stands out. His booklet of Hebrew Christian prayers is unique in terms of a memorial for favors received from Mary, as it is a votive offering, and for the incorporation of Marian iconography. Two identical pictures of the Virgin and Child are included, is placed after the preface and again later in the book (MDZ, image no. 4 and 22, see fig. 6.6). This is the only grammar book with Marian iconography. Adrianus's second woodcut (MDZ, image no. 34; see fig. 6.7) shows him kneeling and praying the rosary. This illustration is also a hint at Adrianus's vagrant life as he is depicted as an itinerant with stick and spur. One may assume that the translator/editor made sure that this illustration in his own book actually depicts him lifelike; and thus we have a portrait, perhaps the only one, of him who cited himself in the accompanying text with this humble prayer in Latin and Hebrew: "I beseech you, O Blessed one among women, that you do not despise the little work of your Matthew."[18]

He offered the following four Marian prayers in Hebrew: *Salutatio angelica* (Hail Mary; image no. 6), *Salve Regina* (Hail Holy Queen; image nos. 6–7), the *Magnificat* (image nos. 7–9), and one less known prayer which is not explicitly mentioned in his preface, and which opens with these honorific Marian titles: "Hail most holy Mary, Mother of God, Queen of Heaven, Gate of Paradise, Ruler [*domina*] of the World (*Ave sanctissima Maria dei mater regina coeli porta paradisi domina mundi*; MDZ, image no. 5).[19]

17. Posset 2015, 102–6.

18. Latin: *Obsecro te o benedicta in mulieribus ne despicas opusculum Matthaei tui*; fig. 6.7.

19. This less known prayer to Mary reads in English translation as follows: "Hail most holy Mary, mother of God, queen of heaven, gate of paradise, ruler [*domina*] of the world. You are a uniquely pure virgin. You conceived Jesus without sin. You bore

Those Marian prayers are followed by the Our Father (image nos. 9–10) and the two official creeds of the Church (MDZ, image nos. 10–14). The latter are a very special treat insofar as no other translator of his time offers the then less known Nicene Creed in Hebrew. At that time only the Apostles' Creed was used during Holy Mass,[20] which explains that this creed was translated into Hebrew also by other Hebraists.

Here, we limit ourselves to the Hebrew Our Father. Adrianus used Manutius's line-by-line approach for his display of the prayers:

1. the Latin liturgical wording,

2. the vocalized Hebrew,

3. the transliteration of the Hebrew with Roman letters.

A comparison of Adrianus's Hebrew with that of Manutius (and thus of Marschalk and of Tissardus) shows great similarities, likely direct dependency. But apparently Adrianus has reworked some of the expressions; for instance, Adrianus has Hebrew *iehi* where Manutius has *iehase* for Latin *fiat* (in "thy will be done").

A note to scholars interested in the pronunciations of the Hebrew at that time: The transliterations in Roman letters differ at times. As samples, here are the five versions of the beginning of the Our Father ("Our Father who art in heaven, hallowed by Thy name, Thy kingdom come") in Hebrew transliterations and in chronological order:

1. Manutius, Venice 1500 (from right to left):

    malchuthah iauo scimcha iithcadas sebasamaiim auinu.

2. Marschalk, Erfurt 1502 (from right to left) with the two printing mistakes (shown in bold print):

    malchuthah iauo scimcha iithcaas dsebasamaiim auinu.

3. Tissardus, Paris 1508 (from the right column, close to Manutius):

---

the creator and savior of the world in whom I do not doubt. Pray for me to Jesus, your beloved son, and free me from all evil."

20. Apostles' Creed in Latin: *Credo in Deum Patrem omnipotentem, Creatorem caeli et terrae. Et in Iesum Christum, Filium eius unicum, Dominum nostrum, qui conceptus est de Spiritu Sancto, natus ex Maria Virgine, passus sub Pontio Pilato, crucifixus, mortuus, et sepultus, descendit ad inferos, tertia die resurrexit a mortuis, ascendit ad caelos, sedet ad dexteram Dei Patris omnipotentis, inde venturus est iudicare vivos et mortuos. Credo in Spiritum Sanctum, sanctam Ecclesiam catholicam, sanctorum communionem, remissionem peccatorum, carnis resurrectionem, vitam aeternam. Amen.*

Malchuthach Iauo Schimcha Iithcadasch Schebasamaim Auinu

4. Pfefferkorn, Cologne 1508 (from right to left, with *Iauo* being a printing mistake in bold print; it should be *iauo*):

   melchuscha asonu Iauo schymcha gysskadasch' baschomagym attho escher Auinu.

5. Adrianus, Tübingen 1513 (from right to left):

   malchutcha iabo simcha itkadas sebasamaim Abinu.

   NB: Boeschenstain has no transliterations of his Hebrew translations.

6. Johann Boeschenstain, 1514

Johann Boeschenstain (or, Böschenstein, 1472–ca. 1540) was a diocesan priest from Esslingen, near Stuttgart.[21] As one of the three leading Christian Hebraists from Swabia he networked with the other two, Johann Reuchlin and Friar Caspar Amman.[22] Boeschenstain's contemporaries often assumed that he was of Jewish descent and forced him to leave Ingolstadt in 1514. He went to Augsburg where he worked as an independent scholar. In 1518 he produced a broadsheet with his cabalistic interpretation of the Tetragram; it may have been printed by Erhard Öglin in Augsburg.[23] Since rumors about his Jewish descent persisted, he was prompted to publish a pamphlet in 1524 to the contrary. He insisted that he was not Jewish, but born of Christian parents at Esslingen.[24]

---

21. Gerald Dörner, "Böschenstein" in Walther Killy, ed., *Literaturlexikon*, vol. 2, 52–53.

22. Posset 2015, 76. On Amman, see Posset, 2015c, 51–105.

23. Anselm Schubert, "Die Wittenberger Reformation und die christliche Kabbala (1516–1524)," in *Anwälte der Freiheit! Humanisten und Reformatoren im Dialog. Begleitband zur Ausstellung im Reuchlinhaus Pforzheim, 20. September bis 8. November 2015. Im Auftrag der Stadt Pforzheim*, ed. Matthias Dall'Asta (Heidelberg: Winter, 2015), 167–80, here 172–76, including the reproduction of Boeschenstain's broadsheet (fig. 5).

24. *Ain Diemietige Uersprechung durch Johann Böschenstain, geborn von Christenlichen öltern, aus der stat Esslingen, wider etlich die von jm sagen, er seye von Jüdischen stämen* (Augsburg: Philipp Ulhart, 1524).

Fig. 6.8. Portrait of Johann Bo[e]schenstain by Hieronymus Hopfer, ca. 1530; with caption in Hebrew of Ps 7:18) ("I praise the justice of the Lord; I celebrate the name of the Lord") combined with words from Ps 119:15 ("though you afflict me, you are faithful").

RESPECT FOR THE JEWS

אָבִינוּ שֶׁבַּשָּׁמַיִם	Pater noster qui es in celis sāctificetur nomē tuū adueni at regnū tuum fiat uolūtas tua. Sicut in celo & in terra. Panē nr̄m quotidianū da nobis hodie & dimitte nobis debita nr̄a sic̄ & nos dimittimus debitoꝛb9 nr̄is & ne nos inducas in tentationē Sed libera nos a malo. Amen.	Vater vnser der du bist in den himeln gehailiget werd dein nam zū kum dein reich deyn will geschech als in hymel/vñ auff erd vnnser täglich brot gib vns heūt vñ vgib vns vnser schuld als vnd wir vergeben vnsein schuldigern vnnd nit für vnns in versuchung. Sonn der erlöß vns võ übel Amen.
יִתְקַדֵּשׁ שְׁמֹךָ תָּבֹא מַלְכוּתֶךָ יְהִי רְצֹנְךָ כְּבַשָּׁמַיִם וּבָאָרֶץ לַחְמֵנוּ תָּמִידִי תֵּן לָנוּ הַיּוֹם וּמְחוֹל לָנוּ חוֹבוֹתֵינוּ כְּמוֹ שֶׁאָנוּ מוֹחֲלִים חוֹבֵינוּ וְאַל תְּבִיאֵנוּ בְּנִסָּיוֹן אֶלָּא הַצִּילֵנוּ מֵרַע אָמֵן		

הֲעֲלוּזִי מִרְיָם חֵן מָלְאָה יְהֹוָה עִמֵּךְ בְּרוּכָה אַתְּ בַּנָּשִׁים וּמְבוֹרָךְ	Aue maria gratia plena dominus tecum benedicta tu in mulieribus & benedictus fructus	Gegrüßt seyest du maria vol genaden ð her mit dir dā bist gesegnet in den weiben vnnd gesegnet ist die frucht

Fig. 6.9. The Our Father in Hebrew, Latin, and German, in: Boeschenstain, *Elementale introductoriu[m]* in column format (but without transliteration in Roman letters). Augsburg: Erhard Öglin, 1514.

Boeschenstain's table of contents indicates the following texts:

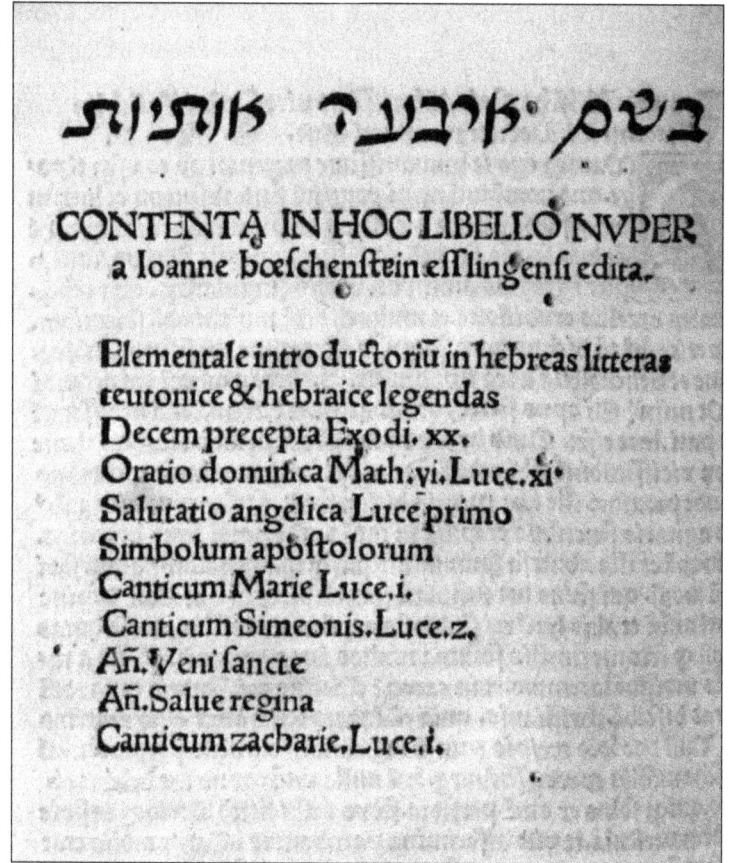

Fig. 6.10. Table of Contents of Boeschenstain's Trilingual Texts.

1. Ten Commandments, Exod 20
2. Our Father, Matt 6 and Luke 11
3. The Angel's Greeting (*Angelus*), Luke 1
4. Apostles' Creed
5. Canticle of Mary, Luke 1
6. Canticle of Simeon, Luke 2
7. Hymn *Veni sancte*
8. Hymn *Salve Regina*

9. Canticle of Zechariah, Luke 1

The title of his trilingual booklet about the "basic introduction to the Hebrew letters" with readings in German and Hebrew"[25] and its table of contents indicate that he offers the texts in Hebrew and German (but, of course, also in Latin). The texts he selected are always given in three columns (from left to right):

1. Vocalized Hebrew,
2. Latin, and
3. German dialect.

Further investigations are needed to determine the origin of his German wordings, whether they are his own, in the Swabian dialect of his hometown, or in another south German dialect such as the one of the printer's location (Augsburg?). The book has to be read from "back to front" in the way Jewish books are being read. After his introductory section with the explanations of the individual Hebrew letters and some grammatical features (comprising five pages), he offers the following texts in the said three languages:

1. Ten Commandments according to Exod 20:2–17 (which he needed not to retranslate into Hebrew, but copy from a Hebrew Bible; MDZ, image nos. 13–12);

2. Our Father according to the Gospels (Matt 6 and Luke 11; MDZ, image no. 11);

3. Hail Mary according to Luke 1 (*Salutatio angelica Luce primo*, actually in the liturgical wording which paraphrases Luke 1:28–29, MDZ, image nos. 11–10);

4. Apostles' Creed (MDZ, image nos. 10–9);

5. Canticle of Mary (*Canticum Mariae = Magnificat*, of Luke 1:46–56, with the liturgical conclusion of "Glory be to the Father, etc."; MDZ, image nos. 9–7). Also from Luke's Gospel (in Latin) are taken the

---

25. *Contenta In Hoc Libello Nvper a Ioanne boeschenstein esslingensi edita, Elementale introductoriu[m] in hebreas litteras teutonice&hebraice legendas Decem precepta Exodi xx. Oratio dominica Math. vi. Luce xi. Salutatio angelica Luce primo. Simbolum apostolorum* ... ; online: http://www.mdz-nbn-resolving.de/urn/resolver.pl?urn=urn:nbn:de:bvb:12-bsb10981642-9 (Signatur: 831303 4 A.lat.b. 256#Beibd.5 831303 4 A.lat.b. 256#Beibd.5).

two hymns of praise, both with the liturgical ending of "Glory be to the Father";

6. Canticle of Simeon (Luke 2:29–32; MDZ, image no. 7);

7. A prayer to the Holy Spirit (*an[tiphon] Veni sancte*, i.e., the *Magnificat*-antiphon, which is not to be confused with the liturgical sequence *Veni Sancte Spiritus*). The Latin antiphon which he presents here in the two other languages is well-known under the same title *Veni sancte Spiritus* (MDZ, image nos. 7–6). It reads as follows: "Come Holy Spirit, fill the hearts of your faithful and kindle in them the fire of your love; you have gathered the nations together in the unity of faith. Alleluia, Alleluia."[26]

8. Among the Marian prayers he also includes the non-biblical antiphon *Salve Regina* (*Hail Holy Queen*, MDZ, image nos. 6–5);

9. Canticle of Zechariah (Luke 1:68–79; MDZ, image nos. 5–3).

Boeschenstain dedicated his work to Johann Reuchlin (MDZ, image no. 23). His grammar book is unique in including the translations of the prayers and other religious texts into German and of omitting the transliterations of the Hebrew words. One can only speculate why this is so, since Boeschenstain definitely wanted to provide a basic introduction to the Hebrew language (*Elementale introductorium in hebreas litteras*) for which a beginner would have needed the transliterations in Roman letters. Boeschenstain may have had readers in mind with an advanced knowledge of Hebrew; for them the transliterations would not have been as crucial as for beginners.

His Hebrew version of the Our Father is not dependent upon others. As a priest he worked from the standard Latin liturgical version and thus does not follow the suggested emendation found in Manutius, Marschalk, and Tissardus.

Conclusion

In investigating the situation at the beginning of the sixteenth century with respect to scholars interested in devotional *Hebraica*, we encounter the strange phenomenon that their early Hebrew grammar books contain

---

26. Original Latin version: *Veni Sancte Spiritus, reple tuorum corda fidelium, et tui amoris in eis ignem accende, qui per diversitatem linguarum cunctarum gentes in unitate fidei congregasti, alleluia, alleluia.* MDZ, image nos. 7–6.

various traditional Christian prayers in Hebrew translation, usually in the punctated (vocalized) form and with transliteration in Roman letters in order to facilitate pronunciation for the uninitiated. The authors under consideration here all worked and published their efforts during the time period of 1502 to 1514, of what may be called the eve of the Reformation. From the given time period, we found that all five books for learning Hebrew contain the Our Father. Those books are called *Introductio* (Manutius, Marschalk, Boeschenstain) or *Grammatica* (Tissardus), while Pfefferkorn's broadsheet lacks a formal title. Adrianus calls his work of 1512/1513 a *Libellus* (booklet) with a lengthy description of its content, but refraining from labeling it a grammar book or an introduction to Hebrew.

Besides the various Hebrew versions of the Our Father, the following other liturgical or devotional prayers became known in Hebrew through their publication efforts: Apostles' Creed, Nicene Creed, the antiphon *Veni sancte* (only in Boeschenstain), the Holy Holy Holy of the Roman liturgy, Hail Mary (*Ave Maria*), Hail Holy Queen (*Salve Regina*), the songs of the Greek New Testament, i.e., the Canticle of Mary (*Magnificat*), the Canticle of Simeon, and the Canticle of Zechariah, usually with the customary liturgical ending of the "Glory be to the Father . . ." Any given author may include his own selection of additional texts, be they biblical or Bible-related, creedal or devotional texts: Boeschenstain chose the Ten Commandments while Tissardus the "genealogy of the blessed and immaculate Mary, mother of God." Adrianus is the only one who translated the Nicene Creed and the antiphon *Veni sancte*. He distinguished himself also with the Hebrew translation of the "Hail most holy Mary, Mother of God. . . ." All the translators investigated here include at least one, or more, prayers to the Virgin Mary, mostly the biblically based Hail Mary (*Ave Maria*) which then was called also the Angelic Salutation (Adrianus and Boeschenstain). Adrianus in addition is a singular, because personal, case. In his book of 1512/1513 he assembled his Hebrew translations, especially of the traditional Marian prayers, as a votive offering to the Virgin Mary. He wanted to honor her and give thanks to her for the protection she provided him when he was in personal danger. He added among other prayers the Our Father. All the translators share in the Catholic Marian spirituality since they incorporate the Marian component in their publications.

The inclusion of the Hebrew Our Father (and other prayers) in grammar books apparently provided an opportunity for a student's "exercise" in learning the rudiments of this sacred language. Research shows that there was no one agreed-upon Hebrew rendering of the prayers. The famous Venetian printer Aldus Manutius turned out to be the trendsetter since 1500. Marschalk in Erfurt, Adrianus in Tübingen, Boeschenstain in Augsburg, and Tissarus in Paris largely followed him. Yet, each translator added a personal touch in that he made minor changes here and there. No clearly missionary purpose (mission to the Jews) can be ascertained for their grammar books. Only Pfefferkorn with his broadsheet comprising three prayers had mission to the Jews as the chief motivation in mind. Pfefferkorn may have used his broadsheet as a "cheat sheet" in disputations with Jews or as a catechetical aid in training new Christian missionaries to the Jews.

7

In Search of an Explanation for the Suffering of the Jews

Johann Reuchlin's Open Letter of 1505

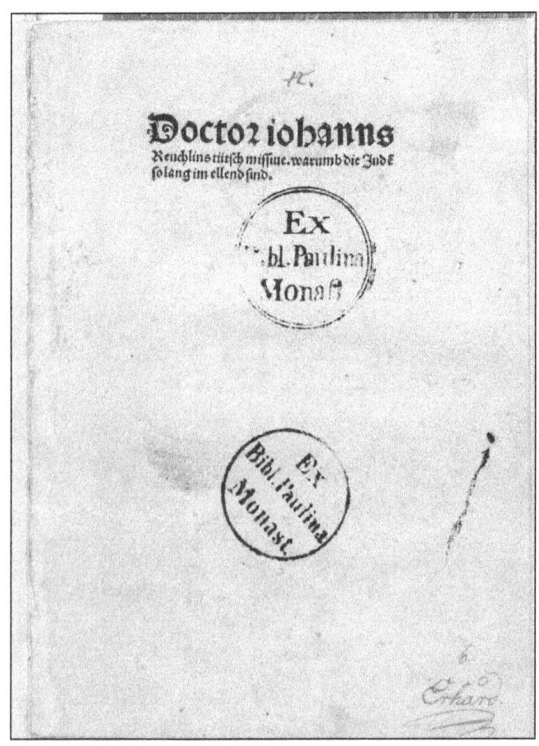

Fig. 7.1. *Doctor iohanns Reuchlins tütsch missiue, warumb die Juden so lang im ellend sind.* Reuchlin's *Missiue* of 1505.

1. In Context

IN 1505, THE HUMANIST Johann Reuchlin published a booklet titled *Doctor iohanns Reuchlins tütsch missiue, warumb die Juden so lang im ellend sind*[1] (Johann Reuchlin's German open letter [discussing] why the Jews have been in "exile"[2] so long). One may debate whether or not Reuchlin's "German open letter" is to be understood as merely repeating the "conventional view that they [the Jews] were suffering for the sins of their forefathers who had murdered Jesus."[3] However, such an interpretation is a far too simplified summary of this rather unusual, "somewhat mysterious tract."[4] Reuchlin felt sincere concern over the continued suffering of the Jews and sought to understand it for many years.

First of all, Reuchlin's macaronic text is far from "conventional" as it is very unusual for a non-Jewish author of that time to use Hebrew phrases, given in Hebrew characters,[5] within the Early New High German text. If Reuchlin had written the text in Latin as one scholar to another, it might not be particularly exceptional, but he writes in 1505 in the then non-scholarly vernacular language. The only other document of the very early sixteenth century written in German and Hebrew is the pamphlet by the former Jew Johann Pfefferkorn (1469–1523), titled *The Enemy of the Jews* and published in 1509,[6] i.e., four years after the *Missiue*. Pfefferkorn may have deliberately mimicked Reuchlin.

Second, in terms of content, Reuchlin's *Missiue* represents more of an expression of "philosemitism" (for lack of a better word)[7] than of conven-

---

1. Reuchlin finished this work after Christmas 1505 and had it printed by Thomas Anshelm in his home town, Pforzheim, as is indicated in the colophon. *Missiue* in SW 4-1: 1–12.

2. The English translation of *ellend/elend* is "exile"; see West, *Early New High German/English Dictionary Part E*, avaiable online at http://www.germanstudies.org.uk/enhg_dic/enhg_dice.htm. Max Brod translated *ellend* as "Exil" in Brod 1965, 170. *Ellend* also carries the modern German connotation of *Elend* (misery); see Erika Rummel, "Why the Jews Have Lived in Misery for So Long," in Rummel 2002, 7.

3. Rummel 2002, 7.

4. Price 1978, 179:237.

5. Earlier writers (such as Nigri) used transliterations of Hebrew phrases.

6. *Ich bin ain Buchlinn der Juden veindt ist mein namen* (Augsburg 1509).

7. One may question Heiko A. Oberman's assertion that philosemitism did not exist in the sixteenth century, but one may simultaneously agree that Christians as "friends of Jews" were rare exceptions; see Oberman 1981, 101; and the critical comments by Burnett 2009, 135.

tional antijudaism. It seems misplaced among *adversos iudaeos* (Against the Jews) texts. Reuchlin is admittedly a rare exception to contemporary (i.e., pre-Reformational), antagonistic attitudes toward Jews. While more commonly discussed in connection to his role in the controversy over Jewish books (that would erupt about four years later, often referred to as the Reuchlin affair), his attitude to Jews can also be demonstrated from his *Missiue*, our focus here.

The *Missiue* (and Reuchlin's other works) is better placed within a minority medieval tradition that was guided by tolerance, exemplified by Gilbert Crispin (ca. 1046–1117), a Benedictine monk at Westminster.[8] In his own time, Reuchlin's *Missiue* reflects the influence of the benevolent attitude toward the Jews of Emperor Frederick III (1440–1493).[9] Coming of age in this imperial milieu, Reuchlin apparently had no personal bias against Jews. This allowed Reuchlin and his work to play an important role in the beginnings of changes in social attitudes toward the Jews.

The tendency to understand Reuchlin as sharing in the prejudices of his age and social class, and to find proof of this in his *Missiue*, began almost as soon as it was published. This understanding, though, accepts the perspective of Johann Pfefferkorn. He found certain passages in it to his liking and quoted from it for his own purposes in his *Hand Mirror* (1511), *Fire Mirror* (1512), and *Compassionate Complaint over all Complaints* (1521),[10] as part of his self-appointed task to convince Christians to eliminate Jewish books as an aid to converting all Jews to Christianity. Reuchlin's *Missiue* appears to have been the main reason that Pfefferkorn submitted Reuchlin's name to Emperor Maximilian I (1493–1519) as a potential expert on the books of the Jews.[11] Some passages in Reuchlin's early work *On the Wonder-Working Word* (*De verbo mirifico*, 1494; reprinted 1514)[12] may also have been to the liking of the anti-Jewish Christian convert Pfefferkorn. The fact that Pfefferkorn could read (or better, misread) Reuchlin in this way may indeed have something to do with passages in Reuchlin's work that appear to be open to a variety of interpretations. However, the overriding tone and

8. Wilhelm and Wilhelmi 2005; Thienhaus 2006. As the prior of the abbey Crispin offered a Jewish scholar the opportunity to dialogue and conduct a rare, respectful exchange of ideas concerning the interpretation of the Hebrew Bible.

9. On Emperor Frederick, see Heinig 1997. For other aspects of this time period, see Bell 2007; Bell and Burnett 2006.

10. Kirn 1989, 184.

11. See Matthias Dall'Asta and Gerald Dörner, introduction to RBW 3: xiv.

12. SW 1-1: 106–9.

style of the *Missiue* demonstrate Reuchlin much more to be a friend of the Jews than their enemy, as is consistent with his overall biography.

To understand Reuchlin's *Missiue* adequately, it is crucial to avoid two errors in interpreting it. First, Reuchlin lists three talking points that must be read within their context in the document itself. If one isolates these three points, one ends up reading the text as if based exclusively upon them, and then the entire document does indeed wrongly appear "conventional." Second, the *Missiue* must be contextualized within the rather benevolent imperial attitude toward the Jews that dominated the reign of Emperor Frederick III and that presumably continued for some time after his death in 1493. Otherwise, one may mistakenly read the *Missiue* as just another expression of antisemitism. The medieval, anti-Jewish tradition of Western Christianity admittedly regained influence during the time of Frederick's successor, Maximilian I, but did not necessarily shape Reuchlin's own understandings.

2. Motivation for Composing the Text

Some suggest that Reuchlin's *Missiue* was his response to the request of a nobleman looking for help "on how to convert Jews."[13] However, neither the text of the *Missiue* itself nor Reuchlin's other writings support such a claim. In his *Defensio* of 1513, Reuchlin recalls the *Sitz im Leben* from which the question had arisen, "Why are the Jews in exile for so long?" Reuchlin explains that in early 1493,[14] an unnamed nobleman had asked him what he should talk about with "his Jews" during times of leisure, but without giving cause for scandal.[15] There is no mention of a question of "How to convert Jews."

In response, Reuchlin composed "something short in which you in times of leisure may want to talk about with your Jews which would not cause offense, but real improvement."[16] Reuchlin encourages dialogue. The

---

13. Hsia 1988, 119. Eckert 1989, 493, 504. Zika 1998, 128–30, wants to see a connection between Reuchlin's *Missiue* and Pico's concept of employing the Cabala as a "weapon against the Jews." This appears to be more an *eisegesis* than an *exegesis* of the given source.

14. About half a year before Emperor Frederick III died on August 19, 1493, at Linz, Austria, in Reuchlin's presence.

15. ... *et ad dispuationem multa formavi argumenta, hinc inde tam gravia quam levia, qualia poteram excogitare, quorum sibi iusseram postulare solutiones* (*Defensio*); SW 4-1: 370.5–7.

16. *Etwas kurtz zů verzeichnen, dar inn ir euch zů müssigen zyten mitt ewern Juden*

nobleman should ask the Jews themselves what the main reason is why they must suffer "imprisonment" (exile) for such a long time. Reuchlin then primarily delves into pertinent passages of the Scriptures in order to tackle this issue. Reuchlin hopes that he may find answers from dialoging on the controversial biblical texts. Reuchlin envisioned a friendly and private atmosphere in which his specific talking points would provide substance. This was its primary purpose. He apparently did not want to present theological theses in the style of Martin Luther's so-called "95 Theses" of 1517. Reuchlin's *Missiue* was also not meant for use in formal, public disputations, like, for example, the famous Leipzig Disputation of 1519 in which Martin Luther and Johann Eck (1486–1543) attacked each other. In Reuchlin's *Defensio*, he points out that in the *Missiue* of eight years earlier he did not intend to provide dogmatic theological determinations or definite conclusions on faith-decisions.[17] This disclaimer suggests that he felt compelled to safeguard himself against potential heresy charges that might result from his over-friendly views of the Jews.

Thus, it is fully legitimate to place the origins of Reuchlin's *Missiue* in the spiritual climate that had developed during the reign of Emperor Frederick III, one that was not poisoned by hatred of Jews.[18] In this rather relaxed atmosphere, conversations concerning the lives and the fate of Jews could address the key question that Reuchlin indicated in the title of his *Missiue*, the length of Jewish exile. Providing assistance "on how to convert Jews" was at best a secondary goal.[19] The *Missiue* is a letter with discussion points meant for use in private. It was made public in order to aid others like Reuchlin's anonymous nobleman who found themselves in similar situations. For such private talks with "his" Jews, noblemen could rely on the talking points that Reuchlin offered.

3. "A Moment of World-Historical Significance"

Reuchlin's study of Hebrew began or continued at the court of Emperor Frederick III in 1492 with the emperor's Jewish physician, Jacob Jehiel

---

möchten ersprachen, dar uß kein ergernüß, sunder mercklich besserung entstünde; SW 4-1: 5.

17. SW 4-1: 370.6–12.

18. Graetz 1956, 293; Baron 1965, 31, 167–68.

19. This does not mean that one should take the *Missiue* as a document of tolerance. There was no tolerance in the modern sense of the word.

Loans (Lohans) (d. 1505) as his teacher. Reuchlin's acquaintance with Loans, whom the emperor greatly favored and knighted, forms the immediate backdrop for the *Missiue*. Frederick's favor to Jews, especially to Loans, including his instruction to his son, co-regent, and successor Maximilian I to "do good to Jews,"[20] may have been a decisive factor influencing Reuchlin. Loans was also aware of Reuchlin's interests in *Hebraica*. In the spring of 1492 Loans arranged that Reuchlin received from the emperor a particularly valuable twelfth/thirteenth-century Bible manuscript, a parchment codex of the Pentateuch in Hebrew with the Aramaic translation Targum Onqelos. This priceless codex was the emperor's farewell present to Reuchlin who received it at the end of his diplomatic mission at the imperial court in Linz.[21] The encounter between Reuchlin and Loans, which evidently developed into friendship, is a "moment of world-historical significance," as Ludwig Geiger convincingly wrote in his Reuchlin biography of 1871.[22] Reuchlin's *Missiue*, written in the year of Loans's death in 1505, may be Reuchlin's literary monument to the memory of his Jewish friend. Whether or not it specifically referred to this friendship, the thorny question about the long Jewish exile raised in the title required an answer.

4. An Open Letter in German and Hebrew

Reuchlin's *Missiue* is probably best defined as an "open letter" or a pamphlet in which he shared his benevolent thoughts on the "Jewish Question" in German interspersed on every single page with numerous Hebrew phrases. For each Hebrew phrase Reuchlin provides a German translation. Such a mix of languages, i.e., of the vernacular with Hebrew, is quite rare in sixteenth-century texts written by non-Jews (while the mix of Latin and Hebrew is more common). Apparently, Reuchlin employed the so-called "Rashi script" for his Hebrew words, while in his later *Rudiments of Hebrew* he applied the common square form of the Hebrew alphabet.[23] A decade earlier, Reuchlin's *De verbo mirifico* had been printed without Hebrew or Greek characters (by Amerbach in Basel).

---

20. As was rumored among the Jews themselves. See Baron 1965, IX: 168.

21. Now known as *Codex Reuchlin 1* or the "Reuchlin Bible." See Greschat 2007, 69–72, 92 (with illustrations).

22. Geiger 1871, 105.

23. *Raschischrift*, Brod 1965, 174.

The use of Hebrew characters makes one also wonder whether, indeed, this letter was meant as an answer to the question of a real or of an imagined German nobleman. The readers would also have to be familiar with the Cabala, something that cannot be expected from an ordinary German nobleman of the time. Words given in Hebrew characters were not something even a highly educated German nobleman would have been able to decipher. It is not inconceivable, then, that the anonymous nobleman is a literary fiction or represents Reuchlin himself. Emperor Frederick III had elevated him to the rank of nobility in 1492. However, Reuchlin's description of the situation at Frederick's court supports his claim that a real person had asked him to suggest discussion points for conversation with Jews.

5. Content

For the imagined, private conversations that make up the *Missive*, Reuchlin presents a series of talking points which are allegations to which he hopes Jews will be able to respond properly. Reuchlin's Christian nobleman should propose to the Jews the following allegations as talking points.[24]

1. This Jewish exile is lasting longer than the Babylonian captivity. Therefore, the sin which led to this punishment must be yet greater.

2. God has promised to punish a person's misdeed only up to the third and fourth generation. Yet, the punishment of the Jews has now endured for more than one hundred generations. Evidently, this sin cannot be that of an individual, but rather that of the entire nation.

3. The reason why the Jews cannot recognize the reason for their punishment is that God himself has made them obdurate.

Reuchlin comes up with the following explanations to prove that the Jewish people have sinned collectively:

First, Reuchlin cites Deut 25:2 (in Hebrew with his own German translation added). A guilty person is to receive the number of stripes his guilt deserves. Evidently the greater the sin the greater the punishment

---

24. *Dar vff moegen ir inen fürwerfen dry gegründte wahrhsafftige meinungen nemlich wie hernach volget*; SW 4-1: 5.11–12.

should be.²⁵ However, God grants mercy (*begnadet*), as Ps 106:43-46 and Neh 9:16-20 teach.²⁶

Second, and in contrast, God gave them notice that he is a jealous God who does not tolerate idol worship; for this he will punish the children down to the third and fourth generation (Exod 20:5 and 34:7). The present day Jews are punished not only to the fourth generation, but down to the hundredth generation. From this fact, one must derive that these sins were not committed by just one or two Jews. If the sin were that of one person, the saying of Ezek 18:20 would apply: "Only the soul of the one who sins shall die. The son shall not be charged with the misdeed of the father."

Reuchlin seeks to harmonize these conflicting words of God. If it is true that an innocent child should not be charged with his parent's sin, then some other sin must have been committed, i.e., by all Jews, based upon the obvious experience that Jews suffer continuously. He calls the sin under consideration the *gemeine sünd*, by which he means a sin which was committed publicly by an entire nation including all its members.²⁷ How is the Early New High German adjective *gemein* to be translated into English? The Latin equivalent is *communis*. In contemporary German it is *allgemein*, or perhaps, *gemeinsam* ("common") as it has something to do with "community" (*Gemeinde*).²⁸ Thus, Reuchlin's choice of words, *gemeine sünd*, means the common sin that is publicly committed by the community as a whole; thus it is a universal, general, or, "collective sin" of all generations (parents and children). It should not be translated, however, with "collective guilt,"²⁹ because Reuchlin explicitly uses *sünd* and not *schuld*, although these may at times function as synonyms.

In Reuchlin's view, another biblical saying applies to the situation of a collective sin, namely that God punishes the children down to the third and fourth generation (Exod 20:5). However, this applies only if the children

---

25. *Ye groesser die sünd ist ye mer die zal der straff soll sin*; SW 4-1: 5.24.

26. SW 4-1: 5.30-33.

27. . . . *Darumb so müß es ein gemeine sünd syn . . . eins gantzen volcks mit allenn iren glidern*; SW 4-1: 6.18.

28. But the expression has nothing to do with contemporary German *gemein* or *Gemeinheit* which means "mean" and "meanness."

29. As found in Oberman 1981, 28. Whereas one may agree that the translation of "collective" for *gemein* is not controversial, this is not necessarily the case for the translation of *sünd* as "guilt." A theological discussion of the distinction between sin and guilt would go beyond the scope of this study. For the non-theologian, sin and guilt may be the same. The philological fact remains that Reuchlin used *sünd*, not *schuld*.

are following the misdeeds of their fathers. The *targum* on Exod 20:5 establishes this condition, which Reuchlin quotes in Hebrew characters along with the comments by Rashi (1040–1105)[30] and Nahmanides, whom he calls Moses Gerundensis (1194–1270)[31] on the same verses (Exod 20:5 and Exod 32:34).[32] These authors had connected the ancient crime of the golden calf with the Jews' miserable imprisonment in their day. Reuchlin disagrees with the interpretation by the great Jewish masters, on biblical grounds, because their view contradicts both Ezek 18:20 and Neh 9:16–20. The latter reads:[33]

> But they, our fathers, proved to be insolent; they held their necks stiff and would not obey your commandments. They refused to obey and no longer remembered the miracles you had worked for them. They stiffened their necks and turned their heads to return to their slavery in Egypt. But you are a God of pardons, gracious and compassionate, slow to anger and rich in mercy; you did not forsake them. Though they made for themselves a molten calf, and proclaimed, "Here is your God who brought you up out of Egypt," and were guilty of great effronteries, yet in your great mercy you did not forsake them in the desert. The column of cloud did not cease to lead them by day on their journey, nor did the column of fire by night cease to light for them the way by which they were to travel. Your good spirit you bestowed on them, to give them understanding.

With this gift of the "good spirit," God forgave them all their sins of any kind. Furthermore, not all Jews sinned, as one finds among them those who hate sin. Nevertheless, the fact remains that the entire Jewish people finds itself in miserable exile. Reuchlin concludes from this that the sin for which they were dispersed is a different category of sin, the *gemeine sünd* of the entire people to which all Jews belong "as long as they are Jews."[34] Reuchlin seems to imply the element of an "inherited sin," perhaps implying

---

30. The commentary on the Pentateuch by Rabbi Solomon of Troyes, who is known as Rashi, is now lost from Reuchlin's library; see Abel and Leicht 2005, no. 24.

31. Moses ben Na[c]hman; Rambon, Ramban, Moyses Gerundensis, Gerondi, i.e., from Gerona; Spanish, Talmudist, Cabalist and commentator on the Pentateuch; on him, see Abel and Leicht 2005, 228.

32. SW 4-1: 6.22–31.

33. New American Bible translation.

34. *Ein gemein sünd deß gantzen geschlechts . . . , darin all Juden verharren so lang sie iuden sind*; SW 4-1: 7.17–19.

the German term *Erbsünde* (inherited sin) usually translated with "original sin" (which does not evoke the element of inheritance present in the German). The theological concept of "original sin" refers to the general sinfulness that every human being inherits from Adam and his first (i.e., original) sin described in Gen 3. However, although Reuchlin discusses all kinds of biblical passages in his *Missiue*, the biblical story of Gen 3, the classical source of original sin is not among them. Nor does he use the technical language that points to this concept.

Reuchlin's third deliberation about the sin for which the Jews have suffered for so long a time results in the statement that it must be the greatest sin that ever was. It was a *gemeine sünd*, and it was a sin that they themselves do not consider a sin. Were they to recognize it as the sin for which they were being punished, they would cease doing it in order that they might return home. But they remain blind, and such blindness is God's special punishment. They do not want to recognize their sin. You can tell them whatever you want; they do not want to hear any of it, as is written in Job 21:14, "They say to God, 'Depart from us, for we do not like to know your ways.'" Even Isaiah was told to tell the people that they had become sluggish (Isa 6:8–10). Even though God's word to Isaiah was communicated in its literal sense,[35] Reuchlin argues that according to cabalistic learning, it is to be understood as applying to Jesus.[36]

Reuchlin's reference to Cabala draws from traditional Christian hermeneutics of the Hebrew Bible and he understands by "cabalistic interpretation" the christianized (christological) version. Through this lens, the prophetic words are spoken as if addressed to "Jesus our Lord God." Only "the learned Jew" (*der gelert iud*) may understand this if he knows the

---

35. *Nach dem buochstaben*; SW 4-1: 8.7.

36. "*Inn der hohen heimlichkeit verstanden vff Jeschuh vnsern hern got.*" SW 4-1: 8.8–9, spelled here as *haimlichkeit*. Reuchlin's Early New High German keyword *heimlichkeit* should be rendered in English as having something to do primarily with *heim* (English home) and *Heimat*. *Heim* is the realm which only members of the household are familiar with; to others it is unfamiliar, secret (i.e., *heimlich*). In medieval German it had the meaning of "familiarity," "pleasantness," and "joy." See *Der Große Duden: Etymologie*, s. v. *heimlich/Heimlichkeit*. The original meaning is not "secrecy"; it has nothing to do with occultism. In medieval spirituality, *heimlichkeit* is a significant concept; see Heimbach-Steins 1995, 71–86. The expression *hohe heimlichkeit* is a synonym for Cabala, as Reuchlin defines Cabala with exactly this term in his *Expert Opinion* (*Ratschlag*) about Jewish books and he writes in his *Eye Mirror*, SW IV, 1: 28.27–28: *Zum dritten find ich die hohe haimlichhait der reden vnd woerter gottes / die sie haissent Cabala.*

"familiar art" (*heimliche kunst*).³⁷ He will understand that "God Jesus" (*got Jeschuh*)³⁸ is the same one who said to his heavenly Father, "Send me" (the words of Isa 6:8). It becomes clear, then, that Reuchlin's vernacular expression (*inn der hohen heimlichkeit verstanden*) is based upon the traditional Christian hermeneutics of the Hebrew Bible and it means the "cabalistic interpretation" in the christianized (christological) version.

In Reuchlin's macaronic language mix, his *German* sentence includes the Hebrew characters for God's name (*Tetragrammaton*, YHVH). As Reuchlin explains, by inserting the Hebrew consonant ש (*shin*) it becomes the Hebrew name for Jesus יהשוה (YHShVH, *Iehoshuha*).³⁹ This insight allows Reuchlin to understand that the heavenly Father told Jesus to make the hearts of the people sluggish. The Messiah as the Son of God, sent by God, is thus the source of the Jews' trouble (*plag*, plague). Jews of their own free will (*vß eigem frien willen*) are blind and obstinate, with the fatal consequence that they do not acknowledge the sinful obstinacy for which they are punished. The highly learned Rabbi David Kimhi had understood this very well in his commentary on Isa 6, says Reuchlin.⁴⁰

Reuchlin sums up his thoughts: You heard three essential reasons (*drüw wesenlich stück*) about the sin for which God punished the Jews for such a long time, a sin that was the greatest sin there ever was: it was a *gemeine sünd*; it was a sin that they themselves did not consider a sin; and it is the sin of blasphemy which their forefathers committed against the true Messiah, our Lord Jesus, and which their children perpetuate, up to this day.⁴¹ Reuchlin further elaborates on the charge of blasphemy as he continues with his christological interpretation of Ps 37:32 that "the wicked man spies on the just [Jesus] and seeks to slay him." The fact that Jesus indeed was a just man was witnessed by Pilate according to Luke 23:14–15.⁴² The Jews' sin of blasphemy was that they supposedly labeled Jesus both a sinner and sorcerer (*ein sünder vnd ein zouberer*) who was hanged and the Virgin *Maria* as a *haria*. Reuchlin gives this word in transliteration, not in Hebrew

---

37. Not to be misunderstood as "occult practices."

38. SW 4-1: 8.11.

39. Reuchlin proclaimed this discovery first in 1494 in his book on the Wonder-Working Word, *De verbo mirifico*. It is not the place here to discuss the flaws in Reuchlin's philology and theology.

40. He cites the original Hebrew and then translates it; SW 4-1: 8.3–19.

41. SW 4-1: 9.6–30.

42. SW 4-1: 9.31—10.2.

letters; etymologically it stems from the Hebrew word for "getting angry," חרה. It is a deliberate play of words (Maria—haria), i.e., (M)aria [Mary], the one "who is full of anger" which in Reuchlin's vernacular is rendered with *ein wüterin*. In addition, they call Jesus' disciples "heretics" (*ketzer*) and us Christians a "non-people" (*ein vnfolck oder nit volck*) and foolish heathens.[43] All Jews as long as they are Jews "participate" in this blasphemy.[44] After Reuchlin sums up all the essential talking points he offers some concluding thoughts which he draws from a great Jewish master.

6. Reuchlin's Concluding Thoughts

Toward the end of the *Missiue* (for the first time in Reuchlin's entire opus), the work מורה הנבוכים (*Guide for the Perplexed*) of the famous Jewish philosopher and theologian, Maimonides (d. 1204) shows its impact as Reuchlin quotes it by its Hebrew title.[45] Reuchlin introduces Maimonides as the highly respected and learned master, *Rabi Mose*, the Jew from Egypt,[46] and gives two quotations in Hebrew characters from the *Guide for the Perplexed* III:23. We do not know from which version Reuchlin took them. We do know that Maimonides's book was available in print by 1480,[47] but it is not found in Reuchlin's library, and it remains a puzzle from whence Reuchlin would have copied these quotations or if he even knew the *Guide* firsthand. The fact that Reuchlin quotes Maimonides in his concluding deliberations signals to the reader that Reuchlin identifies with the wisdom of this medieval Jewish sage and that Reuchlin considers Maimonides's words to be the best answer to his question about the reasons for the continued suffering

---

43. SW 4-1: 11.1–4.

44. *An soelcher gotzlesterung teilhafftig syen*, SW 4-1: 11.9. Reuchlin refers to these statements in his *Eye Mirror* for further clarification, when he talks about Pfefferkorn's twenty-seventh lie; SW 4-1: 163.19—164.3.

45. SW 4-1:11.24–26.

46. *Als do schreibt der hochgelert meister Rabi Mose, der Jud von Egiptten inn dem buch genannt* מורה הנבוכים *libro iij, capitulo xxiiij . . .* ; SW 4-1:11.24–29. Maimonides is referred to in *Eye Mirror* (1511), SW 4-1: 40.32; 114.19; 153.24; and again in Reuchlin's Preface of the Seven Penitential Psalms (1512), but there, too, on a different subject, namely, on the purity of Hebrew; RBW 2: 325.143 (no. 206).

47. Leicht 2005, 414. Reuchlin makes use of Maimonides's book also in his commentary on Athanasius (1519); I am grateful to Dr. Matthias Dall' Asta (Germany) for pointing this out to me.

of the Jews. He cites only two brief passages.[48] The first states, "Whoever commits evil must suffer condemnation."[49] The second reads, "Everything that happens to a person happens in justice, but we lack the knowledge of our defects for which we are punished."[50] Reuchlin, the conservative Christian Hebraist, may have considered these two phrases by Maimonides good summaries of the issues that had been raised.

Without starting a new paragraph, Reuchlin immediately connects the two Maimonides quotations with his prayer for the Jews: "I pray that God may enlighten them and convert them to the right faith so that they may be liberated from the devil's prison, as the community of the Christian Church devoutly prays for them on Good Friday."[51] Once the Jews recognize Jesus as the right Messiah everything will be fine here in this world and in eternity. However, Reuchlin's prayer is not so much a proof for his conscientiousness as a Christian missionary, but more an expression of his own Catholic faith conviction. He remains a Christian who is ready to discuss theological issues with the Jews. He is somewhat anxious to ask them for explanations of how they themselves see things and how they interpret the biblical texts which he cited. But Reuchlin does not do this with the zeal of a missionary like, for instance, Pfefferkorn. Reuchlin has a sincere desire to understand better the fate of the Jews while simultaneously thinking that it would be so much easier if all Jews would become Christians.

---

48. Although Reuchlin has: *capitulo xxiiij*.

49. *Wer boeß tůt der můß verdamnus liden*; SW 4-1: 11.20–21. He does not identify the reference to Daniel.

50. *Vnsere gebrechenheitten alle, daruff die ver damnus gesetzt Ist verborgen vor vns ir missetat*; SW 4-1: 11.26–29. Other possible translations could be: The fate of man is the result of justice, but we do not know all our shortcomings for which we are punished; or, Any definite insights into all our failings and sins, for which we deserve to be punished, remain hidden from us.

51. *Jch bit gott er woell sye erlüchten vnd bekern zů dem rechten glouben, das sye von der gefencknüs des düfels erledigt werden, als die gemeinschafft der Christenlichen kirchen an dem karfritag andechtiglich für sye bitt*, SW 4-1: 11.29–31. Five years later, in his *Expert Opinion* of 1510, Reuchlin will view the Good Friday intercession somewhat differently, i.e., from the Jewish perspective, as a "public scolding" (*offenlich schelten*) which causes the Jews to defend themselves against Christian slander: *Dan die weil wir sy alle iar ierlichs inn vnsern kirchenn am karfreitag offenlich scheltten perfidos iudeos* (*Eye Mirror*, SW 4-1: 53.20–21); on this, see Lotter 1993, 86.

7. Reuchlin's Postscript

In the final paragraph, clearly set apart typographically, Reuchlin states that this letter represents what he wants the (anonymous) nobleman to discuss with his Jews.[52] His final words are an offer himself to talk with any Jew who really wishes to be instructed about the Messiah and "our true faith" (*vnnserm rechten glauben*). He is more than ready to help such a person, who would then not need to worry about temporal food, but would be able to serve God in peace and be free from all concerns (*vnd aller sorg fry syn*).[53] These are the last words of Reuchlin's *Missiue*. Apparently the wealthy Reuchlin himself was offering financial support to any Jewish dialogue partner in order to exchange ideas on the unsolved mystery of continued Jewish suffering. Dialogue, not mission, was his goal. It would be an over-interpretation to view him only as being in search of Jews for the purpose of preaching to them about Christian theological claims.

Conclusions

As Reuchlin had written at the beginning of the *Missiue*, his intention was not to "cause offense," but to achieve "real improvement" (*mercklich besserung*).[54] Improvement and reform of the relations between Christians and Jews appears to be the best interpretation of this phrase in this context. In other words, Reuchlin's booklet (and we must recall that it is in German, not Latin) likely functioned as a manual for non-theologians (primarily Christians but perhaps also Jews)[55] who wanted to prepare for dialoguing about the serious question that preoccupied Reuchlin and that he articulated in the title. The *primary* motivation, however, appears not to be the conversion of Jews to the Christian faith. Reuchlin's *Missiue* and the rest of his works are situated better in the minority medieval tradition of relaxed relations between Christians and Jews.

---

52. *Das hab ich eüch für des erst woellen endecken mit inen zů redden*, SW 4-1: 12.2.

53. SW 4-1: 12.2–6.

54. As to Reuchlin's noun *besserung*: it is connected to the verb *bessern* which means "to improve." The noun *besserung* also carries the meaning of "repentance" or "reformation"; see Jonathan West, "Early New High German/English Dictionary Part B/P," http://www.germanstudies.org.uk/enhg_dic/enhg_dicbp.htm.

55. The fact that in his text so many phrases are given in Hebrew letters may lead even to the surmise that Reuchlin is offering a manual for Jews who are able to read Hebrew and who want to familiarize themselves with Christian thinking on the issue.

Reuchlin was a staunch Catholic, very convinced of his own faith. However, to see his *Missiue* simply as an instrument of converting Jews would mean to agree with Reuchlin's adversary, the converted Jew, Pfefferkorn. He read the pamphlet this way. Because such a misreading of his *Missiue* was possible Reuchlin was forced to clarify his position and his opposition to Pfefferkorn's claims. He refused to identify with the familiar accusations against the Jews that he had listed in the *Missiue* (that the Jews blaspheme Jesus, the Son of God, and that they enjoy such blasphemy) and expressed more clearly his real motivation, i.e., to improve relations between Jews and Christians (what he calls *mercklich besserung*). Pfefferkorn became very upset and completely frustrated with Reuchlin's unexpected clarification and total opposition. As late as in his *Compassionate Complaint over all Complaints* (*Ein mitleidliche clag*) of 1521 Pfefferkorn quoted Reuchlin's *Missiue* of 1505 as a proof for his own claims.[56] Pfefferkorn had been convinced that Reuchlin originally himself was convinced that the Jews blaspheme Jesus, the Son of God, and that they enjoy such blasphemy—accusations that Pfefferkorn kept quoting from the *Missiue*. Pfefferkorn declared Reuchlin a "Judas" for disavowing this position, describing Reuchlin as a man who betrayed him "more than Judas betrayed the dear Lord God."[57]

In his *Missiue*, Reuchlin reviewed the critical, contradictory biblical texts that needed to be discussed in a Jewish-Christian dialogue. He interpreted them as a Christian lay theologian. Puzzled by his excellent personal experience with honorable Jewish men who did not personally deserve divine punishment, he reflected on the traditional biblical reasoning why Jews lived in miserable exile. The answer Reuchlin came up with in this regard was that "collective sin" (*gemeine sünd*) was the root cause. This, he articulated through quotations from Maimonides.

The concept of a "collective sin," which Reuchlin had introduced in his open letter of 1505, does not emerge elsewhere in his works or in his correspondence. The issue was satisfactorily settled, at least in Reuchlin's mind. His motivation and his wishes appear far from "conventional." Reuchlin's unconventional approach caused Pfefferkorn's increased distress.

56. *Fur das erst so zeych ich an ein Epistel die Reuchlin eine[m] Edelma[n] vnder ander[e]n worten[n] zo geschriebe[n] hat waru[m]b die Jude[n] so la[n]g in de[m] ellendt seint* . . . ; *Ein mitleidliche clag*, fol. B ii; digitized edition at MDZ: http://daten.digitale-sammlungen.de/~db/0002/bsb00025516/image_1 (digital pages 19–20).

57. *So hat er [Reuchlin] mich . . . schalckhafftiger vn[d] luge[n]hafftiger verrate[n] dan[n] Judas vnsern liebe[n] hern gott* . . . ; *Ein mitleidliche clag*, fol. B ii, [digital page 19].

Pfefferkorn preferred Reuchlin to have had retained the position that he thought Reuchlin had expressed in the *Missiue*. It fitted his purposes so much better.

8

In Search of the Historical Pfefferkorn

The Missionary to the Jews, 1507–1508

THE YEAR 2015 MARKED the fiftieth anniversary of the Catholic Church ushering in a new epoch of Catholic-Jewish relations with the October 28, 1965, declaration of the Second Vatican Council's *Nostra Aetate*, also known as the *Declaration on the Relation of the Church to Non-Christian Religions*, and followed-up by *Guidelines on Religious Relations with the Jews* of December 1, 1974. The Church no longer works with the concept of a "mission to the Jews," a notion absent from the documents of the Second Vatican Council, but one that was very much present in the mind of Johann Pfefferkorn. This *Declaration* was, is, and will be an inspiration to all, both Christians and Jews. Rabbi Noam Marans put it this way: "The document transformed not only Catholic-Jewish relations and wider Christian-Jewish relations, but even Jewish history, all for the better. *Nostra Aetate*'s power is not limited to the past, but rather ongoing, in the present and the future."[1] This *Declaration* thus is not a "disavowal" (in the sense of a denial or negation of the Holocaust) as some who have not read the *Declaration* might assume.

A complete biography of Johann Pfefferkorn does not exist. There is no critical edition of his works; but, there is one in the making as part of

---

1. Marans, "From Regret to Claim: A Jewish Reaction To Nostra Aetate," in *Celebrating 50 Years of the Catholic Church's Dialogue with Jews* (Washington, DC: Catholic University of America, May 20, 2015), https://www.ajc.org/news/from-regret-to-acclaim-a-jewish-reaction-to-nostra-aetate.

the critical edition of Johann Reuchlin's collected works.² Researchers apparently have come to the insight that in order to understand Reuchlin one must understand Pfefferkorn and vice versa. With the critical edition of Pfefferkorn's works a comprehensive biography of him will become possible. Until then, one depends mostly on the image of Pfefferkorn that was launched by the Reuchlinists, i.e., the friends and followers of Reuchlin in the sixteenth century and beyond. They and their opponents often employed some form of mudslinging, a popular activity at that time according to the saying: "Throw plenty of dirt and some of it will be sure to stick."

First of all, since the sixteenth century the image of Pfefferkorn has been highly distorted. "Cockfights" occurred between the two Catholic laymen, Reuchlin and Pfefferkorn (each with their supporters). Each claimed in all sincerity to be a good Catholic, something that a historian can very well deduce from the available source material. It is not the place here to decide in this inner-ecclesiastical battle who was the better Catholic. It is also not the place to be apologetic, neither in favor of Reuchlin nor in favor of Pfefferkorn. And, one needs to remain aware of the fact that only one aspect of Pfefferkorn's self-understanding can come into focus here: Pfefferkorn as the self-appointed Christian lay missionary to the Jews in 1507–1508, i.e., prior to the great controversy over the confiscation, destruction, and burning of all Jewish books.

It would be a total misreading if anyone would want to see the following contribution as an attempt at rehabilitating Pfefferkorn and of exonerating him from charges of malicious and hateful rhetoric in his later years. He is guilty of throwing plenty of dirt at the Jews (just as Martin Luther did a few years later). But scholarly integrity requires that one does not exclusively take the side of the Reuchlinists in the assumption that their view represents the truth, and nothing but the truth; and further, to imply that we see the whole historical picture when we only see it through the tainted eyeglasses of the Reuchlinists. One must take the self-understanding of both, Pfefferkorn and Reuchlin, into consideration, not just uncritically accept what the Reuchlinists propagated about Pfefferkorn.

Furthermore, this article draws attention to the illustrations that the media-savvy missionary used for the title pages of his pamphlets. One may argue that Pfefferkorn played no role at all in their selection or design. Such an argument may be proposed in order to ascribe a greater role to the friars in Cologne and to belittle Pfefferkorn's expertise (just like the Reuchlinists

2. SW 4-2 (in preparation).

denigrated Pfefferkorn as an ignoramus). Since we do not know whether there was any discussion at all about the selection or design of the illustrations or what transpired in the printing-house in this regard, it must be left undecided as to who the original designer of the images for the title pages of the pamphlets may have been. But it would be preposterous to imply that Pfefferkorn had no role in deciding which specific illustrations that directly relate to his texts should be chosen.

In searching for the historical Pfefferkorn, one is faced with the numerous negative portrayals of him promoted by his adversaries. Ludwig Geiger, the author of an impressive nineteenth-century biography of Johann Reuchlin, wondered how Pfefferkorn's opponents managed to declare him a "butcher."[3] Certainly, one must ask: can Pfefferkorn simultaneously be viewed both as nothing more than a "butcher" and an invincible "nemesis" of the most learned man of his time, Johann Reuchlin?[4]

Also in the search for the historical Pfefferkorn, one encounters unverified statements about him, generally presented as if they represent a scholarly consensus; namely, that not only was Pfefferkorn a butcher, but that he also had been convicted of burglary and theft and allegedly only converted to the Christian faith in Cologne shortly after his release from prison in 1504.[5] The fact that Emperor Maximilian I (1455–1519) saw in Pfefferkorn a very learned citizen of Cologne, one of Jewish descent, in whose expertise he could trust in matters of the Jewish faith, and whom he therefore appointed as imperial solicitor on the issue of whether or not all Jewish books should be confiscated and burned, is usually overlooked or downplayed.[6] Even recently (2011), Pfefferkorn has been described as an "uneducated Jew."[7] It is more likely that Pfefferkorn was a learned man, and that opinion underlies the approach taken in this study, which will focus exclusively on Pfefferkorn's earliest texts, written in 1507–1508.

3. Geiger 1869, 298.
4. As he was described in Bell 2001, 213.
5. Bell 2001, 213.
6. Posset 2015, 330–31.
7. Reventlow 2011, 32.

1. Distorted Portrayals of Pfefferkorn

In his 1513 *Defensio*, rebutting those who were slandering him in Cologne, Johann Reuchlin called Pfefferkorn a "banausic butcher" (*banausus lanius*).⁸ Reuchlin, in defending his own good name, evidently felt it necessary to besmirch the good name of his well-educated opponent. In Reuchlin's view, Pfefferkorn remained nothing more than a baptized butcher, because books like his "are not signs of a true Christian."⁹ Pfefferkorn was only interested in making money with his writings. One should do with him what the ancient writer Apuleius recommended for people of his kind, namely, "cut the tongue out of his throat."¹⁰

Ulrich von Hutten attacked Pfefferkorn with an anonymous three-and-a-half-page pamphlet entitled Pfefferkorn's "story and confession" (ca. 1514) that included a woodcut.¹¹ In it Hutten had Pfefferkorn "admit" that he had acted as a priest for twenty years without proper ordination, and that during that time he had desecrated Eucharistic hosts, drawing blood from the holy bread, pretended to be the Messiah, changed water into wine, raised people from the dead, and poisoned sick patients, among other horrors.¹²

Reuchlin's supporters liked to present Pfefferkorn as an ignoramus, a money-hungry impostor, an opportunist, a fake convert, and a criminal who deserved the gallows. A contemporaneous, anonymous "wanted poster," entitled *Des Pfefferkorns Leben* (The life of Pfefferkorn), from ca. 1515, cemented this inflammatory image of Pfefferkorn. The picture shows the gallows awaiting Pfefferkorn's execution.¹³ It is safe to say that this so-called "life" has nothing to do with the historical Pfefferkorn.

---

8. Reuchlin, *Defensio Ioannis Reuchlin Phorcensis*, 1513; SW 4-1: 21–224 (no. 7). For excerpts in English translation, see Rummel 2002, 98–108, here 102.

9. SW 4-1: 165 (no. 12).

10. SW 4-1: 152 (nos. 23–24); Apuleius, *Florida*, 12. 29.

11. Pfefferkorn allegedly confessed this in prison. Hutten, *Die geschicht vnnd bekantnuß des getaufften Juden genannt Johannes Pfefferkorn*, 1514, extant at Württembergische Landesbibliothek Stuttgart and on microfiche (3352, no. 2313) at Library of the University of Wisconsin in Madison; Posset 2015, 584–88.

12. Some scholars have argued that the pamphlet is about an entirely different Johannes Pfefferkorn (Pfaff Rapp). See Schudt 1714-1718, vol. 1, 355–56 (§§ 5–6); Trachtenberg 1943, 82–83; Adams 2013, 88–89n4.

13. Original in Hebrew Union College, CIN Special Collections, A-85 1196, A-85 1197; Posset 2015, 585–87 (for English translation); Adams and Heß 2017, fig. 1.1 (for depiction).

The Reuchlinists, particularly the authors of the notorious, fictitious *Letters of Obscure Men* (more accurately, *Letters of Unknown Men*), are responsible for spreading the negative image of Pfefferkorn after 1515. Some of Pfefferkorn's detractors portrayed him as a Christian in name only, and in doing so exposed themselves as racists by saying: just as an animal cannot change its nature, a Jew cannot change his, and even if you boil a rock in water for three days, the rock will never be cooked.[14] There is another slanderous document from that period (1516) presenting the same invectives. (fig 8.1) The broadsheet depicts a Dominican friar (right) and Pfefferkorn (center), both facing Reuchlin (left). Pfefferkorn is represented not as a Christian, but as a Jew who still wears the Jewish identification badge in the shape of a circle or ring (*rotulus*) on his clothing. The artist portrays him pointing at this badge with an elongated finger. In this way, the anonymous creator of this broadsheet denied Pfefferkorn his Christian faith. The poem of 1516 speaks of Pfefferkorn as an opportunistic convert and an ignorant baptized Jew, who is the precursor of the Antichrist. Pfefferkorn is accused of having egged on the theologians to oppose the pious man Reuchlin (*frommen man, frum Roechlin*).[15]

Fig. 8.1. Detail, single folio from 1516 with a poem in German (*O welt wie bist so gar verkert*) against Pfefferkorn (center figure).

14. Stokes 1964, 47 (epist. 2); Posset 2015, 584.

15. *O welt wie bist so gar verkert* (1516): "Das ein tauffter judd ongelert. ... Er ist des Antecristes vorbott. ... Die glerten auch bracht vff die ban, Das jm ettlich Theologi Mit irer kunst gstanden by." The original broadsheet is in Nuremberg, Germanisches Nationalmuseum, Einzelblatt Mp 19671 Mappe 34, the entire sheet is reproduced in Posset 2015, 837 fig. 29.

Philip Melanchthon (1497–1560) is responsible for the most enduring misrepresentation of Pfefferkorn's life, displayed in his influential commemorative speech about Reuchlin in 1552, i.e., thirty years after his great-uncle's death. Melanchthon's character assassination is often treated as a reliable historical source, although Melanchthon even failed to provide the correct year of Reuchlin's death (which is 1522); he wrote that Reuchlin died "anno 1521."[16] Melanchthon portrayed Pfefferkorn as a close collaborator of the inquisitor and Dominican friar Jakob van Hoogstraeten (ca. 1460–1527).

In a recent publication (2015), Pfefferkorn is once again referred to as the "assistant of the inquisitor" in Cologne,[17] without any evidence being presented; perhaps this author's source is Melanchthon. Pfefferkorn is frequently seen as the puppet and mouthpiece of the Dominican friars of Cologne, especially of Inquisitor Hoogstraeten, whose protection he supposedly sought.[18] It is also alleged that the Dominicans employed Pfefferkorn as administrator at a supposed Dominican hospital in Cologne.[19] However, the Dominicans did not own hospital a hospital in Cologne. The truth is that the city council of Cologne appointed Pfefferkorn as the administrator of the hospital owned by the city. Pfefferkorn's sponsor was Councilman Johann Byse (dates unknown), who donated a large sum of money to the hospital on the condition that Pfefferkorn and his entire family be allowed to stay there in perpetuity. Pfefferkorn's wife, Anna, was to run the large kitchen that served more than fifty patients.[20] Pfefferkorn held his position from no later than 1513 until his death.[21]

The gross distortions in Melanchthon's biographical sketch of Pfefferkorn as a low-life good-for-nothing generally served as the dark backdrop against which the Reuchlinists and others could present their hero, Reuchlin, allowing him to shine even more brightly. This set the stage for centuries to come: the battle between the villain Pfefferkorn and the victim Reuchlin.

16. CR 11: 1009: "ex hac vita decessit."
17. Sam Wellman, *Frederick the Wise*, 2nd ed. (Saint Louis: Concordia, 2015), 162.
18. Frey 1990, 179.
19. Rummel 2002, 107n19, assumed that Pfefferkorn was a "warden at the Dominicans' hospital."
20. Jütte 2012, 153–57.
21. Geiger 1869, 299.

2. Pfefferkorn: A Well-Educated, Sincere Catholic of Jewish Descent

It might still take a very long time to compose a balanced image of Pfefferkorn. This does not mean, however, that one must agree with Pfefferkorn's misguided efforts and ill-conceived tactics as a missionary to the Jews; not to speak of his vicious attacks on them in later pamphlets (not taken into consideration here).

2.1. A Contemporaneous, Respectful Portrait of Pfefferkorn (1515)

An exceptional contemporaneous and positive depiction of Pfefferkorn exists, but is virtually unknown today. It is an early sixteenth-century portrait that depicts him with some *gravitas*, at the age of forty-six.[22] The abbreviation on the right side *I.P.AN 46* may mean I[OANNES] P[FEFFERKORN] AN[NORUM] 46.

---

22. The picture only has the initials I.P. The etching is reprinted in Posset 2015, 295 fig. 22.

Fig. 8.2. Likely a portrait of Iohann Pfefferkorn by Hieronymus Hopfer. Herzog Anton Ulrich Museum, Virtuelles Kupferstichkabinett, Braunschweig.

This is the only non-polemical, contemporaneous portrait of the historical Pfefferkorn. It is not clear who commissioned it and where the original came from. The artist is Hieronymus Hopfer (1500–after 1550), a famous south German engraver. Assuming that Pfefferkorn was born in 1469, this clue suggests the year 1515. Thus, this etching was created at the height of the battle between Pfefferkorn and Reuchlin (of whom, by the way, there is, surprisingly, no reliable contemporaneous portrait). Obviously, the existence of this Pfefferkorn portrait demonstrates that the vilification of

Pfefferkorn by the Reuchlinists was not a unanimous opinion at the time. Evidently, the (later) famous Hieronymus Hopfer,[23] who, among other things, produced a portrait of Martin Luther (a woodcut image) that circulated before and after the Diet of Worms in 1521, deemed Pfefferkorn a worthy subject for a portrait.

2.2. The Well-Educated Convert

In our search for the historical Pfefferkorn, a more objective starting point, or baseline, is Pfefferkorn's autobiographical note in his *Handt Spiegel* (Hand mirror) of 1511. In it, he states that as a Jew he gained much of his insight into Jewish traditions and the Talmud from a relative (*vetter*, which at that time meant any male relative)[24] by the name of Rabbi Mer Pfefferkorn (for whom no exact dates are known). Johann Pfefferkorn described his Jewish upbringing and the background of his writings as follows:

> Aber als jch daruon schreib / hab ich von jrem hoechsten / groß geachtetein [sic] fürst des Talmuds / vnnd ist mein angeborner vetter sein namen Rabi Mer pfefferkornn ... bey dem selbigenn rabi bin jch von jugent vff erwachsen / sein junger gewest / von jme gehoert / gelernet gesehen / vnd gelesen hab.[25]

> [Translation:] But what I write I have [learned] from their [the Jews'] highest, very esteemed *fürst* [prince] of the Talmud, who is my *vetter* [i.e., uncle, relative] whose name is Rabbi Mer Pfefferkorn ... ; from my youth on I grew up with him, was his student, listened to him, learned from him, watched him, and read him.

A Rabbi Mer (or Meir) Pfefferkorn is known to have lived in Prague. He must have been his uncle.[26] According to *A Hebrew Chronicle from Prague* (ca. 1615), this uncle was the most learned rabbi of his time,[27] being the *dayan* of Prague, i.e., a judge in a Jewish religious court and a person

---

23. However, a caveat is in order. If the etching is correctly ascribed to Hieronymus Hopfer (and nobody doubts this), it would mean that the artist was very young at the time that he created this portrait (about fifteen years old).

24. Drosdowski, *Duden. Etymologie*, 1997, s.v. "Vetter."

25. *Handt Spiegel*, 1511, fol. E1r; available online at http://daten.digitale-sammlungen.de/bsb00004425/image_33.

26. Meier Spanier, "Zur Charakteristik Johannes Pfefferkorns," *Zeitschrift für die Geschichte der Juden in Deutschland* 6 (1936), 209–29.

27. David 1993, 23; Posset 2015, 297.

knowledgeable in Talmudic law, whose advice on religious questions is often sought by other rabbis.

There is no reason to doubt Pfefferkorn's autobiographical statement of 1511, nor that in his 1516 *Streydtpuechlyn* (*Battle Pamphlet for Truth*) about his Christian baptism and mission. He account of a serious illness from which he had suffered. On his sickbed, his thoughts turned to God. As a devout Catholic, he wished to die in the Christian faith, and he felt that his life was coming to an end, which prompted him to renew the vows that he had taken as an adult during the baptismal liturgy. These vows included rejecting Satan, confessing and acknowledging his faith in Jesus Christ, and affirming the Creed of the Church. Pfefferkorn continued: "The tyrants of the world may take away [literally, 'eat'] my flesh and blood, but my faith and my good will they cannot take away from me. The truth shall rule in all eternity."[28]

Fig. 8.3. *Der Joeden spiegel*, September 3, 1507 (P 2299).
University and City Library of Cologne.

28. *Streydtpuechlyn*, 1516, fol. G4r: "Die Tyrannen der welt essen myr ab mein fleisch vnd blůt. Aber meynen glaůben vnd gůten wyllen kunnen sy myr nit essen. die warheit sol bleyben in der ehigkeyt." The image is available online at http://sammlungen.ulb.uni-muenster.de/hd/content/titleinfo/1578412 (image no. 55).

His adversary's disciples, the Reuchlinists, never accepted Pfefferkorn's claim to be a sincere Christian believer. They always saw him as a Jewish opportunist who was faking his Christian faith. Besides Pfefferkorn's own autobiographical remarks about his baptism, there is one other historical document that attests to his baptism in Cologne. This document was issued on August 25, 1506, by a representative of the higher nobility, *Pfalzgraf* (Count Palatine) Philip, and states that Johann Pfefferkorn had "turned from Jewish blindness to the Christian faith and accepted holy baptism in Cologne."[29] Pfefferkorn is an apt representative of what one might call the "convert culture" of his day.[30]

3. The Media-Savvy Missionary and Expert in Christian Iconography: The Mirror of the Jews (1507)

As we look at Pfefferkorn's own publications, it becomes clear that he was an educated Christian of Jewish descent who acquired considerable insight into Christian iconography. We will focus on the title page of *The Mirror of the Jews* of 1507–1508,[31] which appeared in several editions in both German (Cologne, Braunschweig, and Nuremberg) and Latin (Cologne and Speyer) during those years.[32] The German versions do not have the extended title "to convert to Christ" that is found in the Latin editions. His title page shows him to have been an effective communicator who employed visual aids very skillfully. The unique Christian iconography on the title page of his mission booklet is unparalleled. The image presents a clear missionary message: the Crucified Christ is the Savior. Pfefferkorn was obviously a media-savvy missionary.

---

29. Quoted in Geiger 1869, 296: "von judischer plentheit [Blindheit] zu christlichem glauben gekert den heyligen Tauff zu Colen angenommen."

30. Carlebach 2001.

31. The complete text of *Der Joeden spiegel* is edited by Flörken 2014, 39–77. An English translation (Cape 2011) is available, but it is based upon the modern German translation by Kirn 1989, 205–30. The book cover of the English translation shows the title page of the Nuremberg edition of 1507.

32. *Der Joeden spiegel*, 1507; *Der Jodenspiegel*, 1507; *Der Juden Spiegel*, 1507; *Speculum adhortationis Judaice ad Christum*, 1507; *Speculum adhortationis iudaice ad Christum*, 1507.

3.1. The Crucified Christ Removes His Hands from the Crossbeam

The iconographic element of Christ removing his hands from the cross in order to stretch out toward the believer emerged in medieval times with the motif known as *Amplexus Bernardi*, an element in the iconography of St Bernard of Clairvaux. A single folio from ca. 1450 shows the Crucified Christ embracing St Bernard, with his feet still nailed to the vertical crossbeam. Angels hover above the vertical beam, just as on Pfefferkorn's title page. However, where Pfefferkorn's picture shows Christ holding the nails in his fists, the older 1450 single folio shows them still nailed into the crossbeam. Both depictions share a focus on the salvific death of Christ on the cross.

3.2. Participation in Eternal Salvation through Baptism

Christ's "rose-colored blood" (as Pfefferkorn twice referred to it) is gushing from his hands, feet, and side into the baptismal font located directly under the crossbeam, to the right. Christ has suffered on the cross, shedding his blood for the salvation of all. Participation in eternal salvation requires baptism. The baptismal water is shown here as being sanctified by Christ's blood mixing with the water. Baptism is a sacramental washing in the blood of Christ. According to Rev 1:5: "Christ ... has loved us and washed us from our sins in his own blood." The baptismal font is the well of grace, an additional iconographic motif that is part of this title page. All in all, however, one does not get the impression that the people depicted here are being "forced into the font."[33]

3.3. The Circumcision Scene as Prefiguration of Baptism

Pfefferkorn has the Jewish circumcision scene incorporated into the picture; he understood circumcision as an Old Testament prefiguring of baptism, i.e., in its role as a sacrament of initiation. According to Thomas Aquinas, circumcision is a "figure of baptism."[34] Fleshly circumcision is a figure of the "circumcision of the heart" (Rom 2:29). Pfefferkorn prefers the Christian spiritual reading of the Scriptures; in his preface, he asserts that the Scriptures must be understood according to the spirit and not

---

33. This expression is favored in Colish 2014.
34. Thomas Aquinas, *Summa Theologiae*, 1941, vol. 4.3 (*quaestio 70*), cols. 2898b–99b.

according to the flesh. A demon, holding a bowl (of coins?) and tapping the person to be baptized on the shoulder, makes one last attempt to lure him away from Christian baptism by offering him money.

3.4. The "Handicapped Jew"

At the foot of the cross, a demon carries a (money?) purse, which he apparently intends to use to bribe the person who is limping along on crutches, either to go back to the scene of the circumcision or to remain there. The depiction of a Jewish figure with crutches is a source of further reflection. The crutches may not just indicate a disability. A Jew in need of crutches or a cane could be taken as a visual representation of the concept of an inner, spiritual disability or deformation. Pfefferkorn, whose book, significantly enough, is entitled *The Mirror of the Jews*, hopes to make the Jews aware of their spiritual handicap with this representation that is meant to serve as a "mirror." As such, Jews are portrayed as handicapped by their old and "outdated" religion, which from a Christian polemical point of view is sponsored by the devil. That is why the Jew on crutches is depicted as being led by a demon. There is no need to identify this person explicitly as Jewish (normally done by showing the person with a pointed hat or a badge); the crutches tell it all. Remarkably, none of the figures on this title page is explicitly identified as a Jew, whereas on the cover page of *In Praise and Honour of Emperor Maximilian*, another one of Pfefferkorn's books, the handicapped person is clearly identified as Jewish, with the badge in the shape of a ring, as well as with a crutch and a cane.[35]

3.5. Desecrated Communion Wafers on the Floor?

The frontispiece of what is presumably the first edition of *The Mirror of the Jews* (vernacular and Latin versions, Cologne 1507) shows what looks like four wafers or Holy Communion hosts lying on the ground by the feet of the demon, who is standing under the cross near the circumcision scene. At first sight, one might indeed think of Communion hosts with a

---

35. This can be compared to the frontispiece of Petrus Nigri's *Stern des Meschiach* (Petrus Nigri, *In aller übung der vernunft ist die czu preysen vnd czu loben*, 1477), where Jews are identified by yellow badges and depicted as ugly and disabled. The image is available online at http://www.smu.edu/Bridwell/SpecialCollectionsandArchives/Exhibitions/InventionDiscovery/PrintinginGermany/Niger.

cross imprinted on them. Perhaps the creator of this frontispiece had been instructed to make them look like Communion hosts. However, when reworking or copying the title page for the Nuremberg edition, this is not what the Nuremberg artist saw; his reproduction of the illustration shows three pebbles instead.[36]

3.6. Pfefferkorn's Traditional Image of Mary as Mother of Mercy

The left-hand side of the 1507 frontispiece includes the conspicuous figure of the Virgin Mary as "Mother of Mercy" (*Schutzmantelmadonna*). She is directing the figures under her protective cloak toward Christ. They are ordinary folks, young and old, who find protection under her care as they gaze up at the Crucified while approaching the baptismal font—with Mary to Christ, according to traditional Catholic Marian spirituality. Pfefferkorn, the missionary, may have intentionally shown some ordinary folks under Mary's protection to make his message more appealing to the common people—somewhat in contrast to the frontispiece of his *Wie die blinden Juden yr Ostern halten*, 1509 (P 2290). In it we see the highest authorities in the Church and society under Mary's protection: emperor and king (right), pope and cardinal (with red hat; left). Pfefferkorn may have been inspired by the painting in Cologne's Dominican St Andrew's Church (*Dominikanerkirche St. Andreas*). The Marian motifs of the "Mother of Mercy" and the "Queen of the Rosary" were very popular in the Dominican Order, as well as being part of Christian piety in general. The combination of the two is based on the medieval hymn *Salve Regina, Mater Misericordiae*. The title page echoes the words of this traditional hymn: "Hail, Holy Queen enthroned above, O Maria! Mother of Mercy and of Love." In the painting at Cologne's Dominican church, Mary's cloak is being held on each side by Dominicans. Dominican friars kneel behind the pope, in this case Pope Sixtus IV (a Franciscan in office 1471–1484), and his legate, Alessandro Numai, the bishop of Forlì.[37] On the opposite side, under Mary's mantle, the worldly powers, represented by Emperor Frederick III and his son, King Maximilian, kneel in veneration. Their entourage includes the estates (*Stände*) of Cologne. Presumably, they are all praying the rosary.

---

36. The version with three pebbles can be seen on the book cover of Cape 2011.

37. The image is available online at http://gemeinden.erzbistum-koeln.de/st_andreas_koeln/kirche/schutzmantelTriptychon/index.html.

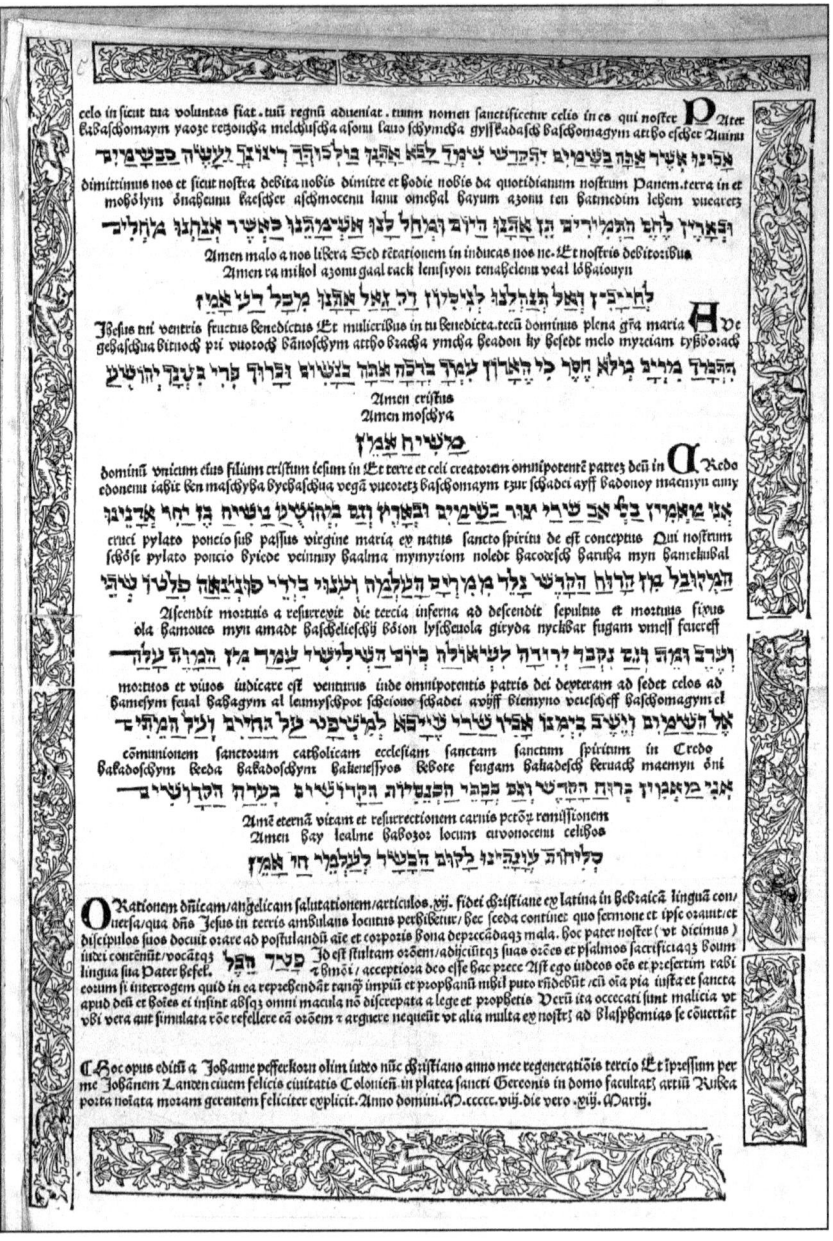

Fig. 8.4. Single folio print of Pfefferkorn's three bilingual texts: Hebrew Version of the Lord's Prayer, Hail Mary, and Creed (Cologne: Johannes Landen, 1508). Niedersächsische Staats- und Universitätsbibliothek Göttingen.

The frontispiece of Pfefferkorn's *The Mirror of the Jews* (1507) is both a conglomerate of motifs from Christian iconography and a summary of his mission program. Space does not permit us to undertake an analysis of the booklet's content. Nonetheless, this much can be said: it is unlikely that Pfefferkorn conceived of this text as a "sermon," as has been suggested.[38] A layman was not permitted to preach sermons.

4. Pfefferkorn's Teaching Material for Disputations and/or for the Training of Missionaries to the Jews

Around 1500, Christian prayer texts appeared in Hebrew translation as part of a six-page grammar booklet for the study of biblical language. In 1502, the German Nicolaus Marschalk (ca. 1470–1525) edited a grammar book (originally by Aldus Manutius of Venice), *Introductio ad litteras hebraicas*, in which he published the bilingual *Our Father*, in Latin and Hebrew, line by line on one page.[39] The first line gives the beginning of the *Pater noster*, the second line shows the transliteration of the Hebrew words, the third line presents the vocalized Hebrew translation of the prayer. Whereas the first two lines are printed in red, the Hebrew words are printed in black.[40]

Pfefferkorn does not draw upon Marschalk's edition, either with respect to layout or translation. With his Hebrew translation, Pfefferkorn played a central role in redirecting the use of Hebrew versions of key Christian prayers away from simply being a means of learning Hebrew *per se* toward a missionary purpose. Pfefferkorn used traditional catechetical teaching material—*Pater noster*, *Ave Maria*, and *Credo*—all in Hebrew translation. He assembled them on a broadsheet, printed by Johannes Landen of Cologne and dated March 13, 1508.[41] Apparently, by 1508, Pfefferkorn already anticipated the expert opinion that the theological faculty

38. Frey 1990, 180: "Die Schrift ist als Predigt konzipiert."

39. The image is available online at http://digital.staatsbibliothek-berlin.de/werkansicht/?PPN=PPN815418078&PHYSID=PHYS_0015 (image no. 12). Marschalk's emended Latin version deviates from the standard reading, as he has "sicut et nos dimittimus qui nobis debent iis" where the traditional petition reads "sicut et nos dimittimus debitoribus nostris"; and thus the choice of Hebrew words may have changed accordingly. Marschalk includes the inscription over the cross in Greek, Latin, and Hebrew according to John; image no. 14.

40. Posset (2015), 305–7.

41. See fig. 8.4. I am grateful to Bärbel Mund (Göttingen Library) for providing a digital image of the only extant copy of this text.

of Cologne offered the emperor in 1510 concerning the "Question of the Jewish books": The Jews need to be "taught in their own language by experienced converts about the true law and the prophets" for the glory of God and their own salvation.[42]

Evidently, Pfefferkorn's printer was already able to print Hebrew characters. He had the three Christian prayer texts laid out on a single sheet in Latin and Hebrew, line by line, in the style used by Marschalk to present the *Pater noster* in 1502. Pfefferkorn's printer did not, however, use two different colors. Pfefferkorn had marked the beginning of each of the three prayers with oversized capital letters: *Pater noster*, *Ave Maria*, and *Credo*.

Below is a sample of the opening of the *Our Father* ("Our Father who art in heaven, hallowed be thy name. Thy kingdom come, thy will be done [on earth as it is] in heaven") from Pfefferkorn's broadsheet. The Latin words and transcription are also arranged in the Hebrew style, written from right to left:

1. The first line is given in Latin:

    celo in sicut tua voluntas fiat, tuu*m* regnu*m* adueniat, tuum nomen sanctificetur celis in es qui noster Pater

    heaven in as thy will be done, thy kingdom come, thy name be hallowed, heaven in art who our Father

2. The second line is given in a Roman-letter transliteration of the Hebrew words (reflecting some odd pronunciation practices among the Cologne Jewry):

    kabaschomaym yaoze retzoncha melchuscha asonu lauo schymcha gysskadasch baschomagym attho escher Auinu

3. The third line has the fully vocalized Hebrew version of the beginning of this prayer:[43]

    .כְּבַשָּׁמַיִם יַעָשֶׂה רְצוֹנְךָ מַלְכוּתְךָ אָתָנוּ לָבֹא שְׁמֶךָ יִתְקַדַּשׁ בַּשָּׁמַיִם אַתָּה אֲשֶׁר אָבִינוּ

In Pfefferkorn's prayers, the first lines are always in Latin, indicating an assumption that the addressees knew Latin. The second lines give a transliteration of the Hebrew in Roman letters, based on the presumption that the reader would need this help (as a beginner in the Hebrew language might

---

42. "The Report on the Question of the Jewish Books," Rummel 2002, 133, Document 7); Posset 2015, 369.

43. I am grateful to Yaacov Deutsch for help with transcribing the Hebrew.

need it, where a Jew would not). The third lines show the Hebrew rendering in Hebrew characters with proper vocalization. The latter is obviously helpful to those who have recently learned this language, for example, future Christian missionaries to the Jews. It is also possible that Pfefferkorn used this print as a "cheat sheet" during disputations with Jews, i.e., disputations with the goal of converting them. A missive from that time indicates that he planned to engage in just such a "disputation" during the Frankfurt Book Fair (*Messe Inn der loblichenn statt frannckfurt*) in the spring of 1508.[44] On April 14, 1508, the city council had given Pfefferkorn permission for such an event.[45] Pfefferkorn would have come to this event well prepared, i.e., with his "cheat sheet," which had been printed a month earlier, on March 13, 1508.[46]

5. Pfefferkorn as Trainer of Missionaries to the Jews

If Jews were the intended readership for this broadsheet, they would have had to have been fairly well educated and able to read and understand the Latin versions of the prayers. One could hazard the assumption that Pfefferkorn meant to use the text to teach Jewish converts a few standard Latin prayers. However, one must then ask: why would those same Jews need a transliteration in Roman letters and the vocalization of the Hebrew texts? They could have read Hebrew without such props. On that basis, the question arises as to whether the Jews were the immediate target group for the text. One possible explanation is that the handout was meant for Christians knowledgeable in Latin, but requiring help to read Hebrew. In that case, the added transliterations of the Hebrew words would have been for their benefit.

Apparently, Pfefferkorn did not create the broadsheet for Christians who wanted to learn Hebrew, but had a more specific purpose in mind; he needed a teaching aid for Christian missionaries, who most likely only had a rudimentary knowledge of Hebrew. This bilingual text would enable him and other Christian missionaries to present the Hebrew version of three important Christian prayers in both Latin and Hebrew. The inclusion of

---

44. The missive is held by the Frankfurt City Archives (Institut für Stadtgeschichte); printed in Frey 1990, 173.

45. Frey 1990, 180.

46. The date is provided at the end of the print: "Anno domini. M.cccc.viij.die vero xiij. Martij."

the transliterations for the proper reading of the Hebrew would prevent the missionaries from embarrassing themselves when reading the prayers, and would allow them to pretend that they had a certain command of the language.

Pfefferkorn's remark at the bottom of his print—"The Jews question the *Pater noster* (as we call it)"—supports the view that his text was a handout intended for future Christian missionaries to the Jews. He wanted to alert them to and prepare them for any Jewish objections. He further warns the missionaries-to-be that in their own language the Jews call the Lord's Prayer a foolish prayer: "Pater hefel. הבל פטר Id est stultam orationem" (Pater of emptiness, *Pater hevel*, that is a foolish prayer). This polemical note[47] was meant to prepare the missionaries for potential objections and resistance they would encounter among their Jewish target groups.

Pfefferkorn's use of classical catechetical material (the Lord's Prayer and the Apostles' Creed) for training future missionaries took place in 1507–1508, during his intense conversion efforts.[48] It should be noted that the *Ave Maria* was not normally part of the classical catechetical material. Its inclusion here may mirror Pfefferkorn's conspicuous Marian devotion, which was always connected to the Christological issues that needed to be addressed when presenting Mary as the mother of the Son of God.

Pfefferkorn could not have foreseen himself performing all the necessary mission work in the German lands. His handout was not so much intended for classes with his own converts as it was for training sessions for missionaries to the Jews. Pfefferkorn's translation of the Christian prayers into Hebrew (as flawed as they may have been in the eyes of some) had ramifications for years thereafter. Armed with a Hebrew version of the prayers, he had no further interest in promoting the study of the Hebrew language *per se*, but instead intended to make use of them either for disputations with Jews or for training catechists and missionaries to the Jews.

As we have seen, the evidence provided by his earliest texts (1507–1508), which were produced as part of his mission work among the Jews, repudiates the picture of Pfefferkorn as an uneducated *banausus*. A critical biography of the historical Pfefferkorn remains *a desideratum* and will be possible once the critical edition of Pfefferkorn's texts become available.

---

47. Kirn 2013, 437.
48. Posset 2015, 305–7.

9

We Love This People

Afterword

BY MARTIN LUTHER

INSTEAD OF A SUMMARY, I want to conclude with a thought-provoking statement which Luther made in June 1540 with a touch of respect for the ancient people of Israel.

From reading Luther's authentic works one surely must arrive at the conclusion that he detested the Jews. However, from a Table Talk, rarely read or quoted, one may learn that the *grobian* Luther also had made, at least once, a surprising statement about the people of Israel, surprising if it was actually ever spoken by him (being mindful that Luther's Table Talk is often unreliable in terms of good historical source material): "We love this people." This is a sort of exclamation which should not be taken out of context, however.

The talk is listed under the heading "Jews." Luther alludes to Saint Paul's metaphor of the roots, the trunk, and the branches: "But if some branches were broken off, and you, a wild olive shoot, were grafted in their place and have come to share in the rich root of the olive tree, do not boast against the branches" (from Rom 11:16–20, here v. 17). Luther makes use of the imagery of "trunk" (*truncum*) and "branches" (*rami*); and of the participle "grafted" (*insiti*) from the Latin verb *inserere*. He embellishes the Pauline expression "trunk" by saying that the Jews are the "true trunk." He alludes to Jer 11:16 with his choice of words of the "beautiful green twig" (using the Latin *virga pulchra*) and the "beautiful plant" (using the Early New High German *schones gewechs*; in contemporary German it would be *schönes Gewächs*). Here follows the original wording of the macaronic talk (in a Latin and German mix; with the German words given in italics) and my translation:

Iudaei. Nos amamus hunc populum, et illi sunt tam superbi et fastuosi. Certe hic populus longe superavit nos magnis viris. Habuit enim hic populus Abraham, Isaac, Iacob, Ioseph, Moses, Dauid, Daniel, Salomon. Paulum doluit gentem tantam perire.... *Drum sein wir woll* rami insiti in verum truncum [cf. Rom 11:17]. Prophetae appellant Iudaeos et maxime lineam Abrahami virgam pulchram, et Christus est flos, *der muste aus dem schonen gewechs komen*. WA.TR 4: 652.5–13 (no. 5089).	Jews. We love this people; and nevertheless they [the Jews] are haughty and fastidious. Surely, this people surpassed us by far with their great men. For [this people] had Abraham, Isaac, Jacob, Joseph, Moses, David, Daniel, and Solomon. It pained Paul that such a great nation perishes.... We may well be the branches that are grafted into the true trunk [see Rom 11:17]. The Prophets called the Jews with full right the beautiful green twig of Abraham's lineage; and Christ is the flower head who had to come forth from this beautiful plant.

This book has been finalized at the end of October / beginning of November 2018, during the time of the worst anti-Semitic massacre in American history, at Tree of Life Synagogue in Pittsburgh, where eleven senior citizens were murdered at worship on October 27. May their memory be for a blessing.

It is also the eightieth anniversary of The Night When the Synagogues Were Burning throughout Germany, November 9/10, 1938 (*Reichskristallnacht*, also known as the Night of Broken Glass) during the terror regime of Adolf Hitler and his National Socialist German Workers' Party.

November 10 is the birthday of Martin Luther, who was born in 1483 or 1484.

Bibliography

Abel, Wolfgang von, and Leicht, Reimund, eds. *Verzeichnis der Hebraica in der Bibliothek Johannes Reuchlins*. Ostfildern: Jan Thorbecke Verlag, 2005.
Adams, Jonathan. *Lessons in Contempt: Paul Raeff's Translation and Publication of Johannes Pfefferkorn's The Confessions of the Jews*. Odense: University Press of Southern Denmark, 2013.
Adams, Jonathan, and Cordelia Heß, eds. *Revealing the Secrets of the Jews: Johannes Pfefferkorn and Christian Writings about Jewish Life and Literature in Early Modern Europe*. Berlin: de Gruyter, 2017.
Apostolos-Cappadona, Diane. *Dictionary of Christian Art*. New York: Continuum, 1994.
Apuleius. *Florida*. Available online at http://www.attalus.org/translate/florida.html.
Aquinas, Thomas. *Summa Theologiae, Tomus Qvartvs completens Tertiam Partem*. Ottawa: Studii Generalis O. Pr., 1941.
Augustijn, Cornelis. *Humanismus*. Translated into German by Hinrich Stoevesandt. Die Kirche in ihrer Geschichte. Ein Handbuch 2. Göttingen: Vandenhoek & Ruprecht, 2003.
Bärenfänger, Katharina, et al., eds *Martin Luthers Tischreden: Neuansätze der Forschung*. Tübingen: Mohr Siebeck, 2013.
Baron, Salo Wittmayer. *A Social and Religious History of the Jews: Late Middle Ages and the Era of European Expansion, 1200–1650*. 2nd ed. New York: Columbia University Press, 1969.
Bauch, Gustav. "Die Einführung des Hebräischen in Wittenberg mit Berücksichtigung der Vorgeschichte des Studiums der Sprache in Deutschland." *Monatsschrift für Geschichte und Wissenschaft des Judentums* 48 (1904).
Bell, Dean Phillip. *Jewish Identity in Early Modern Germany: Memory, Power and Community*. Aldershot, UK: Ashgate, 2007.
———. *Sacred Communities: Jewish and Christian Identities in Fifteenth-Century Germany*. Leiden: Brill, 2001.
Bell, Dean Phillip, and Burnett, Stephen G., eds. *Jews, Judaism, and the Reformation in Sixteenth-Century Germany*. Leiden: Brill, 2006.
Bell, Theo. *Divus Bernhardus. Bernhard von Clairvaux in Martin Luthers Schriften*. Mainz: Philip von Zabern, 1993.
Bernardo di Chiaravalle nell'arte italiana dal XIV al XVII seculo. Edited by Laura Dal Prà. Milan: Electa, 1990.
Black, Crofton. *The Heptaplus of Giovanni Pico della Mirandola and Biblical Hermeneutics*. Leiden: Brill, 2006.

BIBLIOGRAPHY

Böning, Adalbert. *Georg Witzel (1501–1573) als Hebraist und seine Lobrede auf die Hebräische Sprache*. Schwerte, Germany: Katholische Akademie, 2004.

Botterill, Steven. *Dante and the Mystical Tradition: Bernard of Clairvaux in the Commedia*. Cambridge: Cambridge University Press, 1994.

Brod, Max. *Johannes Reuchlin und sein Kampf. Eine historische Monographie*: Kohlhammer, 1965; reprint Wiesbaden, 1988.

Burnett, Stephen G. *Christian Hebraism in the Reformation Era (1500–1660): Authors, Books, and the Transmission of Jewish Learning*. Leiden: Brill, 2012.

———. "Philosemitism and Christian Hebraism in the Reformation Era (1500–1620)." In Irene A. Diekmann and Elke-Vera Kotowski, eds., *Geliebter Feind, gehasster Freund: Antisemitismus und Philosemitismus in Geschichte und Gegenwart: Festschrift zum 65. Geburtstag von Julius Schoeps*. Berlin: Verlag für Berlin-Brandenburg, 2009.

Cape, Ruth I., trans. *The Jews' Mirror (Der Juden Spiegel) by Johannes Pfefferkorn*. Historical introduction by Maria Diemling. Tempe: Arizona Center for Medieval and Renaissance Studies, 2011.

Colish, Marcia L. *Faith, Fiction, and Force in Medieval Baptismal Debates*. Washington, DC: Catholic University of America Press, 2014.

David, Abraham, ed. *A Hebrew Chronicle from Prague, c. 1615*. Tuscaloosa: University of Alabama Press, 1993.

De Boer, Jan-Hendryk. *Unerwartete Absichten—Genealogie des Reuchlinkonflikts*. Tübingen: Mohr Siebeck, 2016.

Deutsch, Yaacov. *Judaism in Christian Eyes: Ethnographic Descriptions of Jews and Judaism in Early Modern Europe*. Oxford: Oxford University Press, 2012.

Dinzelbacher, Peter. "Der hl. Johannes von Kapistran und die Breslauer Juden 1453." *Jahrbuch für Antisemitismusforschung* 22 (2013) 163–78.

Dörner, Gerald. "Böschenstein." In Walther Killy, ed., *Literaturlexikon*, 2:52–53. Berlin: de Gruyter, 2008.

Dolan, John P. "Witzel, Georg." In *Oxford Encyclopedia of the Reformation* (1996), 4:287–88.

Ebeling, Gerhard. *The Word of God and Tradition: Historical Studies Interpreting the Divisions of Christianity*, translated by S. H. Hooks. Philadelphia: Fortress, 1968.

Eckert, Willehad Paul. "Die Universität Köln und die Juden im späten Mittelalter." In *Die Kölner Universität im Mittelalter: Geistige Wurzeln und soziale Wirklichkeit*, edited by Albert Zimmermann. Berlin: de Gruyter, 1989.

Flörken, Norbert. *Der Streit um die Bücher der Juden (1505–1521). Ein Lesebuch*. Cologne: Universitäts- und Stadtbibliothek, 2014.

France, James. *Medieval Images of Saint Bernard of Clairvaux*. Kalamazoo, MI: Cistercian Publications, 2007 (with DVD).

Frey, Winfried. "Der 'Juden Spiegel'. Johannes Pfefferkorn und die Volksfrömmigkeit." In *Volksreligion im hohen und späten Mittelalter*, edited by Peter Dinzelbacher and Dieter R. Bauer, 173–93. Paderborn, Germany: Ferdinand Schöningh, 1990.

Füllenbach, Elias H., and Gianfranco Miletto, eds. *Dominikaner und Juden / Dominicans and Jews Personen, Konflikte und Perspektiven vom 13. bis zum 20. Jahrhundert / Personalities, Conflicts, and Perspectives from the 13th to the 20th Century*. Berlin: de Gruyter, 2015.

Garin, Eugenio. "L'humanesimo italiano e la cultura ebraica." In Corrado Vivanti, ed., *Storia d'Italia*, Annali 11—Gli Ebrei in Italia, 361–83. Torino: Einaudi, 1996.

BIBLIOGRAPHY

———, ed. *Pico della Mirandola, Giovanni. De hominis dignitate; Heptaplus; De ente et uno; E scritti vari*. Edizione Nazionale dei Classici del Pensiero Italiano 1. Florence: Vallecchi, 1942.

Geiger, Ludwig. "Johannes Pfefferkorn. Ein Beitrag zur Geschichte der Juden und zur Charakteristik des Reuchlin'schen Streites." *Jüdische Zeitschrift für Wissenschaft und Leben* 7 (1869) 293–309.

———. *Johann Reuchlin: Sein Leben und seine Werke*. Leipzig: Duncker & Humblot, 1871; reprint Elibron Classics, 2007.

Gerhard, Johann. *Theological Commonplaces: On the Nature of Theology and On Scripture*. Translated by Richard J. Dinda. St. Louis: Concordia, 2006.

Graetz, Heinrich. *History of the Jews* Vol. 4, *From the Rise of the Kabbala (1270 C.E.) to the Permanent Settlement of the Marranos in Holland (1618 C.E.)*. Philadelphia: Jewish Publication Society of America, 1956; 1st English ed., 1894.

Greschat, Isabel. *Johannes Reuchlins Bibliothek Gestern & Heute. Schätze und Schicksal einer Büchersammlung der Renaissance*. Heidelberg: Verlag Regionalkultur, 2007.

Hagen, Kenneth. "Luther's So-Called *Judenschriften*: A Genre Approach." *Archive for Reformation History* 90 (1999) 130–57. Reprinted in Kenneth Hagen, *The Word Does Everything: Key Concepts of Luther on Testament, Scripture, Vocation, Cross, and Worm; Also on Method and on Catholicism*, 399–429. Milwaukee: Marquette University Press, 2016.

———. "What Did the Term *Commentarius* Mean to Sixteenth-Century Theologians?" In *Théorie et pratique de l'exégèse. Actes du troisième colloque international sur l'histoire de l'exégèse au XVIe siecle (1988)*, edited by Irena Backus and Francis Higman, 13–38. Geneva: Droz, 1990. Reprinted in Kenneth Hagen, *The Word Does Everything: Key Concepts of Luther on Testament, Scripture, Vocation, Cross, and Worm; Also on Method and on Catholicism*, 149–68. Milwaukee: Marquette University Press, 2016.

Hamm, Bernd. *Frömmigkeitstheologie am Anfang des 16. Jahrhunderts: Studien zu Johannes von Paltz und seinem Umkreis*. Tübingen: Mohr, 1982.

Hammer, Gabriel. *Bernhard von Clairvaux in der Buchmalerei. Darstellungen des Zisterzienserabtes in Handschriften von 1135–1630*. Regensburg, Schnell und Steiner, 2009.

Harrowitz, Nancy A., ed. *Tainted Greatness: Antisemitism and Cultural Heroes*. Philadelphia: Temple University Press, 1994.

Heinig, Paul-Joachim. *Kaiser Friedrich III. (1440–1493): Hof, Regierung und Politik*. Cologne: Böhlau, 1997.

Helmer, Christine. "Luther in America." In Melloni, *Martin Luther*, 3:1277–93.

Heimbach-Steins, Marianne. "Gottes und des Menschen 'heimlichkeit': Zu einem Zentralbegriff der mystischen Theologie Mechthilds von Magdeburg." In Claudia Brinkler et al., eds., *Contemplata aliis tradere. Studien zum Verhältnis von Literatur und Spiritualität. Für Alois M. Haas*. Bern: Lang, 1995.

Hobbs, R. Gerald. "*Hebraica Veritas* and *Traditio Apostolica*: Saint Paul and the Interpretation of the Psalms in the Sixteenth Century." In David Steinmetz, ed., *The Bible in the Sixteenth Century*, 83–99. Durham: Duke University Press, 1990.

Höss, Irmgard. "Witzel." In *Contemporaries of Erasmus: A Biographical Register of the Renaissance and Reformation*, edited by Peter G. Bietenholz and Thomas Brian Deutscher. Toronto: University of Toronto Press, 2003.

Hsia, Ronnie Po-chia. *The Myth of Ritual Murder: Jews and Magic in Reformation Germany*. New Haven: Yale University Press, 1988.

Hutten, Ulrich von. *Die geschicht vnnd bekantnuß des getaufften Juden genannt Johannes Pfefferkorn.* Strasbourg: Knobloch, ca. 1514.

Idel, Moshe. "Jewish Kabbalah in Christian Garb: Some Phenomenological Remarks." In *The Hebrew Renaissance*, edited by Michael Terry, 14–15. Chicago: Newberry Library, 1997.

———. *Kabbalah in Italy, 1280–1510: A Survey.* New Haven: Yale University Press, 2011.

Joldersma, Hermina. "Specific or Generic 'Gentile Tale'? Sources on Breslau Host Desecration (1453) Reconsidered." *Archive for Reformation History* 95 (2004) 6–34.

Junghans, Helmar. "Aurifaber, Johannes (1519–1579)." *Theologische Realenzyklopädie* 4 (1979) 752–55.

———. "Die Tischreden Martin Luthers." In Helmar Junghans, *Spätmittelalter, Luthers Reformation, Kirche in Sachsen. Ausgewählte Aufsätze*, edited by Michael Beyer and Günther Wartenberg, 154–76. Leipzig: Evangelische Verlagsanstalt, 2001.

Jütte, Robert. "Ein Leben als Konvertit. Johannes Pfefferkorn als Spitalmeister in Köln." In Nathanael Riemer, ed., *Jewish Lifeworlds and Jewish Thought: Festschrift presented to Karl E. Grözinger on the Occasion of his 70th Birthday*, 153–57. Wiesbaden: Harrassowitz, 2012.

Kamin, Sara. "The Theological Significance of the Hebraica Veritas in Jerome's Thought." In Michael A. Fishbane and Emmanuel Tov, eds., *Sha'arei Talmon: Studies in the Bible, Qumran, and the Ancient Near East presented to Shemaryahu Talmon*, 243–53. Winona Lake, IN: Eisenbrauns, 1992.

Karp, Jonathan, and Adam Sutcliffe, eds. *Philosemitism in History.* Cambridge: Cambridge University Press, 2011.

Kaufmann, Thomas. *Luther's Jews: A Journey into Anti-Semitism.* Oxford: Oxford University Press, 2017.

Kidwell, Carol. *Pietro Bembo: Lover, Linguist, Cardinal.* Montreal: McGill-Queen's University Press, 2004.

Kirn, Hans-Martin. *Das Bild vom Juden im Deutschland des frühen 16. Jahrhunderts, dargestellt an den Schriften Johannes Pfefferkorns.* Tübingen: Mohr Siebeck, 1989.

———. "Pfefferkorn (Pfeffer-, Peppericornus), Johannes." In *Deutscher Humanismus 1480–1520. Verfasserlexikon*, edited by Franz Josef Worstbrock et al., 434–41. Berlin: de Gruyter, 2013.

Klitzsch, Ingo. "'Luthers Juden' in Aurifabers Tischredensammlung." In *Luther Verstehen. Person—Werk—Wirkung*, edited by Markus Buntfuß and Friedemann Barniske, 147–99. Leipzig: Evangelische Verlagsanstalt, 2016.

Konrad, Paul. "Dr. Ambrosius Moibanus: ein Beitrag zur Geschichte der Kirche und Schule Schlesiens im Reformationszeitalter." In *Schriften des Vereins für Reformationsgeschichte* 34. Halle, 1891.

Kristeller, Paul Oskar. *Renaissance Thought and Its Sources.* New York: Columbia University Press, 1979; first printed 1961.

Leicht, Reimund. "Johannes Reuchlin—der erste christliche Leser des hebräischen *More Nevukhim.*" In *The Trias of Maimonides: Jewish, Arabic, and Ancient Culture of Knowledge / Die Trias des Maimonides: Jüdische, Arabische und Antike Wissenskultur*, edited by Georges Tamer, 411–27. Berlin: de Gruyter, 2005.

———. "'Von allen vnd yegklichen iuden büchern vnd schrifften nichts vßgenommen'— Johannes Reuchlin und die 'Bücher der Juden' am Vorabend des Bücherstreits." In *Reuchlins Freunde und Gegner. Kommunikative Konstellationen eines frühneuzeitlichen*

Medienereignisses, edited by Wilhelm Kühlmann, 45-68. Ostfildern: Jan Thorbecke, 2010.

Lloyd Jones, Gareth. *The Discovery of Hebrew in Tudor England: A Third Language.* Manchester: Manchester University Press, 1983.

———, ed. *Robert Wakefield: On the Three Languages.* 1524. Binghamton, NY: Medieval & Renaissance Texts & Studies in conjunction with the Renaissance Society of America, 1989.

Lohse, Bernhard. *Martin Luther's Theology: Its Historical and Systematic Development.* Minneapolis: Augsburg Fortress, 2011.

Lorenz, Sönke, and Dieter Mertens. *Johannes Reuchlin und der "Judenbücherstreit."* Redaction by Friedrich Seck. Ostfildern: Jan Thorbecke, 2013.

Lotter, Friedrich. "Der Rechtsstatus der Juden in den Schriften Reuchlins zum Pfefferkornstreit." In Arno Herzig and Julius H. Schoeps, eds., *Reuchlin und die Juden*, 65-88. Sigmaringen, Germany: Jan Thorbecke, 1993.

Mansch, Larry D., and Curtis Peters. *Martin Luther: The Life and Lessons.* Jefferson, NC: McFarland, 2016.

Markwald, Rudolf K., and Marilynn Morris Markwald. *Katharina von Bora: A Reformation Life.* St. Louis: Concordia, 2002.

Marschalk, Nicolaus. *Introductio ad litteras hebraicas. Vtilissima. Alphabetum hebraicum & eius lectura. Vocalium hebraicarum characteres. Vocalium cum consonantibus combinationes. Oratio dominica hebraice: & iuxta latine. Emendata quaedam quae leguntur deprauate. Et alia Titulus saluatoris nostri graece latine & hebraice.* Erfurt, Germany: Henricus Sertorius, 1502.

Melloni, Alberto, ed. *Martin Luther: A Christian between Reforms and Modernity (1517-2017).* 3 vols. Berlin: de Gruyter, 2017.

Mende, Martin. "Der Sumarius und die Judenverfolgung 1510. Zur Geschichte einer der ältesten Druckschriften Brandenburgs." *Mitteilungen des Vereins für die Geschichte Berlins* 1 (2011). Available online at http://www.diegeschichteberlins.de/geschichteberlins/berlin-abc/stichworteot/687-der-sumarius-und-die-judenverfolgung-1510.html.

Miletto, Gianfranco. "Die 'Hebraica Veritas' in S. Hieronymus." In Helmut Merklein et al., eds., *Bibel in jüdischer und christlicher Tradition: Festschrift für Johann Maier zum 60. Geburtstag*, 56-65. Frankfurt: Anton Hain, 1993.

Mühle, Eduard. *Breslau. Geschichte einer europäischen Metropole.* Weimar: Böhlau, 2015.

Nestle, Eberhard, ed. *Conradi Pellicani De modo legendi et intelligendi Hebraeum: Deutschland's erstes Lehr-, Lese- und Wörterbuch der hebräischen Sprache verfaßt in Tübingen 1504, gedruckt in Straßburg 1504.* Tübingen: Heckenhauer, 1877.

Nigri, Petrus [Peter Schwartz]. *In aller übung der vernunft ist die czu preysen vnd czu loben.* Esslingen, Germany: Conrad Fyner, December 20, 1477.

Oberman, Heiko A. "The Discovery of Hebrew and the Discrimination of the Jews: The *Veritas Hebraica* as Double-Edged Sword in Renaissance and Reformation." In Andrew C. Fix and Susan C. Karant-Nunn, eds., *Germania Illustrata: Essays on Early Modern Germany Presented to Gerald Strauss*, 19-34. Kirksville, MO: Sixteenth Century Journal Publishers, 1992.

———. *The Roots of Anti-Semitism in the Age of Renaissance and Reformation.* Philadelphia: Fortress, 1981.

O'Callaghan, Daniel. *The Preservation of Jewish Religious Books in Sixteenth-Century Germany: Johannes Reuchlin's Augenspiegel.* Leiden: Brill, 2012.

Olszowy-Schlanger, Judith. "Robert Wakefield and the Medieval Background of Hebrew Scholarship in Renaissance England." In Giulio Busi, ed., *Hebrew to Latin, Latin to Hebrew: The Mirroring of Two Cultures in the Age of Humanism; Colloquium Held at the Warburg Institute London, October 18–19, 2004*, 61–87. Berlin: Freie Universität Berlin, Institut für Judaistik, 2006.

Paas, Steven. *Luther on Jews and Judaism: A Review of His "Judenschriften."* Zurich: LIT Verlag, 2017.

Pettit, Peter A. "Luther, Lutherans, and Jews: Looking to the Second Five Hundred Years." *Studies in Christian-Jewish Relations* 13 (2018) 1–12, https://ejournals.bc.edu/ojs/index.php/scjr/article/view/10569.

Plummer, Marjorie Elizabeth. *From Priest's Whore to Pastor's Wife: Clerical Marriage and the Process of Reform in the Early German Reformation*. Burlington, VT: Ashgate, 2012.

Posset, Franz. "*Amplexus Bernardi*: The Dissemination of a Cistercian Motif in the Later Middle Ages." *Cîteaux* 54 (2003; issued in 2005) 251–400 (*Amplexus Catalogue*).

———. "The Crucified Embraces Saint Bernard: The Beginnings of the *Amplexus Bernardi*." *Cistercian Studies Quarterly* 33 (1998) 289–314.

———. "'The Hebrews Drink from the Source, the Greeks from the Rills and the Latin People from the Puddle': Some Observations on Luther's Table Talk of August 9th, 1532." In *Ad Fontes Witebergenses: Select Proceedings of Lutheranism and the Classics III; Lutherans Read History*, edited by James A. Kellerman et al., 249–62. Minneapolis: Lutheran Press, 2017 (Posset 2017b).

———. "In Search of the Historical Pfefferkorn: The Missionary to the Jews, 1507–1508." In Adams and Heß, *Revealing the Secrets of the Jews* (2017), 43–60 (Posset 2017a).

———. *Johann Reuchlin (1455–1522): A Theological Biography*. Berlin: de Gruyter, 2015 (Posset 2015).

———. *Luther's Catholic Christology according to His Johannine Lectures of 1527*. 1st ed., Milwaukee: Northwestern Publishing House, 1988; reprinted in *Collected Works*, vol. 3, Eugene, OR: Wipf and Stock, 2019.

———. *Luther ist kein Lutheraner: Gesammelte Aufsätze zum historischen Luther in ökumenischer Perspektive*. Paderborn, Germany: Bonifatius, 2019.

———. *Marcus Marulus and the Biblia Latina of 1489: An Approach to His Biblical Hermeneutics*. Cologne: Böhlau, 2013.

———. *Pater Bernhardus: Martin Luther and Bernard of Clairvaux*. Kalamazoo, MI: Cistercian Publications, 1999; reprint in *Collected Works*, vol. 2, Eugene, OR: Wipf and Stock, 2018 (Posset 1999/2018).

———. *The Real Luther: A Friar at Erfurt and Wittenberg, Exploring Luther's Life with Melanchthon as Guide*. St. Louis: Concordia, 2011.

———. *Renaissance Monks: Monastic Humanism in Six Biographical Sketches*. Leiden: Brill, 2005.

———. *Unser Martin: Martin Luther aus der Sicht katholischer Sympathisanten*. Münster: Aschendorff, 2015 (Posset 2015c).

———. "Vom Sumpf und den Bächen zurück zu den Quellen." In *Anwälte der Freiheit! Humanisten und Reformatoren im Dialog*. Begleitband zur Ausstellung im Reuchlinhaus Pforzheim 20. September bis 8. November 2015. Im Auftrag der Stadt Pforzheim, edited by Matthias Dall'Asta, 159–65. Heidelberg: Winter, 2015 (Posset 2015b).

Price, David H. *Johannes Reuchlin and the Campaign to Destroy Jewish Books*. Oxford: Oxford University Press, 2011.

———. "Johannes Reuchlin." In *Dictionary of Literary Biography*, edited by Coeli Fitzpatrick and Dwayne A. Tunstall, 179:231–40. Detroit: Gale Research, 1978.

Puglisi, Catherine R., and William L. Barcham, eds. *New Perspectives on the Man of Sorrows*. Kalamazoo, MI: Medieval Institute, 2013.

Reinhardt, Klaus, and Horacio Santiago-Otero. *Biblioteca bíblica ibérica medieval*. Madrid: Consejo Superior de Investigaciones Científicas, Centro de Estudios Históricos, 1986.

Reuchlin, Johannes. *De arte cabalistica libri tres (1517). Die Kabbalistik*. Latin-German. Edited by Widu-Wolfgang Ehlers and Fritz Felgentreu. Hebrew text edited by Reimund Leicht. SW 2-1. Stuttgart-Bad Cannstatt: Frommann-Holzboog, 2010.

———. *De verbo mirifico. Das wundertätige Wort*. Latin-German. Edited by Widu-Wolfgang Ehlers et al. SW 1-1. Stuttgart-Bad Cannstatt: Frommann-Holzboog, 1996.

———. *Johannes Reuchlin: Briefwechsel*. Edited by Heidelberger Akademie der Wissenschaften in Zusammenarbeit mit der Stadt Pforzheim. 4 vols. Stuttgart-Bad Cannstatt: Frommann-Holzboog, 1999–2013 (RBW).

———. *On the Art of the Kabbalah (De Arte Cabalistica)*. Translated by Martin Goodman and Sarah Goodman. Lincoln: University of Nebraska Press, 1993; 1st ed., 1983.

Reventlow, Henning Graf. *History of Biblical Interpretation*. Vol. 3, *Renaissance, Reformation, Humanism*. Translated by James O. Duke. Atlanta: SBL, 2011.

Ron, Nathan. *Erasmus and the "other": on Turks, Jews, and Indigenous peoples*. Basingstoke, England: Palgrave Macmillan, 2019.

Rösel, Martin. *Adonaj—warum Gott 'Herr' genannt wird*. Forschungen zum Alten Testament 29. Tübingen: Mohr Siebeck, 2000.

Rubin, Miri. *Gentile Tales: The Narrative Assault on Late Medieval Jews*. New Haven: Yale University Press, 1999; University of Pennsylvania Press, 2004.

Rummel, Erika. *The Case against Johann Reuchlin: Religious and Social Controversy in Sixteenth-Century Germany*. Toronto: University of Toronto Press, 2002.

———, ed. *A Companion to Biblical Humanism and Scholasticism in the Age of Erasmus*. Leiden: Brill, 2008.

Santiago-Otero, Horacio. *Manuscritos de autores medievales hispanos*. Madrid: Consejo Superior de Investigaciones Científicas, Centro de Estudios Históricos, 1987.

Scheible, Heinz. "Reuchlins Einfluss auf Melanchthon." In Arno Herzig et al., eds. *Reuchlin und die Juden*, 123–49. Sigmaringen, Germany: Jan Thorbecke, 1993.

Schilling, Heinz. *Martin Luther. Rebell in einer Zeit des Umbruchs. Eine Biographie*. Munich: Beck, 2013. English ed., *Martin Luther: Rebel in an Age of Upheaval*. Oxford: Oxford University Press, 2017.

Schramm, Brooks, and Kirsi I. Stjerna, eds. *Martin Luther, the Bible, and the Jewish People: A Reader*. Minneapolis: Fortress, 2012.

Schudt, Johann Jacob. *Jüdische Merckwürdigkeiten*. 4 vols. Frankfurt and Leipzig: Samuel Tobias Hocker, 1714–1718.

Shamir, Avner. *Christian Conceptions of Jewish Books: The Pfefferkorn Affair*. Copenhagen: Museum Tusculanum Press, University of Copenhagen, 2011.

Spitz, Lewis W. "Reuchlin's Philosophy: Pythagoras and Cabala for Christ." *Archiv für Reformationsgeschichte* 47 (1956) 1–20.

Springer, Carl P. E. "Martin's Martial: Reconsidering Luther's Relationship with the Classics." *International Journal of the Classical Tradition* 14 (2007) 23–50.

Statements from the International Jewish Committee on Interreligious Consultations (IJCIC) and the Lutheran World Federation (LWF) Consultation. Stockholm, 1983.

Stayer, James M. "Luther and the Radical Reformers." In Melloni, *Martin Luther*, 1:451–71.

Stievermann, Dieter. "Marschalk (ca. 1470–1525)." In *Grosse Denker Erfurts und der Erfurter Universität*, edited by Dietmar v. d. Pfordten, 122–26. Göttingen: Wallstein, 2002.

Stokes, Francis Griffin, trans. *On the Eve of the Reformation: "Letters of Obscure Men."* Introduction by Hajo Holborn. New York: Harper & Row, 1964.

Stupperich, Robert. *Reformatorenlexikon.* Gütersloh: Gütersloher Verlagshaus Gerd Mohn, 1984.

Szpiech, Ryan. "Converso Polemic in Naples: The Transmission of Paulus de Sancta Maria's Scrutinium Scripturarum." In *New Studies on Yale Manuscripts from the Late Antique to the Early Modern Period*, edited by Robert G. Babcock, 113–28. New Haven: Beinecke Rare Book and Manuscript Library, 2005.

———. "Scrutinizing History: Exegesis and Polemic in Pablo de Santa María's *Siete edades del mundo*." *Medieval Encounters* 16 (2010) 96–142.

Thienhaus, Ole J. *Jewish-Christian Dialogue: The Example of Gilbert Crispin.* Baltimore: PublishAmerica, 2006.

Vogler, Günter. "Thomas Müntzer's Heritage: An Alternative in the Process of Reformation." In Melloni, *Martin Luther*, 1:431–49.

Vonschott, Hedwig. *Geistiges Leben im Augustinerorden am Ende des Mittelalters und zu Beginn der Neuzeit.* Berlin: Ebering, 1915; Vaduz: Kraus Reprint, 1965.

Voragine, Jacobus de. *The Golden Legend: Readings on the Saints.* Translated by William Granger Ryan. 2 vols. Princeton: Princeton University Press, 1993.

Walter, Peter. "Erasmus of Rotterdam and his Environment." In Melloni, *Martin Luther*, 1:491–507.

Weinstein, Roni. "Jews and Lutheranism: An Ambiguous Silence." In Melloni, *Martin Luther*, 2:635–48.

Wengst, Klaus. "Martin Luther und die Juden. Über theologische Judenfeindschaft als Geburtsfehler des Protestantismus." In Klaus Wengst, *Christsein mit Tora und Evangelium. Beiträge zum Umbau christlicher Theologie im Angesicht Israels.* Stuttgart: Kohlhammer, 2014.

West, Jonathan. *Early New High German-English Dictionary.* 2004–13. Available online at http://www.germanstudies.org.uk/enhg_dic/enhg_dicbp.htm.

Wilhelm, Karl Werner, and Gerhard Wilhelmi, eds. and trans. *Religionsgespräche mit einem Juden und einem Heiden: lateinisch-deutsch.* Freiburg: Herder, 2005.

Wirszubski, Chaim. *Flavius Mithridates Sermo de passione Domini.* Jerusalem: Israel Academy of Sciences and Humanities, 1963.

Wolfson, Elliot R. "Language, Secrecy, and the Mysteries of Law: Theurgy and the Christian Kabbalah of Johannes Reuchlin." *Kabbalah: Journal for the Study of Jewish Mystical Texts* 13 (2005) 7–41.

Wortsman, Peter. *Recommendation Whether to Confiscate, Destroy and Burn All Jewish Books: A Classic Treatise against Anti-Semitism; Johannes Reuchlin.* Translated, edited, and with a foreword by Peter Wortsman. Critical introduction by Elisheva Carlebach. New York: Paulist, 2000.

Yisraeli, Yosi. "Between Jewish and Christian Scholarship in the Fifteenth Century: The Consolidation of a 'Converso Doctrine' in the Theological Writings of Pablo de Santa

María." Doctoral dissertation abstract, University of Tel Aviv, 2015. Available online at http://humanities1.tau.ac.il/history-school/images/Yosi-Yisraeli-E.pdf.

———. "Constructing and Undermining Converso Jewishness: Profiat Duran and Pablo de Santa María." In Miri Rubin and Ira Katznelson, eds., *Religious Conversion: History, Experience and Meaning*, 185–215. Farnham: Ashgate, 2014.

Zika, Charles. *Reuchlin und die okkulte Tradition der Renaissance*. Sigmaringen, Germany: Jan Thorbecke, 1998.

Index of Personal Names

Adam (biblical), 51, 55, 220, 245
Abraham (patriarch), 46, 51, 99, 115, 117, 272
Abraham ben Avigdor (rabbi), 105
Adrianus, Matthaeus (Hebraist), 2, 48, 93-97, 99, 102, 107, 179, 222-228, 234, 235
Agar (biblical, Hagar), 46
Agricola, Phagus (pseudonym Witzel), 103
Agricola, Rudolf (humanist), 48-51, 56
Alexander (Franciscan friar), 29
Ambrose (church father), 181
Ambrosius Moibanus (theologian), 37
Amerbach, Johannes (printer), 64, 93, 241
Amman, Caspar (Augustinian friar, Hebraist), 98, 100, 228
Anaclete (anti-pope), 30
Angelico (Dominican friar, painter), 19, 22, 24
Anshelm, Thomas (printer), 53, 54, 65-67, 76, 89, 94, 209, 224, 237
Apuleius (ancient writer), 255
Aquila of Pontus (translator), 96, 99, 179, 187
Aquinas, Thomas (Dominican friar), 18, 46, 263
Aristotle (philosopher), 135
Athanasius (bishop), 56-58, 247
Augustine of Hippo (church father), 96, 177, 181, 189
Aurifaber, Johannes (theologian), 199-201, 208

Aurogallus, Matthaeus (Goldhahn, Hebraist), 193, 203, 209
Bembo, Pietro (humanist, cardinal), 204, 205
Bernard of Clairvaux (saint), 2, 18, 19, 30, 31, 263
Bernhardus (former rabbi, Jacob Gipher), 102
Besold (copyist), 199
Boeschenstain, Johannes (priest, Hebraist), 94, 193, 223, 228-231, 233-235
Bomberg, Daniel (printer), 81
Brant, Sebastian (writer), 93
Brod, Max (writer), 237
Buchholzer, Georg (pastor), 87, 88
Buchsenstein see Boeschenstain
Burgos, Paul of (bishop, Hebraist), 6, 51, 69, 70-76, 187
Byse, Johann (councilman), 257

Cadmus (inventor of the Greek alphabet), 99, 115
Caedicius (Roman citizen), 149
Calman (rabbi), 100
Calonymus, David (rabbi), 100
Calvin, John (reformer), 84
Campanus, Johannes (anti-Trinitarian), 102
Capito, Wolfgang (reformer), 193
Capnio[n] see Reuchlin
Carben, Victor von (priest, of Jewish descent), 221

INDEX OF PERSONAL NAMES

Carl I of Baden (territorial lord), 62
Cerretani, Bartolomeo (historian), 38, 84
Chalcondyles, Demetrius (Grecian), 64
Cicero, M. Tullius (orator), 99, 137, 141, 203
Clement V (pope), 41, 96
Cordatus, Conrad (theologian), 199, 201
Crispin, Gilbert (Benedictine monk), 238
Crotus, Rubeanus (humanist, theologian), 103
Cyril of Alexandria (patriarch), 62, 73

Dalberg, Johannes von (humanist, bishop), 65
Daniel (prophet), 248, 272
Dante Alighieri (writer), 30-32
David (psalmist), 14, 272
Delitzsch, Franz (theologian), 3
Demosthenes (orator), 99
Denck, Hans 193
Dietrich, Veit (theologian), 199, 201
Dominic (saint), 17, 18, 22-26, 35

Eber see Heber
Eberhard of Württemberg (The Bearded), 27, 62
Eck, Johann (theologian), 240
Egidio of Rome (Augustinian friar), 30
Eleazar (high priest), 177
Ellenbog, Nicolaus (Benedictine monk), 47, 59, 85, 86
Enoch (biblical), 115, 117
Epicurus (philosopher), 137
Erasmus of Rotterdam (humanist), 5, 61, 103, 121, 204
Ermolao Barbaro (humanist), 64
Esra (inventor of the Hebrew letters), 115
Euripides (playwright), 117
Eusebius (bishop), 99, 115, 187
Evander (inventor of Latin alphabet), 115
Eve (biblical), 51
Ezekiel (prophet), 117
Flaccus [Horace] (poet), 155
Forstemius, Johannes (Hebraist), 203, 205, 206, 208
Forster see Forstemius
France, James (art historian), 22

Francis, (pope), 16
Frederick III (emperor), 43, 44, 64, 85, 238-240, 242, 265
Frederick the Wise (elector), 94

Galatinus, Petrus (Franciscan friar), 187
Garin, Eugenio (historian), 27
Geiger, Ludwig (historian), 43, 50, 241, 254
Gemmingen, Uriel von (archbishop, elector), 38
Gerhard, Johann (theologian), 198
Gerundensis, Moses (Hebraist), 244
Gikatilla, Joseph (cabalist), 65
Gipher, Jacob see Bernhardus [Hebraeus]
Goldhahn see Aurogallus
Gray, Robert (bishop), 198
Gritsch, Eric W. (church historian), 7
Grunenberg (printer), 48

Hager see Agar
Heber (biblical), 117
Heman (biblical chanter and musician), 121
Herodotus (father of historiography), 117
Hetzer, Ludwig (theologian), 193
Heydenreich (copyist), 199
Hilary (church father), 181
Hippocrates (physician), 141
Homer (legendary writer), 117
Hoogstraeten, Jacob von (Dominican friar, inquisitor), 77-79, 257
Hopfer, Hieronymus (artist), 229, 259, 260
Hutten, Ulrich von (humanist, poet laureate), 92, 255

Idel, Moshe (historian), 58
Idithun see Jeduthun
Innocent II (pope), 30
Ioachim (Mary's father), 220
Irenaeus (bishop of Lyon), 177, 181
Isaac (patriarch), 51, 272
Isaiah (prophet), 51, 117, 245
Ishmael (biblical), 46

Jacob (patriarch), 51, 272

INDEX OF PERSONAL NAMES

Jeduthun (biblical temple musician), 121
Jerome (church father), 47, 61, 73-75, 93, 96, 141, 161, 171, 181, 183, 185, 189, 199, 208
John (apostle, evangelist), 22, 23, 25, 35, 63, 125, 207
John the Baptist (biblical), 30, 31
Jonas, Justus (canon lawyer), 103
Josel of Rosheim (Jewish leader), 8, 86
Joseph (biblical), 272
Josephus (historian), 115, 117
Julian the Apostate (emperor), 73
Junghans, Helmar (church historian), 200
Justinian (lawmaker), 141

Karpokrates (philosopher), 137
Kaufmann, Thomas (church historian), 7
Kerdon (gnostic), 137
Khummer (copyist), 199
Kimhi, David (Hebraist), 100, 209, 246
Kimhi, Moses (Hebraist), 209
Koenig, Harry C. (church historian), 2
Kunigunde of Bavaria (princess), 14

Lagus (father of King Ptolemy), 177
Landen, Johannes (printer), 221, 266, 267
Lauber, Jacob (Carthusian monk), 62
Lauterbach (copyist), 199
Leo X (pope), 4, 39, 80, 89, 92, 96
Levita, Elias (Hebraist), 100
Linus (mythological musician), 117
Lippi, Filippino (painter), 31, 32
Livy (historian), 117, 147
Loans, Jacob Jehiel (emperor's physician), 43, 64, 65, 241
Lucian (philosopher), 137
Ludwig (son of Eberhard), 64
Luther, Martin (reformer), xiii, 3-15, 30, 37, 54, 61, 84-92, 94, 102-105, 107, 119, 121, 153, 198-211, 240, 253, 260, 271, 272
Lydia (mythical), 171
Lyra, Nicholas de (Franciscan friar), 72, 187, 208

Maimonides (philosopher), 71, 247, 248, 250

Manutius, Aldus (printer), 213-217, 220-222, 227, 233, 235, 267
Marans, Noam (rabbi), 252
Margaritha, Anthonius (Hebraist), 11-13, 15, 87, 193, 211
Margolioth, Jacob (rabbi), 211
Maro (philosopher), 137
Marschalk, Nicolaus (printer), 215-217, 219, 222, 223, 227, 233-235, 267, 268
Marsilius of Padua (philosopher), 30
Mary, Queen of Hungary and Bohemia 14
Mary (Virgin, Mother of God), 22, 23, 25, 29, 31, 34, 35, 62, 220, 225, 226, 231, 232, 234, 247, 265, 270
Mathesius (copyist), 199
Matthew (evangelist), 131
Maximilian I (emperor), 13, 238, 239, 241, 254, 264
Medici (rulers), 2, 27
Medici, Lorenzo (ruler), 27, 62
Medler, Nikolaus (educator, theologian), 199, 201
Melanchthon, Philip (reformer), 90, 92-94, 107, 205, 257
Mithridates, Flavus (Hebraist), 27, 62, 90
Moses (biblical), 10, 51, 97, 99, 115, 119, 179, 202, 209, 272
Münster, Sebastian (Franciscan friar, Hebraist), 100, 191, 193
Müntzer, Thomas (priest, revolutionary), 5
Musaeus (mythological musician), 117

Nahmanides, Moses (rabbi), 244
Nephtalim (Jew at Eisleben), 104
Nestorius (heretic), 62
Noah (biblical), 115
Numai, Alessandro (papal delegate), 265

Öglin, Erhard (printer), 228, 230
Origen (theologian), 96, 187
Orpheus (mythological musician), 117

Pagninus, Santes (Dominican friar, Hebraist), 195

INDEX OF PERSONAL NAMES

Palamedes (inventor of Greek letters), 115
Paul (apostle), 42, 69, 123, 131, 141, 205, 271, 272
Paula (Jerome's disciple), 185
Pellican, Conrad (Franciscan friar, Hebraist), 100, 191, 216
Perugino, Pietro (painter), 22, 25
Petrarch (humanist), 30
Pfefferkorn, Johann (lay theologian, of Jewish descent), 3, 4, 8, 11, 13-15, 36, 76, 77, 86, 87, 211, 221-223, 225, 228, 234, 235, 237, 238, 247, 248, 250-270
Pfefferkorn, Mer (rabbi), 260
Pfenningmann, Leonhard (abbot), 99
Philip (count palatine, elector), 65, 262
Philo (philosopher), 99, 115, 161
Pico della Mirandola, Giovanni (philosopher), 27, 28, 47, 48, 51, 64, 198, 239
Pilate (biblical), 246
Plato (philosopher), 58, 137
Pliny (Roman scholar), 115, 137, 163
Porchetus Salvaticus (Carthusian monk), 87
Potken, Johannes (orientalist), 58
Prochoros (St. John's secretary), 63
Proclus (patriarch), 62
Ptolemy (king), 177
Pythagoras (philosopher), 48, 91

Rabe (copyist), 199
Raida, Balthasar (Raid, Reith, theologian), 103
Rambon, Ramban see Gerundensis
Raphael (archangel), 91
Rhadamantys (judge in the netherworld), 149
Rashi (Hebraist), 241, 244
Recanati, Menachem (cabalist), 28
Reuchlin, Dionysius (brother of J. Reuchlin), 28, 46
Reuchlin, Johann (lay theologian, Hebraist), xiii, 1-4, 8, 11, 13-15, 26-28, 36-82, 84-87, 89-94, 96-101, 105, 107, 157, 179, 187, 198, 199, 205, 209, 211, 219-222, 225, 226, 228, 233, 236-251, 253-257, 259, 260
Rörer, Georg (theologian), 201, 209
Romolo (Cistercian monk), 34
Rustici (goldsmith), 30, 33

Schilling, Heinz (church historian), 7
Schlaginhaufen (copyist), 199
Schlick, Wolfgang (count), 8, 9
Schmidt, Peter (printer), 199
Seth (biblical), 115, 117
Sforno, Obadiah (Hebraist), 65
Shem (biblical), 117
Simeon (biblical), 231, 233, 234
Simonides (poet), 99, 115
Sixtus IV (pope), 62, 265
Socrates (philosopher), 137
Solomon (biblical), 209, 272
Solomon de Troyes (rabbi), see Rashi
Solomon ha Levi see Burgos
Soncino, Joshua Solomon ben Israel (printer), 26
Spalatin, Georg (theologian), 87, 94
Spitz, Lewis W. (historian), 58
Suetonius (historian), 62
Symmachus (translator), 96, 99, 179, 187

Tacitus (historian), 62
Tertullian (theologian), 115
Thaddeus (biblical), 115
Theodotion (translator), 96, 99, 179, 187
Tissardus, Franciscus (Hebraist), 218-223, 227, 233-235

Urbanus, Henricus (Cistercian monk), 90

Valentinus (gnostic), 137
Victor (patron saint of Florence), 30, 31

Vuolrab see Wolrab

Wakefield, Robert (Hebraist), 2, 48, 97, 98, 107
Walch, Johann Georg (historian), 201
Weller (copyist), 199
Wengst, Klaus (theologian), 8

INDEX OF PERSONAL NAMES

Wied, Hermann von (archbishop), 36
Winmann, Nikolaus (Hebraist), 2, 99, 100, 107, 179
Witzel, Georg (Hebraist, theologian), xi, 1, 3, 48, 83, 100-109, 119, 121, 125, 135, 157, 179, 191
Wolrab, Nicolaus (printer), 103, 106

Xenophanes (philosopher), 135

Zechariah (biblical), 232-234
Zenobius (patron saint of Florence), 30, 31
Zwingli, Ulrich (reformer), 84

Index of Biblical References

OLD TESTAMENT

Genesis
1	20
1:1	19, 28
1:1–5	21
1:6–13	21
1:14–31	21
1:28–31	22
2	20
2:1–3	22
3	245
4:25	115
10:21, 25–26	117
16	46
38	10

Exodus
3:14	119
20	231, 232
20:2-17	232
20:5	243, 244
28:33	40
30:1–8	40
32:34	244
34:7	243
39:25	40

Leviticus
16:10	73

Deuteronomy
20:19	72
25:2	242
28:10	51

1 Chronicles
15:16-17	121
25:1-3	121

Nehemiah
9:16-20	243, 244

Psalms
7:18	229
22:2	129
22:17	105
37:32	246
40:5	50
54:3	49, 50, 56
67 [68]:27	93
88:1	121
90	34
106:43-46	243
109	6
109:8	14
109:18	14
109:19	14
110 [111]:10	47, 86
119:15	229

Proverbs

1:7	47, 86

Isaiah

6:8-10	245, 246
25:1	51
63:16	51

Jeremiah

11:16	271

Ezekiel

18:20	243, 244

NEW TESTAMENT

Matthew

1:21	49
5:18	97, 123
6	231, 232
22:23	137
27:46	100

Mark

5:41	129
7:34	129
14:36	129
15:34	100, 129
16:15	37

Luke

1	231, 232
1:28–29	232
1:46–56	232
1:68–79	233
2	231
2:29–32	233
11	231, 232
23:14-15	246

John

4:22	86
5:39	2, 60, 62, 67, 70, 71, 74-76, 78, 81, 82
6:12	200
14:2	149
19:20	97, 100, 125, 216, 220

Acts

4:12	50

Romans

2:29	263
11:11-17	271, 272

1 Corinthians

5:12	42

Hebrews

1:1–12	206

2 Peter

2:12	139

1 John

1:10	207
2:21	207
3:15	207
3:17	207
4:14	121

Jude

14–15	115

Revelation

1:5	263

www.ingramcontent.com/pod-product-compliance
Lightning Source LLC
Chambersburg PA
CBHW071235230426
43668CB00011B/1446